KING PHILIP'S WAR

THE GREAT NARRAGANSETT SWAMP

From the elevated land on the southwest. A line drawn across the swamp on the
right of the picture would pass through the fort about a mile distant

KING PHILIP'S WAR

BASED ON THE ARCHIVES AND RECORDS
OF MASSACHUSETTS, PLYMOUTH, RHODE
ISLAND AND CONNECTICUT, AND CON-
TEMPORARY LETTERS AND ACCOUNTS

WITH BIOGRAPHICAL AND TOPOGRAPHICAL NOTES

BY

GEORGE W. ELLIS

AND

JOHN E. MORRIS

OF THE CONNECTICUT HISTORICAL SOCIETY

THE GRAFTON PRESS

PUBLISHERS   NEW YORK

KING PHILIP'S WAR

By George W. Ellis and John E. Morris

As Published in 1906

Trade Paperback ISBN: 1-58218-430-5
Hardcover ISBN: 1-58218-431-3
eBook ISBN: 1-58218-429-1

Digital Scanning and Publishing is a leader in the electronic republication of historical books and documents. We publish many of our titles as eBooks, as well as traditional hardcover and trade paper editions. DSI is committed to bringing many traditional and little known books back to life, retaining the look and feel of the original work.

©2001 DSI Digital Reproduction
First DSI Printing: June 2001

Published by DIGITAL SCANNING, INC.
Scituate, MA 02066
Toll Free: 888-349-4443
Outside U.S. 781-545-2100
www.digitalscanning.com

PREFACE

THE period marked by the Indian wars of 1675 and 1676, known as King Philip's War, is one of the most interesting and epochal in the early history of the New England colonies.

It was the first great test to which the New England Commonwealths were subjected, and it enforced upon them in blood and fire the necessity of a mutual policy and active co-operation. The lesson that union is strength was learned at that time and was never forgotten. New England after the war, free from fear of any Indian attacks, was able to turn her attention to her own peaceful industrial and political development undisturbed.

However much we must condemn the arbitrary aggressions which drove the Indian tribes into revolt, the historic fact must be accepted that between peoples the fittest only survive, and that as between races ethics rarely exist.

The importance of this conflict in the minds of the early New England people is attested by the great attention paid to it by contemporary New England historians like Mather and Hubbard, and by the voluminous correspondence of the chief men in the colonies.

The correspondence between the Governors and Councils and the commanders in the field in the records and archives of Massachusetts, Rhode Island, and Connecticut, serve as a vast mine for careful exploration of the conflict in almost all its details.

We do not claim for this work that it is an absolutely true history; no absolutely true history is possible on any subject. All the authors claim is that it is the result of a wide and discriminative study of the published and unpublished archives of the New England colonies, and of the contemporary letters found in the Massachusetts and Rhode Island Historical Society collections.

Among other works consulted have been the contemporary accounts of Hubbard, Mather, and the Old Indian Chronicle, Captain Church's Narrative, the Journals of Mrs. Rowlandson and John Easton, Major Gookin's Christian Indians, Wheeler's True Narrative of the Lord's Providence, etc. Liberty has been taken occasionally to abridge involved and verbose quotations.

The authors wish to acknowledge their great indebtedness to the work of Rev. George Bodge, the late Samuel Drake, Sydney S. Rider, and the constant courtesy and help of Mr. Albert C. Bates, librarian of the Connecticut Historical Society, and to the authors of many of the valuable town histories.

The narrative and references are the work of Mr. George W. Ellis, while the biographical and local notes have been supplied by Mr. John E. Morris. Acknowledgment is herewith made to many local antiquarians for their co-operation and courtesy.

CONTENTS

Squaw Magnus and Stone-layer John. Talcott hands over a captive
Indian to his Indian allies. Terrible tortures. Captain Church redux.
His quarrels with the Plymouth authorities. He goes on a mission to
Awashonks, squaw sachem of the Saconets. She tenders her submission. The wanderings of Philip. He endeavors to surprise Bridgewater. The English close in upon him. Despair of the Indians.
Massachusetts and Plymouth offer conditional pardon for submission
within a fortnight. Piteous petition of Sagamore Sam, Muttaump, and
others of the Nipmucks for peace and pardon. It is refused. The
death of Pumham. Matoonas betrayed into the hands of the English
by Sagamore John. His execution. The activities of Captain Church
in hunting down the Wampanoags. Battles in the swamps. Capture
of Philip's wife and child.

CHAPTER XVI   266

The grief and despair of Philip over the loss of his wife and child.
The controversy as to their disposal. Scriptural precedent sought.
The plea of Rev. John Elliot and Reverend Mr. Keith of Bridgewater for
mercy and humane treatment. They are finally sold into slavery. The
death of the Squaw Sachem Weetamoo. The fate of Totoson. Captain Church renews the pursuit of Philip. An Indian traitor. The
death of Philip. His character. The capture of Annawon and the
surrender of Tuspaquin. Church promises them their lives. Their
execution.

CHAPTER XVII   281

Major Talcott's expedition. The refusal of Governor Andros of
New York to surrender the fugitives seeking refuge in New York. The
fate of Monoco and old Jethro, Sagamore Sam, and Muttaump. The
practical extermination of the Indian tribes. The cost of the war.

APPENDIX   293

The war in Maine. News of the uprising. Settlements along the
coast. Tribes inhabiting the district. The first depredations. Attack
on the house of Major Philips. Captain Wincoll's victory. Squando.
Attack on Salmon Falls. Destruction of Plaisted's force. Indians
withdraw to winter quarters. Estimate of losses. Sufferings of Indians.
Armistice. Treaty of peace signed. Broken by Squando. The reason. Attack upon Falmouth. Flight of the inhabitants. Madockawando offended. John Earthy. Temporary peace through his means.
Peace terminated through an act of treachery. William Hammond
killed. Francis Card captured. Attack and capture of Fort at Arrowsick.
Captain Lake killed. Number of casualties. Indians discomfited at

ILLUSTRATIONS

KING PHILIP'S WAR

KING PHILIP'S WAR

CHAPTER I

IN the opening years of the seventeenth century, Verrazzano and Champlain in their explorations along the New England coast, found the land inhabited by a numerous and warlike population. Many a wigwam village with its waving fields of ripening maize and garden patches of beans and squash, lay stretched along the sheltered coves, and the frail barks of the Indian fishermen thronged the inlets of the shore.

Scarcely a generation later Pilgrim and Puritan searching for a habitable site found the coast almost a solitude. A pestilence more fatal to the Indian tribes than their internecine wars had swept over the land. Wigwams had disappeared. Brush and the encroaching forest were fast blotting out the once cultivated fields and the remnants of the tribes had either retired into the forests or remained too broken in power to offer resistance.[1]

In 1675 a traveler following the course of English settlements found no English habitations upon the coast of Maine east of the Penobscot and the gloom of mighty forests reigned undisturbed. The straggling cabins of Pema-

---

[1] The Bradford History, page 123, Planters Plea; Forces Hist. Tracts, Vol. II.

A

quid amidst the stumps of half-cleared pastures along the shore marked the northern limit of English civilization in the New World.

No road as yet traversed the wild hills and forests that intervened between the Connecticut and the Hudson. South and east, save where Long Island gave to the Connecticut shore a narrow strait of quiet water, spread the Atlantic, while north of the Merrimac lay a vast solitude of rugged mountains and slumbering forest reaching to the St. Lawrence. New England was isolated; and was to remain isolated for many a year to come, a fact of tremendous importance in the molding of New England character.

The political and social center of New England life was Boston, where, beyond the shore edged with docks and wharfs, winding streets and crooked alleys, followed the base of the hills with many a turn, or climbed the slope at the easiest angle. The narrow streets near the wharves were paved with cobblestones, and the shops of one or two stories, and dwellings, mostly of wood, with peaked or gambrelled roofs, presented a medley of shapes and colors.[1]

Homespun garments and cloaks of sober hue, set off with white collars, steeple-shaped hats, loose breeches tied at the knee, everywhere met the eye, the gold laced coats of the brighter colors worn by certain individuals, bespeaking a higher station or a taste for finery that the spirit of Puritanism and the statutes had not entirely eliminated.[2]

---

[1] Memorial History of Boston, Vol. I, pages 535-539.
[2] Massachusetts Colony Records, Vol. V, page 59; Connecticut Colony Records, Vol. II, page 283.

Sailors with skirts hanging to the knees, farm laborers in leather or deerskins, Indian converts in English dress from the nearby Christian villages, merchants and magistrates, crowded the narrow streets, and if it was training day the cobblestones awoke to the tread of marching companies of foot equipped with muskets and bandoliers, or rang under the hoofs of troops of horse armed with carbines, pistols, swords, helmets and cuirasses over buff coats.[1]

No card playing or drinking of healths disturbed the decorum of the taverns, arbitrary regulations which made no distinctions between self-regarded sins and crimes against society, were enforced, and liar and idler[2] were terms sufficiently defined for legal regulation.

A democratic theocracy was here building up on its own interpretations of scriptural precedents, a Biblical commonwealth, "a moral oasis in the midst of a world abandoned to sin," the Canaan of a new Israel, where personal calamities were interpreted as the direct judgment of God.

With the theocracy there was no question of non-conformity. It was their purpose, thoroughly carried out, that New England should be made altogether impossible for those who wished the privilege of thinking or acting contrary to the principles and regulations they themselves laid down as necessary for righteousness and social order. "Better tolerate hypocrites and tares than thorns and briars," affirmed Cotton.

It was not religious considerations alone, however, that

---

[1] There were four companies of foot and one of horse. Ed. Randolph to Privy Council for the Colony, Prince Soc., Hutchinson Papers, Vol. II, page 220.

[2] Connecticut Colony Records, Vol. I, page 538.

had caused the people of the old land to seek homes in New England. The profits of the seacoast fisheries and the lumber trade, the opportunity for securing large tracts of fertile land, and the inducement of copartnership in the great joint-stock trading corporations, seemingly enriched by royal charters and monopolies, encouraged many to venture their fortunes in the colonies of New England, while the ambitious saw in the new and undeveloped land that opportunity of bettering their condition denied them by the civil and ecclesiastical aristocracy of England.

From Boston as a radius, like the spokes of a wheel, bringing the outlying settlements in touch with the center, ran out those rough roads, widened Indian trails cut through the forests and made passable along the swamps by foundations of logs and earth. Many led through forests and meadows only a few miles, but several pushed their way to the farther settlements and the Connecticut Path (Bay Trail) wended westward to the towns on the Connecticut.

Within a radius of twenty miles of Boston were a score of small settlements[1] scattered along the coast or in the bottom lands of the Charles, the Concord and the Neponsit, where the soil yielded an abundance of maize,

---

[1] The settlements in all cases did not occupy the site of the present town of the same name. The more recent and larger towns have often usurped the original title, prefixing to the old settlement the designation north, south, or west. A very considerable number of these settlements were townships covering a large tract of country within whose ancient boundaries are to be found many thriving towns and villages. This is particularly the case in the country around Narragansett Bay, and a proper understanding of these changes is of importance in following the operations of the war.

vegetables and hemp, and the meadows once given over to the coarse native grass, grew thick with English hay.

All these settlements were constantly casting off new shoots and reproducing themselves in the still unsettled lands to the north and west. The wide shaded common running the length of the village, the meeting-house and school at one side facing the center; the dingy but often commodious homesteads that look out from the retirement of orchard or garden where tall well-sweeps show among the trees, are familiar to every traveler in New England. Clapboarded houses of two stories, with gambrelled roofs, looked down in 1675 upon rough cabins, surviving relics of earlier days, or vied in picturesque rivalry with the long, quick-falling roofs that cut their neighbor's rear to a single story.[1] Comfort within kept company with appearance without. The windows were paned with glass, the double or single room of the ground floor had developed into a large living room, bedroom, kitchen and pantries. Great chimney-places, with the crane and swinging kettle, swallowed six-foot logs, and high-backed settles protected the back from draughts. The twinkling bayberry dips or candlewood aided the light of blazing logs, while in the chimney corners were the seats for the children, and in the bedrooms feather beds tempered the cold of the long winter nights.

Industries were springing up on every hand and the foundation of New England as a manufacturing community had already been laid. Iron, linen, leather, and

---

[1] Description of the houses of this period will be found in Weeden's Economic and Social History of New England, Vol. I, pages 213-216; Sheldon's Deerfield, etc.

household utensils were being manufactured.[1] Each town had its saw and grist mill. Ropewalks, breweries, and, upon the coast, salt works, were springing into being, and every community, besides its common herdsmen had its artisans and carpenters, and a considerable commerce was rapidly developing with England, the West Indies, and Portugal.

West and north, beyond the bay towns, lay the frontier settlements, Lancaster, Marlboro, Groton and Billerica, beyond whose scattered farms a wilderness of mountain and forest, tenantless save for wandering bands of Indians, or some adventurous trader, extended for three hundred miles to the French settlements on the Chaudière.

Along the roads near the settlements every stage in the process of reclaiming the wilderness met the eye. By some running stream, in a gash cut in the upland wood, a cabin reared its rough features amid freshly hewed stumps; further along fire had completed the work of the axe, and in the fields crops were ripening for harvest.

The settler's habitation in these clearings, and surviving to some extent even in the older communities, were cabins of square-hewn logs,[2] made tight with clay and mortised at the joints, with irregular exterior chimneys of clay and rock rising above a roof thatched with coarse grass.[3]

Within, generally two, but sometimes a single room about eighteen feet square, occupied the first story, whose floor of beaten earth or split logs merged into the stones

---

[1] Weeden's Economic and Social History of New England, Vol. I, pages 306–308.

[2] In Dedham, ninety-five of the original log houses were standing in 1664. Worthington, page 11.

[3] Weeden's Economic and Social History, Vol. I, page 283.

of the great hearth, above whose ample breast hung the long musket, flitches of bacon, and sheaves of corn. Small windows filled with oiled paper and protected with heavy shutters, broke the expanse of wall, while at the end of the room a rough ladder led upward to the loft under the roof.

Plymouth, encompassed by sand, "the ancient mother grown old and deserted by her children," had not been favored with prosperity, and, though the oldest of New England towns, presented an aspect more rough and homely than many of the younger settlements in the neighboring colonies.

Westward, toward Narragansett Bay, lay a country of upland and shallow valleys interspersed with wastes of sandy plain, of pine barrens, wooded swamps, a sad and monotonous landscape, the far flung and scarcely populated frontier of Plymouth colony, where the traveler's horse would probably more than once come to a sudden halt, as the half-naked forms of a hunting band of Indians stole stealthily in single file across the road, leaving a vision of deerskins, of coarse black hair, and eyes full of somber fire that belied the habitual stoicism of their faces.

Along the eastern coast of Narragansett Bay lay the territory of the Pocasset and Sagkonate Indians,[1] while to the west, where a broad point of land extending from the north lifts itself in wooded slopes across the water, stood Mt. Hope, at the north end of which lay the chief village of the Wampanoags.

Across the narrow strait to the south was the island of Rhode Island, with its thriving seaport town of Newport, at that time under the political control of the Quakers,

---

[1] Sub-tribes of the Wampanoags.

and the Antinomian settlement of Portsmouth, where the followers of Mrs. Hutchinson had found the opportunity for biblical interpretation and political dissent denied them in Massachusetts.

At the base of the peninsula, in the meadows along the Warren River was Swansea, a widely scattered settlement of about forty houses on the frontier of Plymouth toward the Wampanoag country to which a bridge thrown across the river afforded access.

At the head of Narragansett Bay, on "Salt River," was Roger Williams's town of Providence, containing some six hundred inhabitants, which with the nearby settlement of old Rehoboth, Warwick, and a few scattered hamlets along the west shore of Narragansett Bay, constituted the colony of Providence Plantations, forming, with Rhode Island, that "nest of pestilential heretics" most abominable in the eyes of the Massachusetts and Plymouth theocracies, Providence supremely so, because its position at the back door of Massachusetts made it at once a sanctuary and a sally port for "every false doctrine that stingeth like a viper."

Never were such a variety of theological cultures collected in so small an area as were found to be in these settlements;[1] the Mecca of every inspired tanner, tailor and woman expounder of Holy Writ, where it was only necessary to announce that a new religion "had come to town" to make it as welcome "as in ancient days was a new philosophy in Athens."

Of all the New England colonies those of Providence

---

[1] Roger Williams himself had by this time embraced the broad liberalism of the Seekers; one who seeks but has not found any true church, ministry and sacrament.

Plantations and Rhode Island were the weakest in population, the most divided in sentiment, and the least effectively organized for the carrying out of any public policy, yet it was at this point that New England came in touch with the most powerful and independent of the Indian tribes. Massachusetts and Plymouth faced the remnants of broken tribes decimated by pestilence and awed by fear of the dreaded Mohawks, while Connecticut, marching hand in hand with the Mohegans, was served by and unconsciously served the designs of Uncas. But Providence Plantations and Rhode Island, excluded from the New England confederation, faced in their political isolation the powerful Narragansetts and the allied tribes of the Wampanoags. Hostilities, occasioned more by the faults of their neighbors than themselves, had more than once threatened, but had been dispelled by the just and conciliatory policy of Roger Williams and his friendship with the sachems of the Narragansetts.

Along the western coast, where stretches of salt marsh ran into meadows, and numerous inlets driving into the shore provided a lair for many a smuggler and pirate,[1] lay the country of the Narragansetts.

Above the navigable waters of the Connecticut River, a score of miles beyond the nearest of the three towns that constituted the heart of the colony of Connecticut, lay Springfield, with over five hundred inhabitants, its situation at the junction of the Valley Trail and the Bay Path giving it an importance in the valley second only to Hartford.

Seventeen miles to the north was the settlement of

[1] Weeden's Economic and Social History of New England, Vol. I, pages 340–345.

Northampton, while across the river in the wide expanse of meadow lay Hadley, looking out across the stream on the north at the hamlet of Hatfield.

The meadows, the sloping uplands, and the glades of the wood where the fires of many years had cleared away the undergrowth, offered good pasturage, and a rich soil for cultivation, while the broken trail fit only for riders or ox teams, the log cabins clinging closely together for protection, and the frequent Indian wigwams were unmistakable tokens of frontier life. Throughout these valley settlements the traveler met frequently with Indians; now the slovenly squaw selling her corn baskets in the villages, or harvesting the crops in the Indian fields; or the warriors themselves, relieving the long periods of indolent loafing with hunting and fishing, or a spasmodic tilling of the white man's field with an eye to the enjoyment of that firewater, which, despite the stringent regulations as to its sale, was already working the ruin of the race.

Northwest of Hadley, near the junction of the Green and Deerfield Rivers, was Deerfield, a rude community of some thirty houses, while a few miles farther up the valley, on the uplands, stood the frontier hamlet of Northfield, amid meadows and fields cleared by former generations of the Squakheags.

Here ended the Valley Trail, and the little hamlet, like a lonely sentinel, faced the encompassing wilderness—three hundred miles of tangled forest and rugged mountains, traversed only by adventurous traders or wandering bands of Indian hunters, until the French settlements, on the St. Francis, were reached.

Fifty thousand settlers,[1] almost exclusively English, of

---

[1] Poole, in his preface to the life of Johnson, quotes an address drawn

the yeomanry and middle classes, and, with the exception
of a few merchants and traders from Devon and Dorset,
representative of the Teutonic stock which predominates
in the western shores of that country, were distributed
among these towns and hamlets, their leaders were almost
all men of education, many of them graduates of the
English universities, particularly of Cambridge.

The suppression of luxury and the penalty against idleness, the supervision of social and business life, and the
geographical isolation which virtually compelled New
England to a life of its own, had already intensified in-
dividuality and concentrated the energies of its people upon
the cultivation of the land and the development of trade.

In his journey through New England the traveler would
have noticed, scattered along the inlets of the coast and
on the banks of the ponds and rivers, many an Indian
village surrounded by clearings and cultivated fields.

Arranged around a center left open for the performance
of the village games and ceremonies, were the wigwams,
constructed of saplings, which, set firmly in the ground
and bent together, were fastened at the top and covered
with bark or mats. Some were cone-shaped, holding only
a single family, while others, resembling a covered arbor,
varied in length from twenty to one hundred feet.[1]

The wigwams were pitched closely together, and the
village seldom occupied more than from three to four
acres. Within the wigwams, and arranged around the

1660 but not sent, congratulating Charles II on his accession, in the
name of 80,000 of his New England subjects; an exaggeration undoubtedly to swell its importance. Ed. Randolph gives 150,000, an enormous
exaggeration. See Hutchinson Papers, Vol. II, Prince Society.

[1] Gookin, I Mass. Hist. Soc. Coll., Vol. I, page 150.

walls, were the woven baskets that held the corn, stone or earthern household utensils, the bark pails and the low raised bunks covered with boughs and skins.[1] In the center blazed the fires, which, either for the purpose of cooking or for warmth, were kept constantly alight, and the smoke from which found its way skyward through a hole in the roof. The life of the inmates, what with the dirt, the fleas, unruly children, yelping dogs and the blinding smoke, which with every gust of wind filled the interior, was one of extreme discomfort.

These villages were seldom permanently located in one place, the scarcity of fish or game in the vicinity, or lack of shelter, of firewood against the winter, leading to a prompt removal of the population to a more favored locality.

On the top of some prominent hill commanding an extensive prospect of the surrounding country, or some swamp-surrounded hillock in the midst of the woods, offering shelter in the severe winter and a refuge in time of war, were the stockaded villages, the headquarters of the sachems.

The men were tall, straight, and admirably proportioned, but the women, short, clumsy, and seldom handsome even in youth, were quickly deprived of every trace of feminine grace by a life of hard labor and mental and moral degradation. The force of natural selection left few weaklings, but the strength of the Indian was that of the hunter rather than the sinewy power of the husbandman.

Smallpox swept their crowded and dirty villages at intervals, with fearful result, the smoke caused blindness to many, and rheumatism and diseases of the lungs were

---

[1] Gookin, I Mass. Hist. Soc. Coll., Vol. I, page 150.

common. Their medicines were concoctions made from roots and herbs, and vapor baths. But even more effective in their eyes were the gorging feasts and the incantations of the medicine men. All manual drudgery, except the cultivation of tobacco, was left to the women, who tilled the fields, cooked the food, cured and fashioned the deerskins and wove the mats, while the warriors, save when engaged in hunting, fishing, or warfare, passed their time at indolent ease,[1] gorging themselves with food, if food was plenty, or gambling with rushes, rude painted pebbles, or in field sports.

Intellectually they were well developed, but being governed by their emotions were as changeful in purpose as children. Poets and artists by nature, their artistic side was well worthy of development. Their sense of humor, it may be safely said, was more developed than their white neighbor's.

In warfare they bore themselves as did the Greek heroes of the Homeric Age, boasted of their own exploits and taunted the foe with sarcastic reflections on his skill and courage. Generosity or chivalrousness toward a discomfited enemy were qualities unknown, and, like Achilles, their triumph was never complete unless they dragged their fallen enemies in the dust, or forced upon them the bitterest dregs of humiliation.

"Their virtues, like their vices, were the product of the state of society in which they lived." Proud, dignified and courteous, they were grateful for favors, nor was kindness ever forgotten. Hospitable to friends and strangers, they were generous to improvidence, and if, despite coolness of temperament, their morals were free

---

[1] Gookin, I Mass. Hist. Soc. Coll., Vol. I, page 149.

and easy and their treatment of their women unchiv-
alrous, they were devoted fathers. Parental authority,
however, was little more than a name, and the boys particularly, were trained to independence rather than restraint.[1]

Dressed in moccasins and small breeches of tanned
deerskin, fringed and embroidered with wampum, the
body left bare above the waist was greased, and, on the
warpath, adorned with grotesque and startling designs in
black, yellow and vermilion, the totemic emblem of their
clan, the bear, wolf, or tortoise being featured on the
breast. The sachems were distinguished by heavy belts
and caps of wampum, and the Indian dandies adorned
themselves with long mantles of multi-colored feathers.
In fall and winter, mantles of fox and beaver, deer and
bearskin, with the hair turned in, were worn.

The hair was arranged in a variety of fashions according to the taste of the individual. Some shaved one side of
the head and let the hair grow long on the other. Some
left only a ridge in the middle extending from the fore-
head to the neck, which, kept short and stiffened with
paint and grease, resembled the crest of a Roman helmet,
while still others shaved all but a small tuft, the scalp-
lock, on the back of the skull.

Their diet consisted chiefly of fish, wild fowl and game,
corn, beans and squash, ground nuts and berries, prepared in a variety of ways without regard to the niceties
of life, the bones and entrails of fish and the smaller animals being seldom removed before cooking.[2]

---

[1] Gookin, Mass. Hist. Soc. Coll., Vol. I, page 149: Roger Williams'
Key, Mass. Hist. Soc. Coll., Vol. III, page 211.

[2] De Forest Hist. of the Indians of Conn. page 11. The Narragansetts were an exception in this respect. A party invited by the

Two of their dishes were early adopted by the whites. Corn mush or samp, consisting of corn meal and currants boiled with water to a paste and served plain or fried in fat. The other was succotash, made of boiled corn, beans and fat, to which fish was sometimes added. The great dish, however, in times of abundance, was a stew of all manner of flesh, fish and vegetables boiled in a common pot and thickened with powdered nuts. The clambake was a favorite way of cooking shell fish, and was early adopted by the whites.

While on the warpath or engaged in hunting, parched corn and maple sugar were carried, and on this coarse food, moistened by water from a spring, they covered long distances. Against the winter they provided stores of parched corn, maize and dried fish, stored in pits (the so-called Indian barns) dug in the slope of a hill and covered with mats and earth.

The Indian mind rarely grasped the essential elements of the Christian faith. Their own gods were not moral preceptors but mere dispensers of good or evil fortune, the last much more to be appeased and regarded than the spirit naturally benign.[1]

Every inanimate as well as animate thing had its spirit. There was the spirit of the deep woods and the flowing river; the spirit of the waterfall, of fire, of cold, of the sea and the tempest.

Said an Indian to Roger Williams, "Fire comes out of the cold stone, it saves us from dying of hunger; if a

---

Nipmucks to attend a feast of lampreys were murdered by their hosts for expressing disgust at the manner of cooking. De Forest's Indians of Conn., page 267.

[1] Gookin, Mass. Hist. Soc. Coll., Vol. I, page 154.

single spark falls in the dry wood it consumes the whole
country. Can anything which is so powerful be anything but a deity?"[1]

They believed in the immortality of the soul which
found beyond the grave a land lying in the southwest[2]
flowing with milk and honey, bright with sunshine, and
where neither disease, old age, nor want were known.

Their Government was monarchial from father to son;
but the mother must be noble, for if the mother is noble
the son is at least half noble. If the mother is ignoble,
the son may not have a drop of noble blood in him.

At the head was the sachem. Attending him, a council of sagamores, distinguished for warlike deeds or wis-
dom. The authority of the sachems was both loose and
strong, as was natural in a state of society where custom
and tradition take the place of law.

The Indian tribes were divided into a number of great
clans or families, each distinguished by a symbolic totem,
like the bear, the wolf, the tortoise. Each clan had its
separate ward in the village, and its warriors marched
together on the warpath. All members of the totemic
clan were as brothers and sisters,—to injure one was to
injure all, but intermarriage was forbidden.

White law demands that brother shall give evidence
against brother in behalf of the State, but the totemic
law exalted the individual. Understanding this we shall
immediately recognize the fundamental divergence of the

---

[1] Roger Williams' Key, Mass. Hist. Soc. Coll., Vol. II, pages 226–229.
[2] Roger Williams' Key, Mass. Hist. Soc. Coll., Vol. III, page 218.
Heaven was in the southwest because the wind from that quarter was
the warmest and pleasantest that blows, and brings fair weather.

savage and civilized points of view. The importance, therefore, of the individual under the totemic system, created among the Indians a closely knit democracy in which all were essentially equal. Insults were never borne except by those too physically weak to revenge them, and the offensive air of superiority assumed by the English settlers stung the Indians to the quick.

Southern New England in the seventeenth century was occupied by five great agricultural tribes of the generic race of the Algonquins, in numbers and lands the greatest of the Indian races of North America, but far inferior in political and military organization to the Five Nations, or Iroquois confederacy, whose hand lay heavy on all the tribes from Hudson Bay to Tennessee.

Of the New England Indians the Massachusetts were broken, enfeebled and largely converted to Christianity, and occupied the country around the Bay towns, many of them living in the stockaded villages[1] established by the Rev. John Eliot.

Along the east coast of Narragansett Bay were the Wampanoags, considerably reduced by pestilence from their former strength when their confederacy comprised the whole Plymouth peninsula, but still numbering about five hundred warriors, while along the west shore of the Bay, and extending to the Pawcatuck River, lay the territory of the formidable Narragansetts who were able to bring about a thousand warriors into the field.[2]

Between the Connecticut River and the Thames were the scattered tribes of the old Pequot confederacy, on whose ruins, Uncas, the son-in-law of the Pequot

---

[1] Gookin, Mass. Hist. Soc. Coll., Vol. I, page 180.
[2] Gookin, Mass. Hist. Soc. Coll., Vol. I, pages 147–148.

B

sachem, Sassacus, had built up the supremacy of the Mohegans.[1]

From Northfield, and extending south and east into Connecticut and Providence Plantations (Rhode Island), were the Nipmucks, or Nipnets (fresh water Indians), whose numerous villages supplied about a thousand warriors, Nashaways, Squakheags, Pocumtucks, Nonotucks, Agawams and Quabaugs.

Each village was politically independent, and the bonds of the old confederacy which had once loosely united them, had completely broken; indeed, even among the Narragansetts, the political adhesion of the different tribal units were falling apart and each local Sagamore had begun to act his own pleasure without reference to his sachem.

Along Cape Cod were the Nausets who formerly owed fealty to the Wampanoags, but whose conversion to Christianity had made them dependent upon the English. They probably numbered less than four hundred men, women, and children. The Pennacooks, tributary to the Nipmucks, held the country along the banks of the Merrimac in northeastern Massachusetts and New Hampshire, while to the east, between the Piscataqua and the Kennebec and stretching northward into Canada were the wandering hunting tribes of the Abenakis or Tarratines. The boundaries of the lands of all these tribes were not set, but overlapped, and the semi if not complete independence of the petty sachem of each village and the lack of political cohesion into which the tribes had fallen, present a confusion of village communities and tribes which it is impossible to disentangle and reduce to accuracy.

[1] De Forest's Indians of Connecticut, page 62.

CHAPTER II

THE intercourse between the Indians and the English had been advantageous to both. The Indians had taught the early settlers to enrich their fields with fish and to raise corn, and had during almost the whole of the first generation been the actual producers of food-stuffs. By the time the industry and improved agricultural methods of the settlers had freed them from this form of dependence, the increased demand for furs still held the Indian temporarily on an economic level with his white neighbor, for furs, fish and lumber were the means by which the colonists made return to the joint-stock corporations and paid for their imports.

The economic relation between the races can be clearly traced by the rise and fall of the value of wampum. Thirty years after the landing of the Pilgrims it had become the accepted currency of New England.[1] It figures in old wills in place of coin. It was made by law legal currency[2] and colonial records are full of acts regulating its value.

About 1662 the fur trade had largely declined and fish had become the great article of export. Silver received from the Indies and Europe in exchange for fish and

---

[1] Weeden, Vol. I, pages 39–44. Wampum made from the whelk shell pierced and polished (black double the value of white), was not only a medium of exchange, but served as a recalling to memory of events, and as an ornament.

[2] Connecticut Colony Records (1649), Vol. I, pages 179, 546.

lumber had come into the colonies, and between 1662 and 1670 wampum gradually ceased to be the medium of exchange. When the Indian had ceased to be either a producer of food or a supplier of furs, the old economic relations perished. No longer necessary to the English he was soon regarded by them as an encumbrance.

The Indian had both profited and been injured by his contact with the English. Civilization increased his comforts but degraded him. The white man's blanket or the gun which made hunting easy, and in the handling of which he early became an expert, had become necessities. He had learned better methods of agriculture and the use of the domestic cattle, while the vicinity of the settlements to the Indian villages mitigated the periodical famines which had fallen so often upon the tribes during the hard New England winters.

The Indian, always an opportunist, was quick to absorb and exaggerate in himself all the vices of the white man, unchecked by religious scruples or civil authority. Gookin draws the sad picture of the general effect of their contact with civilization: "And though all strong drink is prohibited to be sold . . . yet some ill-disposed people, for filthy lucre's sake, do sell unto the Indians secretly, whereby they are made drunk very often, and being drunk they are many times outrageous and mad. This beastly sin of drunkenness could not be charged upon the Indians before . . . the Christian nations came to dwell in America, which nations, especially the English in New England, have cause to be greatly humbled before God."[1]

---

[1] Gookin, Mass. Hist. Soc. Coll., Vol. I, page 151.

The conduct of the New England settlers and the authorities was marked by an evident intention of just dealing. The sale of lands was regulated by law, but unfortunately the Indian's idea of what he sold and the white man's idea of what was bought were entirely at variance. The result was the usual one, the stronger interpreted from its own point of view, and, in the main, to its own satisfaction. The Indian believed that the white man would make such use of the land as he himself made of it; he made free and lavish gifts of it on this account, and the English authorities in many respects were more careful of Indian rights of possession than the Indian himself. Sometimes its transfer was under terms that "whenever the Indian shall remove from a certain place, then and thenceforth the aforesaid settlers shall enter upon the same as their proper right and interest, to them, their heirs and assigns."[1] An elastic deed. Some deeds gave the right to cut grass and graze stock on land not planted by the Indians, while in other cases the Indians retained for themselves the privilege of hunting, fishing, and gathering nuts. While "the Indian little appreciated the value of land until he felt the pressing want of it," there is no doubt but that the English settler was greedy, for "land is one of the Gods of New England, of which the living and most high Eternal" will punish the transgressor, wrote Roger Williams.[2]

It is not always the thing itself as the way a thing is done that leaves the most abiding sense of injustice and resentment behind it, and the provocative attitude, the

---

[1] Baylie's Mem. of Plymouth Col., Vol. II, page 234.

[2] Letter of Roger Williams to Major Mason. Rhode Island Hist. Soc. Coll., Vol. III, page 162.

rough hand and the constant petty interferences in their most trivial affairs, did more to ultimately drive the Indians into hostility than the loss of landed possessions; yet the relations as a whole for many years after the destruction of the Pequots, were friendly. The Indian greeting, "What cheer, friend?" was familiar in every village. The Indian boys and the settler's children played in the village streets, and the squaws, during certain seasons, stored their valuables in the settler's house. "We have found the Indians very faithful to their covenants of peace," wrote Edward Winslow.

Little by little, however, the two races were beginning to approach the narrow causeway where one would have to give way before the other. The point of view of the two races was too far apart for them ever to agree, and, grounded in suspicion, irreconcilable causes, both social and economic, were hurling them into collision. The differences over land have, as a rule, been given too much importance, though the land question was a contributory cause to a growing estrangement, for when the Indian saw that things which, in his own possession, were of little value, as soon as they were transferred to the Englishmen became valuable, it led him naturally to the embittered conclusion, "It is the Indian's property in the white man's hands that gives the white man importance, makes him arrogant and covetous, and he despises the Indian as soon as his ends are met and the Indian has no more to part with."

The Puritan was not of a character, either individually or collectively, with whom men of any other race could be expected to maintain harmonious relations. Amiability was not one of his characteristics, and he was totally lacking in that great gift of humor so essential to friendly association and broad understanding, and, lacking it, he remained devoid of that sympathetic temper necessary to live at peace with and to understand the nature of the savage, so closely akin to that of a child.

The French cherished the Indian and made the fierce hunting tribes of New France an instrument in the building up of French power; the English, failing to make an agricultural laborer out of the more pliable New England Indian, treated him with indifference or contempt and turned him into a sullen enemy.

The narrow determination to regulate the actions of others by their own ideas of what was well ordered led the authorities to interfere even in the most trivial affairs of the tribes and individuals, regardless of Indian traditions and customs, held him to a strict observance of their laws, and constantly punished him for offenses he did not understand.[1] Cotton Mather admirably sums up the general attitude of the English towards the Indians by the unconscious confession, "The heathen people, *whose land the Lord* God has given to us for a rightful possession, have at sundry times been plotting mischievous devises against that part of the English Israel."

Among the causes which inflamed the Indian mind one of the most potent was the well-meant attempt of the just-minded Eliot, and others,[2] to convert them to Chris-

---

[1] We read in the Connecticut Records of one fined forty shillings for breach of the peace in traveling from Springfield to Hartford on Sunday; another for stealing apples and firing a gun on Sunday.

[2] Rev. John Eliot, of Roxbury in 1604, was born at Nazing, England. He matriculated as a pensioner of Jesus College, Cambridge, where he took his degree of A. B. He came in the *Lion* to Boston, 1631, and

tianity. It was customary among the Indians to augment their numbers by the adoption of individuals and even of smaller tribes. Whoever had lost a brother, son or husband, possessed the right, sanctioned by immemorial usage, of extending mercy to a prisoner of war by adopting him. The Christianizing of these Indians therefore, when associated with their separate settlements, assumed a sinister significance, and appeared to the Indian as a form of adoption devised to weaken and break up their tribal relations, while it strengthened the whites. Nor did the English, actuated by a sincere desire to benefit and uplift their neighbors, fail to see a material advantage in that very possibility which so excited the apprehension of the Indians.

The broken tribes around the Bay and on the Cape received Christianity as a passport to the white man's favor, but the others would have none of it. Philip told Roger Williams he cared no more for Christianity than the button on his coat, while Ninigret told those who came to him that "as long as the English could not agree as to what was religion, among themselves, it ill became them to teach others." Even Uncas, subservient in all else, desired no missionaries among his people.

They listened courteously. "It is good for the white man, but we are another people with different customs," they said.

In Massachusetts, fourteen villages, many of them stockaded, told the success of Eliot's efforts among the broken tribes of the Massachusetts and the Nipmucks,

---

was settled as a teacher, and afterwards pastor, in the Roxbury church. He labored for forty years to spread among the aborigines the sentiments, in some degree, of his religion. He died May 20, 1690.—Savage.

while other villages of converts, built up by Mayhew[1] and Bourne,[2] were to be found within the jurisdiction of Plymouth colony and at Martha's Vineyard and Nantucket.

Many of these Christian Indians did credit to their professions, but there were some among the independent tribes who curried favor by playing the rôle of the informer upon the actions of their own people, or took advantage of their position as Christian protéges to escape the consequences of their own evil behavior,[3] and in the frequent bickerings between the Indians on the one hand and the traders on the other, punishment was often meted out with little regard to the source from whence the provocation came.

Traders of the stamp of Stone [4] and Oldham [5] probably

---

[1] Thomas Mayhew, Watertown, born 1591, came to this country in 1631. He was a merchant, active in trade, first at Medford and afterwards at Watertown, but in 1647 removed to Martha's Vineyard where he became a preacher to the Indians and labored in this field more than thirty-three years. He died in 1681 and his work was continued by several generations of his descendants.—Savage.

[2] Richard Bourne of Lynn, 1637, removed to Sandwich and was the first instructor of the Indians at Marshpee, beginning in 1658. He died in 1682.—Savage.

[3] British State Papers, 1665, No. 63: Report of King's Commissioners to the Colonies.

[4] John Stone, captain of a trading vessel from Virginia, was a man of violent temper and intemperate habits. September 3, 1633, he was forbidden by the General Court of Massachusetts to come again within the jurisdiction under penalty of death, "for his outrage committed in confronting authority, abusing Mr. Ludlowe both in words and behavior," etc. Shortly after, he entered the Connecticut River with his vessel, and, being in need of a pilot seized two Pequot Indians, whom he bound and in this condition compelled them to take his vessel to the point he desired to reach. Having been watched through this proceeding by other Indians, that night, when all were asleep, they entered the ship and murdered Stone and his comrades.

[5] John Oldham came to Plymouth in the *Ann* in 1623. He shortly

drew their fate upon themselves by their dishonest and treacherous conduct, and the Pilgrims had punished with death the Indians who had resented the pilfering and the aggressive insolence of Walton's profligate colony at Weymouth. The Puritan temper had not mellowed in fifty years; tares had been mixed with the wheat among the later arrivals and the civil and religious conflict in England and the ecclesiastical quarrels in the colonies had made them more intolerant among themselves. That a serious outbreak had been postponed for so many years was due to the influence of Massasoit, Canonicus[1] and Roger Williams, the memory of the dire fate of the Pequots, the economic benefits of the trade carried on between them and that traditional enmity among the tribes which made concerted action impossible.

Of the sachems of New England, Uncas,[2] the Mohegan,

---

after gave offense through the expression of his religious opinions and was driven to Nantasket and thence went with Roger Conant to Cape Ann. He returned to Plymouth in 1628 and became reconciled with the government and was made freeman May 18, 1631. He removed to Watertown and engaged actively in trade with the Indians, chiefly by means of his shallop, upon which he was killed by the natives near Manisses (Block Island) in July, 1636.

[1] Canonicus, the great sachem of the Narragansetts, was contemporary with Miantonomah who was his nephew. He sold the island of Rhode Island to Roger Williams and others, and was the firm friend of Williams. At the time of the Pequot war, great pains were taken to strengthen the friendship between this sachem and the English. "June 4, 1647. Canonicus, the great sachem of the Narragansetts died, a very old man."—Drake's Book of the Indians.

[2] Uncas was born in the Pequot settlement in Connecticut about 1588. He was Pequot by birth but by reason of rebellion against his chief, Sassacus, he was banished from the tribe, and, gathering about him a band of malcontents, became their head, calling his followers Mohegans, after an ancient name of the Pequot tribe. His lands lay to the north

and Canonicus, who divided the power and sachemship of the Narragansetts with Miantonomah, were the only ones to recognize the full meaning of the English settlements in relation to the fate of their own people. Uncas made use of them to build up his power; Canonicus sought to play off the Dutch against the English and to keep the peace, whereas Massasoit, a thoroughgoing opportunist, welcomed them for the peace they enforced upon his neighbors, the Narragansetts.

In the Mohegans and their chief, Uncas, the Connecticut colony had a constant ally who knew how to make his personal quarrels appear in the eyes of the authorities as drawn upon himself solely as their friend. With rare foresight he had recognized the possibilities of a policy based on an alliance with the whites. Fearless and subtle, uniting in a rare degree the character of statesman and warrior, he had built up the power of the Mohegans on the ruins of the Pequot confederacy, and while constantly provoking the other tribes by his aggressions, he was never at a loss to prove himself the injured party to the satisfaction of his Connecticut allies. However valuable in its results to the Connecticut settlers, this alliance was to be one of the most toward circumstances in destroying the confidence of the tribes in the good faith and justice of the English.

So important is this fact that some explanation of the cause is necessary. A quarrel between the Mohegans

---

and east of Lyme. In the expedition against the Pequots commanded by Captain John Mason, Uncas with his followers accompanied him as allies.

and Narragansetts, arising originally over a division of the Pequot captives on the destruction of that tribe, soon assumed the character of a personal vendetta between Uncas and Miantonomah,[1] and the ears of the authorities were clamorously assailed by their conflicting claims and accusations.

So numerous were the complaints and so constantly did hostilities threaten, that the commissioners of the colonies compelled both sachems to present themselves at Hartford, September 21, 1638, and to enter upon what was known as the tripartite treaty.[2]

"I perceive you have received many accusations and hard conceits of this poor native Miantonomah,"[3] wrote Roger Williams to Governor Winthrop.

In 1640, Miantonomah was accused of conspiring with the Mohawks, and, obeying the orders of Governor Thomas Dudley, presented himself at Boston, where, in punishment for objecting to a Pequot as an interpreter, he was treated as an ill-behaved child. "We would show him no countenance nor admit him to dine at our table as formerly he had done, until he had acknowledged his

---

[1] Miantonomah, sachem of the Narragansetts, was the nephew of Canonicus and associated with him in the government of the tribe, succeeding to full authority in 1636, and from him and his uncle, Roger Williams received the deed to land for his colony at the head of Narragansett Bay.

[2] Its principal clause was as follows:

"If there fall out injuries and wrongs, each to the other or their men, they shall not presently revenge it, but they are to appeal to the English and they are to decide the same, and if one or the other shall refuse to do it, it shall be lawful for the English to compel him and take part if they see cause against the obstinate or refusing party."—R. I. Hist. Soc. Coll., Vol. III, page 177.

[3] Mass. Hist. Soc. Coll. 3, Vol. I, page 166.

failing." His rebuke,—"When your people come to me they are permitted to use their own fashions and I expect the same liberty when I come to you," should have shamed them into courtesy. Such childish treatment of a powerful sachem was an act of inexcusable folly. The charge was easily refuted and Miantonomah allowed to return home.

He continued, however, to be regarded with suspicion, and two years later a widespread belief that he was planning a general conspiracy caused him to be again summoned to Boston.[1]

Clothed in his robes of state, he made his defense before the grim elders of New England so successfully that Governor Winthrop wrote of him as having "shown good understanding in the principles of justice and equity, and to have accommodated himself to our understanding."[2] Most of the charges against the Narragansetts were preferred by Connecticut, and display the deft touch of Uncas turning his influence with the Connecticut authorities to good account.[3] Uncas had cause to fear his rival; it was six of one and half a dozen of the other so far as the desire to injure each other was concerned. That the Massachusetts authorities were not blinded is made evident by their refusal to assent to the request of Connecticut that war be declared against Miantonomah. "All this might have come out of the enmity of Miantonomah and Uncas, who continually sought to discredit each other[4] . . ." and they (Connecticut) were not pleased

---

[1] Winthrop, Vol. II, page 81.
[2] *Ibid.*, page 81.
[3] *Ibid.*, page 82.
[4] *Ibid.*, page 80.

with Massachusetts for refusing, was the comment of Winthrop.[1]

The next year, unfortunately for himself, the Narragansett, by selling the Shawamut peninsula to Samuel Gorton,[2] that "arch heretic, beast and miscreant, whose spirit was struck dumb with blasphemies and insolences," involved himself in the quarrel between Massachusetts and the Gortonists.[3]

Massachusetts, then engaged "in drawing in the last of those parts who now live under another government, but grow very offensive," greatly desired the acquisition of the territory of Narragansett Bay. Urged by the enemies of Gorton, Pumham, the local sachem, laid claim to the ownership of Shawamut and pleaded the inability of Miantonomah and Canonicus to give valid title to

---

[1] Winthrop II., page 83.

[2] Samuel Gorton, born in Gorton, England, about 1600, settled in Boston in 1636. He remained there until religious disputes drove him to Plymouth, where he fared still worse, being fined, imprisoned, and finally expelled. No better fate was in store for him at Newport, where he was publicly whipped, and he moved from place to place until 1642 when he bought lands at Shawamut on the west side of Narragansett Bay. His title to this was disputed by some of the Indians and on the appeal to the authorities at Boston, a military force was sent to arrest him and with ten of his followers he was taken to Boston and tried as "damnable heretics," sentenced to imprisonment and hard labor in irons. After his release in 1644, Gorton went to England to obtain redress and having procured from the Earl of Warwick an order that he should be allowed the peaceable possession of his lands at Shawamut, he returned to his colony in 1648 and renamed it Warwick in honor of the earl. Gorton's religious beliefs were very peculiar, but the sect he founded survived him for about one hundred years. He has been ably defended by the late Chief Justice Brayton of the Rhode Island Supreme Court. Rhode Island Hist. Tracts, No. 17.

[3] Winthrop, Vol. II, page 120.

the lands they had sold.[1] This scheme was successful, and a syndicate composed of Benedict Arnold[2] and other citizens[3] of Rhode Island, standing ready to purchase the land in question it was conveyed to them by Pumham and Sacononoco, who at once offered their allegiance to the Massachusetts colony.

Miantonomah summoned to Boston, could not prove, in the opinion of the authorities, his paramountcy over Pumham and Sacononoco, despite the declaration of Roger Williams, that the authority of the Narragansett sachems over the lands and chiefs in question, had existed as far back as the settlement of Plymouth.

Miantonomah on his return home, learning that one of his subordinates, Sequassen, had been roughly handled by Uncas, took up the quarrel and complaining to Connecticut, received for answer that "the English had no hand in it." He next turned to Massachusetts and "was desirous to know if we would not be offended if he made war upon Uncas." To which Winthrop replied: "If Uncas had done him or his friends harm and would not

---

[1] Clarence S. Brigham in "State of Rhode Island and Providence Plantations," Vol. I, pages 35, 36.

[2] Benedict Arnold was born in England, December 21, 1615. In 1663 he was made by the Royal Charter President of the Rhode Island colony and was continued in this office for eight years. He was reported to be the wealthiest man in the colony. About 1676 he built the "old mill" still standing at Newport, about which traditions of a Norse origin have been thrown. He died in 1678.

[3] The Shawamut lands were held by the Arnold coterie for some years, when, circumstances rendering it desirable for Arnold to again own fealty to Rhode Island, by a petition of his party to the authorities they were granted a discharge from the Massachusetts jurisdiction and Shawamut once again became Rhode Island territory.

give satisfaction, we shall leave him to take his own course."[1]

Believing that he had complied with the terms of the tripartite treaty and was free to make war, he marched upon Uncas, met his surprised rival, who could rally but an inferior force, on the outskirts of the town of Norwich. Uncas, stepping out from the lines, engaged Miantonomah in a parley and challenged him to decide the quarrel by personal combat. On the challenge being refused, in accord with a previously arranged plan, he threw himself on the ground, and his warriors, firing over his body, charged and routed the surprised Narragansetts. In the pursuit, Miantonomah, hampered by a coat of mail, said to have been the gift of Samuel Gorton, was captured.

In accordance with Indian usage his life was forfeited, but Uncas, not knowing how Connecticut and Massachusetts would regard such an act, puzzled by the threat of Gorton forbidding him to injure his captive, and dreading to embroil himself with the Narragansetts unless assured of support, carried his prisoner to Hartford.

On the appeal of Miantonomah, the commissioners of the colonies, brushing aside the communications that had passed between Miantonomah and both Connecticut and Massachusetts, whereby they had themselves failed in their duty under the tripartite treaty, found that the Narragansetts had violated its terms by attacking Uncas suddenly "without denouncing war." Finally, deciding that, though it was not safe to set him at liberty, there was not sufficient ground to put him to death, they turned over

---

[1] Winthrop, Vol. II, page 129.

the matter for advice to a convocation of ministers[1] then in assembly at Boston, five of whose number as a committee, advised that "Uncas, the Englishman's friend, could not be safe while Miantonomah lived, and that he, Uncas, might justly put such a fierce and bloodthirsty enemy to death."

The commissioners therefore ordered Miantonomah to be turned over to Uncas for execution, but if Uncas refused to kill him he was to be sent to Boston by water.[2]

Roger Williams was at this time in England and unable to speak in behalf of the unfortunate sachem, and Uncas, attended by a guard of musketeers, took his captive to Windsor[3] where one of the Mohegans, stepping behind the prisoner, clove his skull with a tomahawk.

---

[1] "Who always to our magistrates
Must be the eyes to see."
  Peter Folger. Looking glass for the times. (About 1670).

[2] The details as to Miantonomah and the action of the commissioners will be found in Hazzard State Papers, Vol. II, page 6; Winthrop, Vol. II, page 131. Acts of the Commissioners of the United Colonies. Plymouth Colony Records, Vol. IX, page 10.

[3] Trumbull, says Norwich, accepted the local tradition. Governor Winthrop of Massachusetts, however gives a very different spot as the place of Miantonomah's execution. When the decision to put him to death had been reached, the commissioners directed that Uncas should conduct his captive "Into the next part of his own government, and there put him to death, provided that some discreet and faithful person of the English accompany them and see the execution, for our more full satisfaction." Uncas promptly obeyed the directions given, taking with him two Hartford men as witnesses. Winthrop continues: "Taking Miantonomah along with him, in the way between Hartford and Windsor, (where Onkus hath some men dwell) Onkus' brother, following after Miantonomah, clave the head with a hatchet." Winthrop who records the event understood, evidently, that the execution took place in this Mohegan claim between Hartford and Windsor, that is, the present East Hartford and East Windsor, and he probably derived his informa-

C

The commissioners undoubtedly found themselves on the horns of a dilemma. Uncas enjoyed the right conferred on a conqueror by Indian usage, of putting his captive to death, but such a course, unsupported by the English, was dangerous in view of the numerical superiority of the Narragansetts.

To free Miantonomah, however, was to take sides against Uncas, and court a continuance of the old quarrel. Connecticut was insistent that their ally should be protected from Miantonomah, and in fact the alliance of the Mohegans seemed more valuable to both Connecticut and Massachusetts than that of the more distant Narragansetts, yet, Roger Williams had informed the general court of Massachusetts some years before, "the Narragansetts have been true in all of the Pequot wars to you. . . . I cannot learn that ever it pleased the Lord to let the Narragansetts stain their hands with any English blood."[1]

The necessity of defending Uncas, whom they believed endangered by Miantonomah's intrigues, the general suspicion that the Narragansetts were dangerous to the peace of New England, were undoubtedly the most potent factors

---

tion from the Englishmen that were designated to witness the act. Miss Frances M. Caulkins, the historian of Norwich, thinks that tradition has become confused between the place of Miantonomah's capture on "Sachem's Plain" near the Shetucket, and the place of his execution, but that the contemporary account of Governor Winthrop must be reliable. The narrative of Winthrop is explicit in stating that Uncas led his captive to this district, and that he was executed suddenly on the way, probably as soon as they had passed the English boundary. Caulkin's History of Norwich, pages 34-38; Winthrop's History of New England, Vol. II, page 134; Stiles' History of Windsor, Vol. I, page 118.

[1] Roger Williams to General Court of Massachusetts. R. I. Hist. Soc. Coll., Vol. III, pages 156, 157.

in deciding the fate of the Narragansett sachem. There is little doubt but that his relations with Gorton weighed heavily in the balance against him. Not only do almost all the Rhode Island historians take this view, but it is supported by the researches of Judge Savage,[1] and by such careful collaborators as Drake and Bodge.

The condemnation and execution of Miantonomah was a clerico-judicial murder.[2] He was judged and condemned to death by the white allies of Uncas. On that day confidence in the white man's justice received its death blow among the Narragansetts who, impotent to save or revenge, could only nourish their wrath with all the passionate remembrance of Indian nature; nor did it pass without notice among the other tribes that Uncas, the hated of all nations had his lips to the ear of the English, who heard no other voice than his.

---

[1] Winthrop's Hist. of New England, Vol. II, page 133; Judge Savage note with reference to Governor Stephen Hopkins (1765), Second Mass. Hist. Soc. Coll., Vol. IX, page 202.

[2] Means would have been found for his preservation had he not encouraged the sale of Shawamut to Gorton and his heterodox associates. —Judge Savage (Winthrop's History).

All that he and old Canonicus had ever done for the English was made but as dust in the balance by his countenance of Gorton. Reichman's Rhode Island, Vol. I, page 191.

CHAPTER III

IN 1662, Massasoit,[1] Sachem of the Wampanoags, the old and faithful friend of the Pilgrims, was gathered to his rest. Forty-one years had passed since he had drunk the great draught of rum that had made him sweat all over and had pledged himself to peace and friendship. Two sons survived him, Wamsutta and Metacom, who, having declared their friendship for the English, had asked that English names be given them, and received those of the Greek conquerors, Alexander and Philip.

The eldest, Alexander, became sachem in the place of his father. He was naturally inclined to continue the policy established by Massasoit towards the English but circumstances, not the least of which was his constant opposition to all attempts to Christianize the Wampanoags, made a continuance of the old relations difficult.

Since the economic dependence of the whites upon the Indians had ceased, the two races had been steadily drifting apart. The Wampanoags, who in former years had exercised sovereignty over the territory stretching south from Plymouth and the head of Narragansett Bay, saw

---

[1] Massasoit, chief of the Wampanoag tribe, was born about 1580. This tribe occupied the country in what is now Massachusetts, between the ocean and Narragansett Bay. It is supposed that the tribe was once numerous but before the landing of the Pilgrims it had been greatly reduced by disease. The residence of Massasoit was at Sowams upon what is now the Warren River. Morton says "he was a very lusty man in his best years, an able body, grave of countenance and spare of speech."

the ruin of their confederacy and power in the gradual
Christianizing of the kindred tribes along Cape Cod,
while they themselves were being slowly separated and
crowded into the peninsulas.

Complaints of trespass, the loss of lands, the effect of
which they had begun to realize, and a feeling of resentment at the constant interference of the English with
their internal affairs, had sown a sullen bitterness in the
Indian breast, which had troubled the last years of Massasoit.

Reports of the unrest and resentment of the Wampanoags, which lost nothing in the telling, were not long in
reaching the ears of the authorities at Boston and Plymouth, borne on the tongues of Christian protéges and
spies, and enhanced whenever the quarrels of the tribes
or chiefs led to mutual accusations of conspiracy in the
endeavor to win the assistance of the English.

Rumors from Boston of his unfriendliness and of negotiations on his part for an alliance with the Narragansetts,
soon found credence in Plymouth, and Alexander was
summoned to appear before the court and explain his
intention. On his failure to attend, an armed force under Major Winslow[1] and Major Bradford was sent to
compel[2] his compliance. Winslow took only ten men,

---

[1] Josiah Winslow of Marshfield, was the son of Governor Edward,
and was born in Plymouth in 1629. He was commissioner of the colonies for thirteen years, was deputy, and many years assistant, till 1673,
when he was elected Governor of Plymouth and held that office until
his death.—Gen. Register, Vol. IV, page 299.

[2] Hubbard says that Major Bradford and his force seized the arms of
the Indians to prevent resistance and compelled Alexander to accompany
them to Plymouth at the muzzle of their guns. We have preferred the
account given in a letter by John Cotton to Increase Mather, who quotes

expecting to recruit more from the towns on the way, but midway between Plymouth and Bridgewater, observing a hunting lodge on Monponsit Pond they rode up to it and found it occupied by Alexander and a number of his men and women. He agreed to return with them giving as his reason for lack of promptness that he had wished first to confer with a friend, Mr. Willet,[1] who was absent in New York.

His explanation seems to have been satisfactory, but, seized with a fever while staying at Major Josiah Winslow's house at Marshfield, he was sent home at his own request and died during the journey, 1662, his sudden death giving birth to a belief among the Indians of his having been poisoned.

His brother Philip, then about twenty-three years of age and by nature less inclined than his brother to accept a position of dependence, succeeded him. A policy of conciliation might have won his good will, but the constant nagging to which he was subjected increased his resentment and nurtured in him a sullen distrust.

Summoned to Plymouth at the beginning of his sachemship, he had renewed the old covenant of peace and friendship. Five years later one of his own subjects accused him of a willingness to join the Dutch and French in order to recover his lands and enrich himself with the goods of the English.[2]

Philip declared the story was a fabrication of Ninigret,[3]

---

the testimony of Major Bradford.—Mass. Hist. Soc. Coll., Vol. VIII, page 233, Fourth Series.

[1] Captain Thomas Willet of Wannamoiset (Riverside, R. I.), afterwards first English Mayor of New York.

[2] Plymouth Records, Vol. IV, pages 151, 164-166.

[3] Ninigret was sachem of the Niantics, a tribe of the Narragansetts

sachem of the Niantics. Both chiefs were consequently summoned to appear at Rehoboth before two commissioners appointed by Plymouth, and though the tale-bearer boldly repeated his accusations, Philip was not held, and at the next meeting of the court the arms he had surrendered were returned to him. In 1669, Governor Lovelace of New York warned Rhode Island that Philip was carrying on an intrigue with Ninigret, but the Niantic cleared both Philip and himself of the charge.[1] Most of these accusations seem to have been based on suspicions inspired by Uncas, and evidence of a trust-worthy character is lacking.

The attitude and measures of Plymouth throughout these transactions and those following were arbitrary and high-handed and were admirably adapted to bring about the very state of affairs they were intended to forestall. Three years later the Plymouth authorities, hearing of warlike preparations among the Wampanoags, the sharpening of hatchets, "the repairing of guns, suspicious assemblings and impertinent bearing towards Englishmen in divers parts of the country," called peremptorily upon Philip to appear before them. Philip was at first uncompromising in his refusal. He demanded hostages as a guarantee for his own safety and even requested that Governor Prince[2] should come to him; finally, on Richard

---

whose principal residence was at Wekapaug, now Westerly, R. I. He was cousin to Miantonomah. At the time of Philip's war he was an old man and took no part in the hostilities, but always professed friendship for the English.

[1] Rhode Island Records, Vol. II, pages 263, 267, 284.

[2] Governor Thomas Prince (Prence) was born in England in 1601. He came to New England, and settled in Duxbury about 1634, but a year previous to that time he was appointed "master" of a trading house

Williams and James Brown remaining as hostages Philip consented to go, but on approaching Taunton, and noting military preparations on the part of the English, he took up his position near a mill on the outskirts with a large and well-armed following, but sent no messengers into the town. The commissioners sent from Massachusetts, William Davis, William Hudson and Thomas Brattle, to mediate between the parties, however, went out to meet him and, after an extended conference, induced him to meet Governor Prince and the Plymouth authorities on the 12th of April, 1671. On that date Philip and his chiefs entered the church at Taunton. "Both parties were armed: the Indians with their faces and bodies painted after their savage manner, with their long bows and quivers of arrows at their backs, with here and there a gun in the hands of those best skilled in the use of them; the English in the Cromwellian habit, slouched hats with broad brims, bandoliers, cuirasses, long swords and unwieldy guns."

Charged with warlike designs, the Wampanoag declared that his preparations were made against the Narragansetts and were entirely defensive, thereby strengthening the suspicions against him, as his relations with the Narragansetts were believed to be friendly.

After a long conference, a partial confession as to his failings and "naughtiness" was wrung from him and he agreed to renew the old covenant of peace and to surrender all firearms into the custody of the English so long

-----

then established near Sowams, the home of Massasoit. He was several times chosen Governor and occupied that office at the time of his death, March 29, 1673.

as any suspicion against him remained.[1] This pledge was valueless; he could have no intention of performing it and placing himself entirely at the mercy of the English, and he could not have carried out such a measure if he had desired. Muskets had become a necessity to the Indian and as the laws in the different colonies against the selling of arms had been gradually relaxed, and in Plymouth had been abolished altogether, the Indians had come in possession of large numbers and regarded them as the most valuable and necessary of their possessions. It is not surprising, therefore, that few arms were handed over; the council took measures to enforce compliance. The arms of the Assowomsett and Middleboro Indians were seized by force and declared to have been "just forfeited," and an order was issued to distribute them among the English towns "proportionately."[2] Here was an end to Philip's hope of their restoration as provided by the Taunton treaty. Whether or not the English would have lived up to this agreement had the Indians quietly delivered up their arms cannot, of course, be determined.

The Sagkonate (Saconet) Indians were also threatened with war unless they complied with the demands made upon them, and finally submitted themselves by treaty.

By September only seventy guns had been handed in and the Plymouth authorities, alarmed at their failure to receive their surrender, and the general attitude of the Indians, again summoned Philip to appear before them on the 13th of that month to give an account of his actions, threatening to employ force unless he complied with their

[1] Plymouth Records, Vol. V, page 63.
[2] Plymouth Records, Vol. V, pages 63–74.

demands and observed his agreements. The towns were ordered to make preparations for furnishing troops and supplies, and the people were bidden to carry their arms to meeting.

Secretary Morton[1] sent word to Massachusetts and Rhode Island of the action taken, requesting advice and assistance,[2] but adding that unless Philip submitted himself they "would send out forces to reduce him to reason," alone if necessary.

Philip, who had no doubt received information of their intentions, arrived at Boston on the same day as this letter and appealed to Massachusetts against the demands and threats of Plymouth, with temporary success. When the letters from Plymouth were read to him he expressed himself before the governor and council as follows: "That his predecessors had been friendly with Plymouth governors and an engagement of that nature was made by his father and renewed by his brother, and (when he took the government) by himself, but they were only agreements for amity and not for subjection. He desired to see a copy of the engagement they spoke of and that the Governor of Massachusetts would procure it for him. He knew not that they were subjects. Praying Indians were subject to Massachusetts and had magistrates and

---

[1] Nathaniel Morton of Plymouth, born in England about 1613, came with his father in the *Ann* in 1623. He became secretary of the colony December 7, 1647, and held that office until his death, June 29, 1685. Almost all of the records of Plymouth colony are in his handwriting. He wrote a valuable history called "New England's Memorial, a brief relation of the most memorable and Remarkable passages of the Providence of God manifested to the Planters of New England." Printed at Cambridge in 1699.—Pope.

[2] Plymouth Records, Vol. V, page 76.

officers appointed; they had no such thing with them and therefore they were not subject."[1]

Massachusetts proposed that the difference be referred to commissioners from Massachusetts and Connecticut. They also took occasion to inquire into the nature of Philip's subjection to the government of Plymouth, and expressed themselves as unable to adopt Plymouth's idea of the matter.

"We do not understand how far he hath subjected himself to you, but the treatment you have given him and proceedings toward him do not render him such a subject as that if there be not a present answering to summons there should presently be a proceeding to hostilities: and the sword once drawn and dipped in blood may make him as independent upon you as you are upon him."

Governor Leverett[2] of Massachusetts, Governor Winthrop[3] of Connecticut, and others of the commissioners,

---

[1] Hutchinson, Vol. I, page 281 note.

[2] Governor John Leverett of Boston was born in England in 1616. He came with his father, Thomas, arriving in Boston September 4, 1633. He was many times chosen delegate and assistant, and on the 7th of May, 1673, was elected Governor and remained in that office until his death, March 16, 1678–79. See New England Register, Vol. IV, page 125.

[3] Governor John Winthrop of Connecticut was the eldest son of Governor John of Massachusetts. He was born at Groton, County Suffolk, and bred at Dublin University, 1622-25. He assisted his father in the work of colonizing Massachusetts; came in the *Lion,* arriving at Boston, November 3, 1631. In 1632 he was chosen an assistant. He was the founder of New London (Conn.) in 1645, though he was for a number of years thereafter an assistant of the Massachusetts Court. He was elected Governor of Connecticut in May, 1657, and every year until his death, April 5, 1676.—Savage.

finally went to Plymouth at the request of Governor Prince and his council, to inquire into the matters.[1]

The charges against Philip were as follows:

1. He had neglected to bring in his arms.

2. He carried himself insolently and proudly, refusing to come down to our court when sent for.

3. He harbored and abetted divers Indians, not his own men, but vagabonds and our professed enemies.

4. That he had endeavored to insinuate himself unto the Massachusetts magistrates and misrepresented matters to them.

5. He had shown great incivility, especially unto Mr. James Brown and Mr. Hugh Cole.[2]

Philip claimed that he and his people were subjects to the king equally with the Plymouth colonists, but were not subjects of Plymouth colony, whereas Plymouth claimed that his acknowledgment of himself as subject to the king made him a subject to the colony. The claim that his refusal to obey his neighbors whenever they had had a mind to command him, and into the justice of whose mandate he was not to inquire, was a hostile act and against the treaties, was a sorry one. Philip's appeal to Massachusetts was in accordance with the terms of the Taunton treaty which had made the Massachusetts council the arbitrator of future misunderstandings. These questions, in view of the practice among all the colonies except Providence Plantations, are largely academical, and Massachusetts and Connecticut were not likely to

---

[1] Plymouth Records, Vol. V, page 78.

[2] Mr. Cole having come upon Philip during a dance is said to have called him to account for some offense, whereupon Philip knocked off his hat.—Letter of James Walker to Governor Prince.

take issue with Plymouth over a self-conferred preroga-
tive that they were themselves continually making use of.

On September 29th a new treaty was entered into and
Philip humbled himself to the court and agreed to pay
tribute of one hundred pounds value in kind, and five
wolves' heads a year, if he could get them, to go to Plymouth in case any differences arose and not to engage in
war with the other Indians or sell any lands without the
consent of the Plymouth government.[1] The question of
guns was allowed to drop, but he was told that "if he
went on his refractory way he must expect to smart for
it."

During the next three years the relations between them
were interrupted by no event of importance, and Narragansetts, Wampanoags and Nipmucks seemed to have
resigned themselves to the inevitable domination of the
English. There were those who suspected that the calm
was that which comes before the storm. Hunters and
Christian Indians spoke of the sullen demeanor of the
independent Indians, but the great body of the colonists
seemed to have been lulled into security; many of the
exposed towns on the frontier had been left unstockaded,
and so low had the interest in military matters fallen in
Massachusetts that the election of military officers had
given place some time before to appointment by the general court.

It is impossible to trace Philip's actions during these
years, but contemporary historians imply that he endeavored to reach some agreement with the sachems of the
Narragansetts and the tribes of the Nipmucks.

To the Narragansetts and Canonchet he could recall

[1] Plymouth Records, Vol. V, pages 77–79.

the death of Miantonomah, awakening the thirst for vengeance. To Weetamoo, queen of the Pocassets and widow of his brother Alexander, he could appeal to the memory of bitter suspicion. With the Nipmucks there were other chords to be touched, and if long-continued feuds and suspicions made any definite or formal alliance almost impossible, yet the voice of an Indian sachem, even of another tribe, calling to mind the high-handed interference, the stern threats, the loss of lands, and their own declining power could not fail to touch a sympathetic chord and inflame the passions of his hearers on subjects long brooded over.

No general conspiracy certainly was entered into. Doubts as to their own power and suspicions of each other made each tribe hesitate to commit itself before the others. Philip himself lacked those personal qualities of leadership which made Pontiac and Tecumseh formidable, and the Indian nature, liable to alternate outbursts of passion and despondency, lacked the genius for combined and concerted effort. Inflammable substances were plentiful, however, and it needed but a spark to fire the train.

CHAPTER IV

THE least suspicion of intrigue could not long escape the notice of those Indian converts who kept the authorities well informed of all that went on. There had been living among the Wampanoags at Nemasket,[1] the daughter of whose chief he had married, an Indian convert of Eliot's, named Sassamon, a Natick, "a cunning and plausible man" Hubbard calls him. This man had accompanied Philip to Boston as interpreter[2] after the death of Alexander and served him for some time thereafter, but having, it is said, been found guilty of some offense, had returned to Natick and again professed Christianity. Associated with Philip on familiar terms, he claimed to have received the sachem's confidences and betrayed them to the settlers under pledge of secrecy; his life would be in danger, he declared, if his connection with the matter were made known. His information (because it had an Indian origin "and one can hardly believe them when they speak truth") was not at first much regarded, but Philip, learning in advance of a summons, of the charges, made haste to Plymouth to free himself from suspicion, and, having given renewed assurances of his friendly intentions, was allowed to return.[3]

---

[1] The Indian village of Nemasket was located about a mile and a half southeasterly from the center of the present village of Middleborough, on the river of that name.

[2] Hubbard, Vol. I, page 60.

[3] Mather's Brief History, page 218.

In the spring of the following year the dead body of Sassamon was discovered in Assowomset Pond.[1] An Indian named David, having discovered some bruises on the body, suspicions were aroused and an investigation led to the belief that Sassamon had been killed while fishing during the winter and his body thrown under the ice. Three Indians, Tobias, Mattaschunanamoo and Wampapaquin, Tobias' son, were arrested on the evidence of an Indian who claimed to have been an eyewitness of the affair.[2] The Indians claimed that Sassamon had been drowned while fishing and that the marks on his body[3] were caused by contact with the ice. They declared that the informer who claimed to have been an eyewitness, "had gambled away his coat and, on its being returned and payment demanded, he had, in order to escape the debt, accused them of the murder knowing it would please the English and cause them to think him the better Christian."[4]

Mather, ever on the watch for the marvelous, declared that the body bled afresh when Tobias approached, a sign then and to a much later day credited as a proof of guilt. The three Wampanoagsfy were convicted by a white jury to which had been added several friendly Indians, and executed, [5] "and though they were all successfully

---

[1] Assowomset Pond is located about four miles south of the present village of Middleborough in Plymouth County in the town of Lakeville. Its neighborhood was a favorite resort of the natives. A few survivors of the Nemasket tribe reside upon the shores of the pond to-day.

[2] Plymouth Records, Vol. V, page 159.

[3] The wounds were enumerated in the Record as bruises, twisted neck, etc. No gunshot or arrow or knife wounds are mentioned.

[4] Easton's Relation, page 4.

[5] Plymouth Records, Vol. V, pages 167, 168. Hubbard declares that

turned off the ladder at the gallows utterly denying the fact, yet the last of them, hoping to break or slip the rope, did before his going off the ladder again confess that the other Indians did really murder John Sassamon, and that he himself, though no actor in it, was yet a looker-on."[1] Wampapaquin was reprieved but shot within the month. No direct proof was produced at the trial to connect Philip with Sassamon's death, but it was widely believed that it had been decreed, according to Indian law, by Philip and his council, as a punishment for his treachery.

The trial and execution of the three Indians aroused the Wampanoag warriors to madness. From all sides came reports to the authorities of excesses on the part of the Wampanoags. Cattle were shot, corn stolen, houses robbed; in some places outbuildings were fired. The attitude of the warriors had become defiant, while spies reported that strange Indians were swarming into Philip's villages and the women and children were being sent to the Narragansetts. Alarm and terror spread among the outlying settlements. Men saw portents that foreboded evil days. Comets in the form of blazing arrows shot athwart the skies, and the northern lights took on strange and awful shapes. Many heard the thunder of hoofs of invisible horsemen, and bullets fired from no earthly weapons whistled through the air.[2]

The authorities held back from all aggressive action, in the belief that such a course would allow the excite-

---

Wampapaquin confessed that Sassamon had been murdered by his father, and implicated Philip, but there is no other contemporary evidence.

[1] Mather's Magnalia, Book VII, page 560.

[2] Mather, Brief History, page 52

D

ment among the warriors time to abate,[1] but as Philip
made no attempt to clear himself, James Brown of Swansea, who had been on friendly terms with him, solicited
and obtained permission to inform Philip that the Plymouth authorities disclaimed all injurious intentions and
urged him to discontinue hostile preparations.[2]

Rhode Island, alarmed at the state of affairs, made
ineffectual attempts to compromise the matter and bring
Philip to an agreement. Deputy Governor Easton[3] of
that colony, and five others, including Samuel Gorton,
met Philip and his chiefs at Bristol Neck Point on the
17th of June, and proposed that the quarrel and all matters in contention should be arbitrated. It might be well,
was the reply, but that all the English agreed against
them. Many square miles of land were taken from them
by English arbitrators. They then went on to recite their
grievances. If they surrendered their arms jealousy might
be removed, but the Englishmen would not deliver them
again as promised until they had paid a fine. They said
they had been the first to do good, the English the first
to do wrong. When the English first came the king's
father was as a great man and the English as a little child.
He constrained other Indians from raiding the English,
gave them seed, showed them how to plant and was free
to do them good, and let them have one hundred times
more land then than now the king had for his own people,

---

[1] Hubbard, Vol. I, page 65.

[2] Hazzard State papers, Vol. II, page 333.

[3] Governor John Easton lived in Newport. He was born in England
in 1621 and came with his father in the *Mary and John* in 1634. He
became Deputy Governor of Rhode Island in 1666 and was Governor of
the colony for five years, 1690-94. He died December 12, 1705.

but the king's brother, when he was king, came miserably
to die, being forced to court, and, as they judged, poisoned.
Another grievance: that if twenty of them testify that the
English had done them wrong, it was nothing, but if ever
one of their worst Indians testified against any Indian or
the king, when it pleased the English it was sufficient.
Englishmen made Indians drunk and cheated them in
bargains. English cattle and horses increased. The Indians could not keep their corn from being spoiled, they
never being used to fences. The English were so eager
to sell Indians liquor that most of the Indians spent much
in drunkenness and then raided upon the sober Indians,
and they did believe often hurt the English cattle and
their king was obliged to sell more land to pay the fines.

The white delegates endeavored to persuade them to
lay down their arms and not to make war, for the English were too strong for them. They said the English
should do to them as they did when they were strong to
the English.[1]

The conference broke up without any agreement having
been reached. Easton states as his belief that the Indians
would have accepted the Governor of New York and an
Indian king as arbitrators and that peace might still have
been preserved. It is more than doubtful. That the
Wampanoags had broken loose from all restraint seems
certain. Philip would at any rate have been glad to gain
time in order to have procured arms and ammunition and

---

[1] Easton's Relations, Hough Edition, page 7. Palfrey questions
whether Governor Easton wrote this narrative ascribed to him on account of its illiteracy. There seems no doubt of it, however. Illiterate
spelling and construction were common. It was not published until
many years after the war. Mather knew of its existence and of some
of its allegations and rushed his own history into print.

to involve more definitely the other tribes, but in the state of mind of his followers no such course was possible; the pent-up passions of many years, fanned into flame, were past suppression.

Captain Benjamin Church[1] of Little Compton, in the territory of the Saconet Indians, attending by invitation of the squaw sachem, Awashonks,[2] a ceremonious dance, June 15th, found on his arrival that it had been given in honor of six ambassadors from Philip, her overlord, to make sure of her co-operation. On her explanation of Philip's overtures he boldly advised her in their presence to knock them on the head and seek refuge with the English. Two days later, near Pocasset, he met Peter Nunnuit,[3] who had married Alexander's widow, Weeta-moo. Peter said he had just come from Mount Hope where Philip had been holding a dance in which Indians from all the Wampanoag tribes had participated; that war was certain, [4] and that Philip had been forced to promise the young men "that on the next Lord's day

---

[1] Captain Benjamin Church was born at Plymouth in 1639 and was a carpenter by trade. He probably lived in Duxbury after his marriage in that town, but later removed to Little Compton, R. I., and afterwards lived for a time in Bristol in the same colony. He subsequently returned to Little Compton and died there January 17, 1717-18. His services during the war are recorded in his "Entertaining History," written by his son from dictation by himself in his last years.

[2] Awashonks, squaw sachem of Sagkonate, was the wife of an Indian called Tolony, of whom but little is known.—Book of the Indians, Vol. III, page 65.

[3] Peter Nunnuit, the husband of Weetamoo, did not concern himself against the English, but, abandoning his wife, joined the enemy against her. After the war he was given command over the prisoners who were permitted to reside in the country between Sepecan and Dartmouth. —Drake's Book of the Indians.

[4] Church's Entertaining History, page 3.

when the English were gone to meeting, they should level their house and from that time forward kill their cattle." He also told them that Samuel Gorton and James Brown of Swansea were at that time at Mount Hope,[1] and that one of the young warriors wanted to kill Brown, but that Philip prevented it saying that his father had charged him to show kindness to Mr. Brown. Church, at the request of Peter, had an interview with Weetamoo, who was near by, and advised her to go over to Rhode Island for security and to send a messenger to the governor immediately. He then hastened with the information he had acquired to Plymouth.

On the afternoon of June 21st, Governor Leverett of Massachusetts received a letter from Governor Winslow informing him of the situation. It was determined in view of the attitude of the Wampanoags, to immediately send a commission consisting of Captain Edward Hutchinson,[2] Seth Perry, and William Powers, to the Narragansetts to find out their intentions and to put them on their good behavior[3]. Acting upon their instructions they stopped at Providence and induced Roger Williams to accompany them to the chief village of the Narragansetts.

At this conference Pessacus,[4] Canonchet and Ninigret seem to have assented to the desires of the Massachusetts authorities and promised to be neutral. The commission-

---

[1] Probably arranging for the conference with the Rhode Island Committee.

[2] Seth Perry was of Boston, a tailor, and was made freeman in 1666. —Savage.

[3] Massachusetts Archives, Vol. 67, page 201.

[4] Pessacus was born about 1623 and was about twenty years of age when his brother, Miantonomah, was killed. He was killed by the Mohawks beyond the Piscataqua River in 1677-78.

ers departed apparently satisfied with the success of their mission, but Williams, who knew the Indian character well, seems to have been suspicious and, on June 27th, wrote to Winthrop that he believed their friendly answers were empty "words of falsehood and treachery." Pessacus, one of the sachems of the Narragansetts, is said to have confessed to several of the men of Newport, that while his heart sorrowed he could not rule the youth or common people or persuade the chiefs. Even before the Massachusetts commission had started on its journey two houses had been burned by the Wampanoags at Mattapoiset, June 19th.

Philip, driven to bay and forced into conflict by the passions he now found himself unable to control, could hardly have plunged into the conflict confident of success. He knew the bitter resentment and the desire of his own warriors for war. The independent tribes of the Nipmucks were ripe for revolt. Initial successes on his part were all that were needed to bring them to his aid, but he knew equally well that sympathy, the sense of common wrongs, and a tentative understanding, were but feeble reeds on which to lean if disaster threatened.[1]

Events had rushed forward faster than his plans or preparations. No general conspiracy had been organized, no concerted action arranged for, and as the old Wampanoag confederacy had fallen into ruins under the pressure of the whites, he could depend with certainty only on his personal following. The Indians, however, did not lack advantages and if once the pent-up fury of the

---

[1] If they (the Pequots) doubt the victory "they would be in hazard of joining with the stronger."—Letter of Rev. James Fitch of Norwich to the Council of Connecticut. Conn. Records, Vol. II, page 337.

different tribes should be loosed upon the long frontier the contest was certain to be long continued. They had become expert in the use of firearms. They knew the fording places of the rivers and every trail, and were acquainted with the daily habits of the settlers. They were adepts in a method of warfare admirably suited to the character of the country. To turn every cover and position to advantage, to strike quickly, to lie patiently in ambuscades, and to draw off rapidly on the failure of an attack with a fleetness in which the heavily armed settler, unaccustomed to forest warfare, could not compete, were formidable tactics in a broken and wooded country of long distances sparsely settled and traversed only by rough trails.

The martial spirit which had distinguished the early generation of colonists had ceased to inspire the new generation.[1] The very spreading out of the settlements offered a wide-flung and weakly settled frontier to the swift moving warriors, while the contempt which had grown up among the settlers in respect to the Indian, both from the result of the Pequot war and the long subservience of the race in later dealings, made it certain that for a time at least, over-confidence and lack of military training would lead to catastrophies.

There were among the settlers, however, many traders well acquainted with Indian ways, and if the great mass of the settlers were untrained to warfare, yet there were those among them who had served as under-officers and captains under Cromwell, in the most perfect army the century had seen. Material for good soldiers was in

---

[1] Conn. Records, Vol. II, page 217. Report on Condition in 1673. The same was true of Massachusetts.

abundance, arms and equipment plentiful, their stockaded towns offered a protection and a base of supplies which the Indian villages could not possibly afford. Many individual Indians were certain to join them and the whole of the Mohegans would be their effective allies, while the numbers, resources and character of the population once brought into the field and trained, made the result of a prolonged campaign certain.

Tradition had attributed to the Indians engaged in the war, between seven and eight thousand fighting men. The swift movements of the war parties, some of whom were able to cover forty miles a day, made their forces appear far greater than was actually the case, and neither the fears of the settlers nor the reports of friendly Indians desirous of enhancing the value of their services were likely to underestimate the number. Their actual number probably did not at most exceed thirty-five hundred. Of these the Wampanoags and their kindred mustered about five hundred; the Nipmucks and the Connecticut River tribes not over eleven hundred; the Abenakis and Tarratines about six hundred; the Narragansetts about one thousand. In addition there were probably some three hundred scattered warriors, roving Indians, small parties from the northern tribes and Christian Indians, throwing in their lot with their kindred either from choice, or, as occurred in more than one instance, driven into revolt by the harsh treatment of the suspicious settlers.

The Wampanoags, in the belief it is said, that the first party to shed blood would be vanquished, had been provoking the settlers by daily outrages to commence hostilities, and on the 18th of June one of a number of Indians was shot and wounded by an irate settler at Swansea.[1] According to John Easton some Indians at Swansea were seen by an old man and a lad, pilfering from houses whose owners were at church, whereupon the old man bade the young one shoot, and one of the Indians fell but got away. Later in the day some of the neighboring Indians came to one of the garrison houses, either Miles's or Bourne's, and asked why they had shot the Indian. In reply to the English question whether he was dead, the Indian said, "yea," on which one of the English remarked that "it was no matter." The other endeavored to convince the Indians that it was but a young man's idle words, but the Indians, returning no answer, went hastily away.[2]

Plymouth colony had already taken precautions in view of the existing conditions. Captain Benjamin Church, at the request of Winslow, had some time before induced the Governor of Rhode Island to provide boats for the patrol of the northern shore in case of an outbreak, and the towns had been warned to be on their guard and prepared to send their contingents into the field at a moment's notice.

Now, on the 20th of June, a messenger brought news to Plymouth that the house of Job Winslow[3] at Swansea had been plundered by Indians on the 18th, and that on

---

[1] Hubbard (Hubbard says the Indian was only wounded, not killed), Vol. I, page 64.

[2] Easton's Relation, page 17.

[3] Job Winslow was the son of Kenelm Winslow. At the outbreak of the war he was living at Swansea and his house was "broken up and rifled" by the Indians. After the close of the war he erected a dwelling-house near the "wading place" at Kickemuit on what is now the farm of Mr. Edward Ennis. It is probable that the house destroyed occupied this same site.—Savage. "Massasoit's Town; Sowams in Pokanoket," by Miss Virginia Baker, page 19.

the 19th several houses, among them that of Hugh Cole, had been burned while the people were attending worship.[1] Captain Church was immediately ordered to collect a force of twenty horsemen at Bridgewater and to proceed to Swansea by way of Taunton, which was appointed as the rendezvous of the Plymouth forces.

The troops were already assembling under Majors James Cudworth[2] and William Bradford[3] and Captains Gorham and Fuller, when Church marched into the place on the 21st, and the next day the whole force proceeded towards Swansea, Church leading the van with his horsemen and a number of friendly Indians,[4] "and to keep so far before as not to be in sight of the army, and so they

---

[1] Records of Commissioners of New England. Plymouth Colony Record, Vol. X; Vol. II, pages 362-364. (Letters of Josiah Winslow and Thomas Hinckley.)

[2] Major James Cudworth came probably from London to Boston in 1632. In 1652 he was captain of the militia at Scituate. In 1649 he was made deputy to the colony court at Plymouth; assistant from 1656 to 1658 and again from 1674 to 1680. In 1675 he was chosen "General and Commander-in-chief of all forces that are or may be sent forth against the enemy," which commission he declined. He was chosen Deputy Governor in 1681 and appointed agent for the colony to England. He died in London of smallpox in 1682. See Deane's History of Scituate, page 245.

[3] Major William Bradford, son of Governor William of Plymouth, was born in Plymouth, June 17, 1624. In 1656-57 he was deputy from Plymouth to the General Court and 1658 became an assistant, in which office he served for twenty-four successive years, and for the remaining ten years of the colony's existence filled the new office of Deputy Governor, save for the years of Andros' reign. For twelve years he was colonial commissioner. He died March 1, 1704. "Governor William Bradford and his son Major William Bradford," by James Shepard, page 78.

[4] Church, page 5.

did for by the way they killed a deer, flayed, roasted, and eat the most of him before the army came up with them."

Panic already reigned among the scattered farmhouses that stretched along the eastern shore, and Major Bradford, with the company from Bridgewater, leaving Swansea on the 23d, marched down to Jared Bourne's[1] stone house at Mattapoiset where nearly seventy people had collected. Everywhere along the march were to be met people flying from their homes, wringing their hands and bewailing their losses. A part of the relieving force was dispatched the next day to escort Mr. John Brown, who had acted as guide, to his home at Wanamoiset, with orders to act strictly on the defensive. Meeting, on their return, a party from the garrison going out with carts to bring in corn from the deserted and outlying houses, they warned them that the Indians were out in force and urged them not to proceed. Confiding in their numbers, however, the foragers continued on their way only to fall into an ambuscade, where, attacked and routed, they were driven back to the garrison with a loss of six killed.[2] The settlement was abandoned the following week, the inhabitants seeking refuge on the island of Rhode Island.

June 24th was the day appointed by the authorities for humiliation and prayer, and as the settlers of Swansea

---

[1] Gerard (Jared) Bourne was of Boston in 1634; made freeman May 6, 1635. He resided at Muddy River (Brookline) and was there a constable. Savage says he removed to Rhode Island in 1665. He was in 1675 the owner of the stone garrison house in Swansea on Mattapoiset (now Gardner's) Neck. This was located one-half mile north of the railway station at South Swansea, on the farm now owned (1904) by Mr. William H. Green, and a few rods in the rear of Mr. Green's dwelling. The old garrison spring may still be found in the meadow.

[2] Old Indian Chronicle, page 109.

were returning from service they were fired upon.[1] One was killed and several wounded. Two of the settlers were dispatched for assistance, to Plymouth. They were never to reach it, for the commissioners, Major Savage[2] and Captain Thomas Brattle,[3] who had been sent by Governor Leverett and the council to treat with Philip, on approaching Swansea in the evening, came upon their bodies weltering in blood upon the highway, and turned back to Boston.[4]

Philip, realizing, it is said, that the first blow, if the warriors took matters into their own hands, would be struck at Swansea and the neighboring towns, ordered no harm should be done to James Brown,[5] Captain Thomas Willet [6]

---

[1] Mather's Magnalia, Vol. VII, page 561.

[2] Major Thomas Savage was born in Taunton, Somerset County, England, and came in the *Planter* to Boston, April, 1635. He was an original member of the Artillery Company and chosen its captain in 1651. He served as representative to the General Court from Boston, Hingham and Andover; he was speaker for a number of terms and assistant from 1680 until his death, which occurred February 14, 1682.—Bodge.

[3] Captain Thomas Brattle was born about 1624. He was a merchant in Boston in 1656, and was of the Artillery Company in 1675. He owned valuable iron works at Concord and was deputy from that town from 1678 to 1681, as he had been from Lancaster in 1671 and 1672. In 1671 he was one of the commissioners sent to treat with Philip at Taunton. He was appointed cornet in the Suffolk troop in 1670, lieutenant in 1675 and captain May 5, 1676. He died April 5, 1683, and left, it is said, the largest estate in New England at that time. Bodge, page 261.—Savage.

[4] Connecticut Records (War Council). Letter of Massachusetts Council to Governor Winthrop Vol. II page 336.

[5] James Brown, son of John, was made freeman at Plymouth in 1636. He was of Rehoboth, 1658. He was for a number of years deputy from Swansea. He twice went to Philip in 1675 "to persuade him to be quiet," but both times found his men in arms and "Philip very high and not persuadable to peace."—History of Barrington, page 580.

[6] Captain Thomas Willet came to Plymouth from Leyden in the spring

and James Leonard.[1] He also sent word to Hugh Cole,[2] who had befriended him to remove lest it should be out of his power to prevent harm befalling him, and extended protection to two small children because "their father sometime showed me kindness."

The news of the attack reached Plymouth before night and messengers were immediately dispatched to Boston for assistance. Both governments took prompt measures. At Boston the drums were beat to assemble the companies and in the late afternoon of the 26th, Captain Daniel Henchman[3] with a company of foot, and Captain

---

of 1630. He was intrusted with the command of the Plymouth trading-house at Kennebec in 1639, from which office he was forcibly ejected by D'Aubrey, the French Lieutenant Governor of Acadia. He was a magistrate in Plymouth from 1651 to 1664, when he accompanied Colonel Nicholson in the reduction of New York, of which city he was the first English mayor. In 1673, the Dutch having again come into posesssion, Mr. Willet retired to Wannamoisett. He died the next year. His wife was the sister of James Brown.—New England Register, Vol. II, page 376.

[1] James Leonard, of Providence, 1645, and Taunton, 1652, came from Pontypool in Wales. The first iron works in the colonies were established in Taunton by his brother Henry, Ralph Russell and himself. Philip was on very friendly terms with the Leonards, visiting them and being received with great consideration. He depended upon Leonard for the repair of his guns and tools. Leonard died before 1691.—Baylie's History of Plymouth.

[2] Hugh Cole, born about 1627, was of Plymouth in 1653. In 1669 Philip sold to him and others five hundred acres of land on the west side of Cole's River in Swansea. During the war his house was destroyed and he removed to Rhode Island. He returned in 1677 and located on the west side of Touiset Neck on the Kickemuit River in Warren. The farm he owned and the well he dug are still in the possession of his lineal descendants. History of Barrington, page 574.

[3] Captain Daniel Henchman was of Boston. He was appointed captain of the 5th Boston Company Colonial Militia, May 12, 1675. He died in Worcester, October 15, 1675.—Bodge, page 45.

Thomas Prentice[1] with a troop of horse, set forth.[2] The infantry were armed with muskets and long knives fitted with handles to fix in the muzzles, and carried a knapsack, six feet of fuse, a pound of powder, a bandoleer passing under the left arm and containing a dozen or more cylinders holding a measured charge of powder, a bag containing three pounds of bullets and a horn of priming powder. The troopers were equipped with a sword and either two pistols or a carbine. All carried in addition a few articles of wearing apparel, a day's provisions and a pound of tobacco.

Prolonging their march well into the evening they were nearing the town of Dedham on the Neponset River, twenty miles from Boston, when the moon was darkened by an eclipse (in Capricorn) "which caused them to halt for a little repose until the moon recovered her light." Some among them imagined they discerned in the moon a black spot resembling the scalp of an Indian, others made out the form of an Indian bow, ominous signs, "but both," writes the chronicler, "might rather have thought of what Marcus Crassus, the Roman general going forth with an army against the Parthians, once wisely replied to a private soldier that would have dissuaded him from marching because of an eclipse of the moon in Capricorn, 'that he was more afraid of Saggitarius (the archer) than of Capricornus,' meaning the arrows of the Parthians."

---

[1] Captain Thomas Prentice was commander of the Middlesex troop of horse. He was born in England about 1620, and settled in Cambridge, N. E. He was appointed captain of the special troop in June, 1675. He died July 7, 1709.—Bodge, page 89.

[2] Hubbard, Vol. I, page 67.

"When the moon had again borrowed her light," and the road once more became distinct, they resumed the march, reaching Attleboro,[1] thirty miles from Boston, early in the morning. Here they rested until the afternoon when Captain Samuel Moseley,[2] with a rough company of volunteers composed of sailors, privateersmen, and several paroled pirates accompanied by a number of hunting dogs, joined them.

The combined force of two hundred and fifty fighting men, besides the teamsters, pushing rapidly on, reached Swansea[3] early in the evening of the 28th and pitched their camp alongside of Major Cudworth, and the Plymouth men near the fortified house of the Rev. Mr. Miles,

---

[1] The march ended at Woodcock's garrison, located nearly a mile north of the center of the present village of North Attleboro, opposite a small burying ground. John Woodcock was the pioneer of Attleboro, and his house was built for defense against the Indians and was also a house of entertainment. It was the only dwelling at the time of its erection between Dedham and Rehoboth (Seekonk). The old house remained until 1806 when it gave way to a large tavern built by Colonel Hatch upon the same site. The cellar hole of the Woodcock garrison may still be seen, as the Hatch tavern has been removed.—Daggett's History of Attleboro.

[2] Captain Moseley was of Boston and by trade a cooper. "This Captain Moseley hath been an old privateer at Jamaica."—Badge, page 59.

[3] This was at what is now the village of Barneyville, about three miles northerly from the village of Warren, R. I., and Miles' bridge crossed the Warren River at that place. The garrison house, or rather what is so considered by some, is still standing, though other antiquarians think this is of a later date than that occupied by the Rev. Mr. Miles in 1675. The population of Swansea was scattered over a wide area of farming territory. There were distinct hamlets and many isolated houses, the whole extending over an irregular trail some ten miles from one extreme to the other.

a Baptist clergyman,[1] which stood a short distance from the bridge leading toward Mount Hope.

Immediately on the arrival, a dozen of Prentice's troopers, impatient of delay, under the command of Quartermaster Joseph Belcher and Corporal John Gill,[2] with Captain Church as a volunteer, sallied over the bridge to explore the country beyond. Hardly had they cleared the bridge when a party of Indians in ambush poured in a volley upon them, killing William Hammond,[3] a guide, wounding Gill and Belcher, and driving the rest back in confusion[4] to the barricade which had been erected around the house of the Rev. Mr. Miles.

Made confident by this success, a number of Indians the next morning showed themselves at the end of the bridge, shouting derisively, while some, more bold than

[1] Rev. John Miles (Myles), a Baptist clergyman, was born in Wales and settled in Swansea in the year 1662. The church in Swansea, Mass., is supposed to have been organized in Swansea, South Wales, Mr. Miles simply removing the church organization from that country. Mr. Miles settled in Rehoboth, now Swansea, in that part known as Barnneyville and his meeting house is said to have been near the One Hundred Acre Cove on the Barrington River. This was included in the destruction of Swansea and after the war Mr. Miles returned to his old field and a church was erected for him at Tyler's Point, New Meadow Neck, opposite Warren, R. I., and in the cemetery at that place Mr. Miles was probably buried.

[2] John Gill was of Dorchester, 1640, and lived in that part of the town which became Milton. He removed to Boston and died in 1678. Quartermaster Joseph Belcher, who was also of Milton, was his son-in-law, having married Gill's daughter Rebecca.—Savage. Dorchester Church Records.

[3] William Hammond went to Swansea with Captain Thomas Prentice's troop, and having been a resident of that town was competent to act as "pilot," or guide, to the troops. His body was taken to Watertown for burial. See The Hammond Genealogies, Vol. I, page 477.

[4] Church, page 5.

MILES GARRISON HOUSE, SWANSEA, MASSACHUSETTS

the rest, even ventured upon the bridge itself. The whole force was immediately drawn up and while the infantry advanced toward the bank of the stream, a troop of horse and a party of volunteers under Moseley rushed furiously down the road upon them and drove them off with loss,[1] losing, however, one of their own number, Ensign Savage,[2] wounded, it is said, by the fire from the infantry on the bank.

On the evening of the 29th which was spent skirmishing with the Indians, came Major Thomas Savage, accompanied by Captain Paige and sixty horse and as many foot, to take over the command of the Massachusetts forces.[3] The force assembled at Swansea now numbered over five hundred men, and, at noon on the following day, leaving a small guard in the garrison, the little army, with Major Cudworth in command, crossed over the bridge, and, throwing out horsemen on the flanks to prevent an ambuscade, pushed on toward Mount Hope.[4]

Here and there, within the boundaries of the Indian country, they saw groups of empty wigwams and fields of corn, the smoking ruins of what had once been the homes of the settlers, and "Bibles torn in pieces in defi-

---

[1] Hubbard, Vol. I, page 69.

[2] Ensign Perez Savage, son of Major Thomas, was born February 17, 1652. He was ensign of Captain Moseley's company, "a noble, heroic, youth," as Church calls him. In addition to the wound received at Swansea he was again badly wounded at the Narragansett Swamp fight, at which time he was a lieutenant. He never married, but removed to London, from which he carried on trade with Spain. His death occurred at Mequinez in Barbary, where he was held in captivity by the Turks. —Savage.

[3] Massachusetts Archives, Vol. 67, page 209.

[4] Hubbard, Vol. I, page 71.

E

ance of our holy religion," while ghastly heads[1] and hands stuck upon stakes bore witness to the fate of the occupants. But, while Philip's wigwam[2] was discovered and the trail of his warriors followed to the shore, not an Indian was to be seen.

Throughout the day the rain had fallen steadily, soaking the troops to the skin, and as evening drew on the Plymouth men, passing over the strait, found shelter on the island of Rhode Island, but Major Savage, with the Massachusetts division, bivouaced in the open fields amid the storm.[3]

With the dawn came rumors that the Indians were in force near Swansea, and Savage, after laying waste the fields of growing corn, hastened back over the route of the day before, but though the force met many Indian dogs deserted by their masters, and saw at times burning dwellings, they came upon no Indians, and the infantry, tired

———

[1] Church, in his narrative, says, in connection with the march under Cudworth to Mount Hope, "They marched until they came to the *narrow of the neck* at a place called Keekamuit where they took down the heads, of eight Englishmen that were killed at the head of Mattapoiset Neck, and set upon poles after the barbarous manner of these Savages." This spot is on the west bank of the Kickemuit River, just above the ancient "wading place," and directly east of Belchers Cove which sets in from the Warren River behind the village of Warren, thus narrowing the Mount Hope Neck to the width of half a mile. The spot is exactly a mile east of Warren.

[2] The term "Mount Hope" was applied to the peninsula between the Warren and Kickemuit Rivers and not to the mountain alone. Philip's Village was not located, as many writers have erroneously stated, upon the mount itself, but about a mile and a half north of it near the "Narrows" of the Kickemuit River where evidences of Indian occupation are still plentiful.—See Massasoit's Town, page 24.

[3] Hubbard, Vol. I, page 72.

SITE OF PHILIP'S VILLAGE, NEAR MOUNT HOPE, RHODE ISLAND

and discouraged, made halt at Swansea.[1] The cavalry,
however, under Prentice, proceeded to scour the country
towards Seekonk and Rehoboth,[2] but discovering no trace
of the enemy finally encamped for the night.

The next morning Prentice, having placed a portion of
his command under Lieutenant Oakes[3] with orders to
march parallel with the main force along another road
in order to cover a wider extent of territory, set out on
his return to Swansea. They had advanced only a short
distance when they came in sight of a party of Indians
burning a house. Prentice was unable to reach them on
account of several intervening fences, but Oakes, continuing along the road, charged upon and put them to flight,
killing several, among them Phoebe,[4] one of their leaders,
and losing one of his own men, John Druce.

Information in the meantime had reached Swansea

----

[1] Hubbard, Vol. I, page 72.

[2] The Rehoboth of King Philip's time was situated about six miles
west of the present village, and very nearly identical with the present
village of East Providence Center. Its western boundary was the Seekonk River, and Seekonk Cove pushed its way inland to a point near the
settlement. On the bank of this cove at one time lived Roger Williams.
The site of an early garrison house is still identified, which was one of
the two houses remaining after the destruction of the town by the Indians.

[3] Lieutenant Edward Oakes was made freeman in Cambridge, May 18,
1642. He was a native of England. He was selectman of Cambridge
for twenty-six years and deputy to the General Court from Cambridge
and Concord for eighteen years. He became lieutenant of Captain Prentice's troop in June, 1675. He died at Concord October 13, 1689.
—Bodge, page 84.

[4] Phoebe, Pebee or Thebe, was a petty Wampanoag sachem, one of
Philip's councilors. He lived at Popanomscut in the southerly section
of Barrington, R. I. This was called Phoebe's Neck by the English
and was located directly opposite the village of Warren and separated
from it by the river.

that Philip had been discovered at Pocasset,[1] but Savage, instead of marching directly toward this point with his whole force, divided his command, sending Henchman and Prentice to scour the woods and swamps along the mainland, while he himself with the commands of Captains Paige[2] and Moseley, marched down to Mount Hope. No signs of Indians were discovered at Mount Hope, and leaving a party to build a fort,[3] despite the earnest entreaty of Church that the whole force should go over to Pocasset and drive Philip from cover, Savage again returned to Swansea.

---

[1] Pocasset was the territory now occupied by the town of Tiverton in Rhode Island, and the city of Fall River in Massachusetts. Its western border rests upon the Taunton River and the arm of Narragansett Bay, known as the Sakonet River.

[2] Captain Nicholas Paige came from Plymouth, England, and was in Boston as early as 1665. June 27, 1675, he was appointed captain of a troop to accompany Major Thomas Savage. He was active in business and in civil affairs; was of the Artillery Company in 1693; later its commander, and a colonel. He died in 1717.—Bodge.

[3] This fort was erected very near Philip's Indian village and in full sight of it, at the Narrows of the Kickemuit. It was built upon the brow of a bluff facing the water, and a comparatively few years ago its remains were visible, but the action of the waves upon the bluff has washed away the site.

CHAPTER V

THE Massachusetts forces, reinforced by a body of Christian Indians raised by Major Gookin and sent down from Boston under Captain Isaac Johnson,[1] were once more at Swansea, where Cudworth and the main body of the Plymouth men soon joined them.

The whole plan of campaign had completely broken down, every movement had been marked by doubt and hesitation and the failure of the authorities to promptly suppress the outbreak was soon to be seen in the growing disaffection of the Nipmucks.

Suspicious of the Narragansetts, among whom it was said the women and children of the Wampanoags had found a refuge,[2] and stirred by the warning letter of Roger Williams before quoted, Governor Leverett and the Council now sent Captain Edward Hutchinson[3] to

---

[1] Captain Isaac Johnson was of Roxbury where he was admitted freeman March 4, 1635. He was of the Artillery Company in 1645 and its captain in 1667. He was early in the service of King Philip's war and is heard of at Mount Hope and Mendon.

[2] Uncas supplied this information. Rev. James Fitch of Norwich quotes him as authority for the statement in a letter to the Connecticut Council. Conn. Records, Vol. II, page 336. Age had not abated his cunning or his enmities.

[3] Captain Edward Hutchinson born about 1608, came to America from Alford in Lincolnshire in 1633. He early settled in Newport but removed to Boston. He soon entered service in the Artillery Company and held a captain's commission in 1657. In 1658 he was elected representative to the General Court. He owned a large farm in the Nipmuck country and he and his family were widely known among the

take the Massachusetts force into the Narragansett country and compel Canonchet to make a treaty and give hostages for the good behavior of his people.

Immediately on the arrival of Hutchinson and Joseph Dudley,[1] a council of war was held and it was resolved to "go make peace with a sword in their hands."

Savage at once began his march by way of Providence, while Moseley and Hutchinson and a party of volunteers accompanied by Roger Williams and Dudley, sailed down the bay to Smith's Landing[2] on the Narragansett shore.

Both parties found the country of the Narragansetts deserted. The wigwams stood empty, and though the

---

Indians with whom he was popular.—New England Register, Vol. I page 299.

[1] Joseph Dudley of Roxbury was the son of Governor Thomas and was born September 23, 1647. Graduated from Harvard College in 1665; was representative 1673-75; Artillery Company in 1677; assistant from 1676 to 1685. He was of Andros' Council and Chief Justice of an unconstitutional Superior Court. After a long imprisonment he went in 1689 to England and became Deputy Governor of the Isle of Wight under Lord Cutts, and came home in 1702 with a commission as Governor in which office he served until 1715. He died April 2, 1720.—Savage.

[2] Smith's Landing. Richard Smith came from Gloucestershire, England, and became a leading man in Taunton. "On account of matters of conscience" he left that place and settled in the Narragansett country. purchasing from the Indians a large tract of land. He built on the banks of the Annoquatucket River a large trading house where he gave free entertainment to travelers. This was located about one mile north of the present village of Wickford, R. I. At this place he had a wharf. His son Richard inherited this property in 1664 and became his father's successor as a trader and prominent citizen. It was burned during the war, but was rebuilt, some of the timbers of the original house being used in the construction of the new. It still stands, in an excellent state of preservation and is known as the Updike house.—Rhode Island Hist. Soc. Coll., Vol. III, page 166.

SITE OF SMITH'S LANDING AND GARRISON HOUSE

Wickford, Rhode Island. The present structure, erected immediately after the destruction of the garrison in King Philip's War, is said to contain some of the timbers of the original house

crops were showing above the soil, men, women and children in fear or hostility had withdrawn into the swamps. Again and again Hutchinson sent for the sachems, but, as Roger Williams wrote to Waite Winthrop[1] at New London, July 7th, a meeting had not been agreed upon, and if it were he feared it "would end in blows and bloodshed."

A few days later Waite Winthrop with a company of Connecticut troops and a number of Mohegans after a march across country, during which Winthrop having met old Ninigret had secured a promise of neutrality,[2] arrived at Smith's Landing and joined the Massachusetts men.

By the 15th a few aged and unimportant Indians had been gathered together and forced to sign a treaty. The totemic marks appearing on the document although designated by the signers of the treaty as counselors and attorneys to Canonicus, Ninigret and Pumham,[3] are those

---

[1] Waitstill Winthrop, sometimes written Waite, was the son of Governor John Winthrop of Connecticut, and was born February 27, 1642. He was one of the commissioners of the New England colonies in 1672 and during the years of Philip's war. He was chosen an assistant in 1692 under the old form of government, ten days before the arrival of Sir William Phips with the new charter, in which he was named by the King one of the Council. He died November 7, 1717.—Savage.

[2] Letter of Waite Winthrop to Governor Winthrop. Conn. Records, Vol. II, page 338.

[3] Pumham was sachem of Shawamut, a part of Narragansett territory, and disputed the deed given by Miantonomah to Samuel Gorton, appealing to Massachusetts for protection. There may still be seen on the banks of Warwick Cove the remains of an earthwork erected by the authorities of the Massachusetts colony as an aid in the resistance of the colony to the demands of Rhode Island, and known as Pumham's fort. See Narragansett Historical Register, Vol. VI, page 137.

of obscure individuals. Not a name of importance appears.

By the terms of this one-sided treaty (here given only in part) the signers on behalf of the Narragansetts agreed:

"I. That all and every of the said sachems shall from time to time carefully seize, and living or dead deliver unto one or other of the above-said governments, all and every one of Sachem Philip's subjects whatsoever, that shall come, or be found within the precincts of any of their lands, and that with the greatest diligence and faithfulness.

"II. That they shall with their utmost ability use all acts of hostility against the said Philip and his subjects, entering his lands or any other lands of the English, to kill and destroy the said enemy, until a cessation from war with the said enemy be concluded by both the above-said colonies.

* * * * * * * *

"VI. The said gentlemen in behalf of the governments to which they do belong, do engage to the said Sachems and their subjects, that if they or any of them shall seize and bring into either the above English governments, or to Mr. Smith, inhabitant of Narragansett, Philip Sachem, alive, he or they so delivering, shall receive for their pains, forty trucking cloth coats; in case they bring his head they shall have twenty like good coats paid them. For every living subject of said Philip's so delivered, the deliverer shall receive two coats, and for every head one coat, as a gratuity for their service herein . . . etc.

"PETTAQUAMSCOT,[1] July 15, 1675."

----

[1] Pettaquamscot was that section of country lying in the southeasterly part of what is now the town of South Kingstown, R. I. It was sepa-

Well might the unfortunate Narragansetts as they contemplated the forceful invasion of their territory and the terms of this treaty extorted by force, which, signed by no sachem, would be held binding upon them, feel that the burden of past wrongs and present injuries was almost too great to be borne.

Of all the New England tribes they indeed were the most deserving of sympathy. The whole conduct of Massachusetts and Connecticut against the Narragansetts had from the first been often unjust, and always aggressive and high-handed. It had never been a wise policy, and now that the bold and warlike Canonchet had succeeded the pacific Canonicus the results were soon to be reaped.

In the meantime Philip, relieved from pressure by the Massachusetts men and the partial inactivity of the Plymouth forces, found refuge in the wooded swamps and thickets that lay in the interior of the Pocasset territory.[1] The Indians along the eastern shore had been forced to join him, and numerous war parties sallying forth ranged the country in all directions, burning solitary farms, shooting at the settlers from ambush and killing the cattle.

Middleboro[2] was devastated and the inhabitants forced

---

rated from Boston Neck by the Pettaquamscot River and Cove. Tower Hill at the southerly end, was the portion of this territory settled by the English.

[1] Although the land of Pocasset along its water front is broken and hilly, behind this ridge and extending the whole length of the territory is an extent of swamp and meadow surrounding Watuppa Pond, among the thickets of which the natives could find shelter from which they could not easily be driven.

[2] Middleboro in Plymouth colony, was so named from the fact that Nemasket, the Indian village of the town, was the halfway or middle place between the settlement at Plymouth and Sowams, the seat of

to take refuge in a mill on the Nemasket River; a few days and this too was deserted and the settlers, abandoning all their possessions, removed to Plymouth. Dartmouth[1] was beset and partly burned during the latter part of July. Taunton also was threatened and travel along the highways ceased, except under escort. Men feared to work in the fields and the inhabitants of all the border towns sought refuge at night in the largest and strongest houses, which were extemporized as garrisons.

Cudworth, unmindful of Church's persistent advice to strike vigorously and with full force at the main body of the Indians, who, he declared, were with Philip at Pocasset, had moved towards Taunton the better to protect that side of the country from the activities of the war parties. Like most of the commanding officers he possessed no experience in warfare and failed to realize that against the Indians a vigorous offensive was the surest means of defense.

Massasoit. The English settlement grew up around the "Four Corners" a mile or two above Nemasket, and is still the central portion of the village. A short distance to the north, on what is now the main street, stood the fort, overlooking the valley of the Nemasket, and opposite the fort lot still stands an ancient house, said to be a survivor of the destruction of the place in Philip's war. The mill, in which the inhabitants took refuge from the Indians, stood on the river at a spot which now forms the northeastern corner of the village and known as the lower factory.

[1] The portion of Dartmouth that suffered most was that located about five miles southwest from New Bedford and called by the Indian name of Apponagansett, on the river still called by that name. At Russell's Orchard, a short distance north of the bridge spanning the river, there stood on the east bank, Russell's garrison house, into which the inhabitants of that section securely retired. This portion of the town is now known as South Dartmouth or Padanaram. The ruined cellars of the garrison were traceable a few years ago.

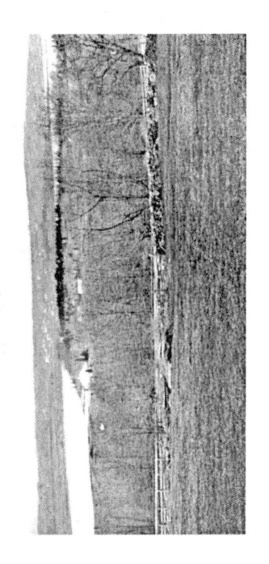

THE POCASSET COUNTRY

Looking across the scene of Cudworth's fight. The exact place of the battle is not known.

In the hope, however, that Church, who was known to possess considerable influence with the Pocasset Indians, would be able to persuade or force them into peace, he dispatched him with a small force of thirty-six men, with Captain Fuller in command, to Pocasset. Unable to get in touch with them, though informed by his Indian scouts that they were in force close by, the captain placed his men along a well-trodden trail and sat down to wait.

Fuller's men were unfortunately seized with an intense desire to smoke, and "this epidemical plague of lust after tobacco"[1] betrayed their presence to a party of Indians coming down the path who instantly turned back.

On their return to the rendezvous certain of the men began to twit Church on his failure to show them any Indians, whereupon he offered to show such as would volunteer to accompany him as many as they desired to see.

It was now determined to divide the force, Fuller marching along the coast, while Church, with nineteen men, moved into the swamp. Fuller had marched only a few miles when he discovered a band of Indians, who had evidently been watching the force for some time, closing in upon him. Urging his men forward he took possession of a deserted house near the water's edge and held his own stoutly until the evening when, a sloop approaching the shore, he embarked his force and passed over to the island of Rhode Island.

Church's party in the meantime marching along the rocky but deeply wooded ground soon came upon a "fresh plain trail," but so infested with rattlesnakes that

---

[1] Church, page 7.

the men were unwilling to proceed. "Had they kept on," says the chronicle, "they would have found enough (Indians) but it is not certain they would have returned to tell how many."[1] The desire of the men to turn back must have been welcome to Church who knew the peril of their position. Retracing their steps a short distance they turned off into a pea field in two divisions. Suddenly two Indians appeared. Church and those with him threw themselves on the ground, but the others discovered themselves and the Indians fled. Deeming their position critical the captain drew his men together and marched toward the shore as the glitter of gun barrels in the sunlight showed them a large force of Indians who soon opened a fierce fire.[2] The little force, keeping well together and taking advantage of the ground, made their way without loss to the beach,[3] and here, burrowing in the sand and lying behind the rocks, they kept the Indians at bay.

For over twenty-four hours the force had been without food, and the boats which they had expected to follow along the shore were seen aground towards Rhode Island. Hard pressed by numbers Church ordered his men to

---

[1] Church, page 8.

[2] Church, page 9.

[3] The scene of Church's exploit is located on Punkatees Neck, sometimes called Pocasset Neck. It is about five miles south of the village of Tiverton and shoots out from the mainland directly opposite the little village of Tiverton Four Corners. The immediate scene of the conflict was on the shore directly opposite Fogland Point, a spur of land pushing out westwardly and then turning to the north, thus forming a cove of which the point is the western boundary. The spring at which Church records himself as quenching his thirst, has disappeared, and it is most probable that the shore on which Church's force actually stood has been encroached upon and swallowed up by the sea.

throw off their outside garments in order that the Rhode Islanders, watching the fight from the opposite shore, might distinguish his meager force by their white shirts, and send assistance.[1]

The Indians had now taken possession of the ruins of a stone house near by, but the English lay close in shelter and their fire accomplished little. The fight continued all of a sultry afternoon, until near evening a sloop, commanded by Captain Golding, came in close to shore and brought them off two at a time in a canoe.

Philip having been definitely located amid the swamps about Pocasset, the Massachusetts troops on their return from the Narragansett country proceeded through Rehoboth to Taunton. On the 18th they were joined by the Plymouth forces under Cudworth and the whole army proceeded into the Pocasset swamp,[2] which they reached after an eighteen-mile march.[3]

Pushing forward in haste and without caution they were met by a murderous volley from a large number of Indians lying in wait for them in a thicket. Five of their number were instantly killed and many were wounded.

---

[1] Church, page 11.

[2] Hubbard, Vol. I, page 84.

[3] The "swamp" here mentioned was rather a thick growth of woods and tangled underbrush than a wet and miry lowland. There is evidence that the encounter was at a point on the eastern shore of the Taunton River directly opposite the present village of Somerset, between the Assonet River and the railroad track leading to Middleboro, and hemmed in on the east by the highway from Fall River to Assonet village. This section of country is rolling, watered by several streams, with occasional marshes. Hubbard characterizes the Pocasset swamp as being seven miles in length, but this only lends probability to the statement made above that the term applied to a tangled and difficult wooded country rather than to a marsh, there being nothing of the latter sort, of anything like that extent, in this whole region.

Before they could rally and assume the offensive, the Indians, leaving their wigwams at the mercy of the English, withdrew farther into the swamp.

Hearing from an old Indian found in one of the wigwams that Philip was near by, the English attempted to follow, but the night was coming on and in the dusk the soldiers began to fire at every stump and waving bush, and many, made nervous and confused by the darkness, shot in the gloom even at their comrades. Orders were given to halt, and the force retreated out of the swamp.

It was now decided, from the belief that Philip and his Wampanoags were finally cornered, to leave Captain Henchman and his company, supported by the Plymouth forces to build a fort which it was supposed would prevent the egress of the Indians and lead eventually to their being starved into submission.

Considering that Philip was as good as taken the main army now disbanded,[1] while Captain Prentice marched towards Mendon where five or six of the inhabitants had been killed while laboring in the fields by a war party of Nipmucks.[2]

Philip was very far from being taken, and, while Henchman was building his fort, evaded the outposts during the night of the 31st of July, and, crossing the Taunton River at low tide by swimming and by rafts,[3] made his escape.

---

[1] Hubbard, Vol. I, page 86.

[2] This was the first attack on any place in the Massachusetts colony, and was led by Matoonas, a Nipmuck chieftain. The wife and son of Matthias Puffer were slain as was also one William Post, and these are the only ones that can now be identified among the victims. The site of the slaughter is marked by a monument.

[3] Hubbard says, "About a hundred or more of the women and children, which were like to be rather burdensome than serviceable, were

He had turned the flank of the colonists and was well on his way to the Nipmuck country before the sun was high. He had outgeneraled his opponents, and could he once pass unmolested through the plains about Rehoboth the whole undefended frontier would be at his mercy.

Fortunately for the settlements Philip's force was discovered while crossing Seekonk Plain by a scouting party from Taunton.

The Reverend Mr. Newman[1] of Rehoboth gathered a company of volunteers, and, reinforced by fifty Mohegans and some Natick Indians returning from Boston under the command of Oneco and two other sons of Uncas,[2] rushed in pursuit. The troops towards Mount Hope and Swansea were notified and the pursuers were soon joined by Lieutenant Thomas[3] with a small force, including some Providence volunteers. Night had fallen, but they continued the chase until notified by the Mohegan scouts that the Wampanoags were near by.

Just before dawn, leaving their horses, the whole force stole upon the Indian encampment and surprised the inmates. It was Weetamoo's camp, and the Indians fled,

---

left behind, who soon after resigned up themselves to the mercy of the English."

[1] Rev. Noah Newman was the son of Rev. Samuel Newman, and succeeded his father in the pastorate of the church at Rehoboth. He died April 26, 1678.—Savage.

[2] Massachusetts Archives, Vol. LXVII, page 215. Curtis' Return and Relation.

[3] Lieutenant Nathaniel Thomas lived at Marshfield, of which town he was representative for eight years from 1672. At the time of Philip's escape from the Pocasset swamp he was stationed at the Mount Hope garrison with twenty men, eleven of whom he took with him on his chase after the other forces, which he overtook at sundown. He died October 22, 1718, in his 76th year.—Bodge. Savage.

leaving several dead. The settlers were following hard upon the heels of the fugitives when suddenly they found themselves confronted by Philip's fighting men.[1]

The fight raged fiercely for some time, both sides losing several killed, among the Wampanoag dead being Woonashun,[2] one of the signers of the treaty of Taunton, but finally the Indians withdrew and the Mohegans, finding the plunder of Weetamoo's camp to their liking, could not be induced to continue the pursuit.

Captain Henchman was still building his fort at Pocasset when the news reached him that Philip had escaped. Embarking his force he crossed the water and soon came up with the Rehoboth men who were returning for their horses left in the rear.

Henchman failed to energetically pursue the retiring Indians although furnished with supplies by Edmonds[3] and Brown.[4] He failed to grasp the importance of an-

---

[1] The place of this encounter was known as Nipsachick. It is located in the northwest corner of the town of Smithfield, R. I., a mile and a half south from the Tarkiln station of the Providence & Springfield R. R. It is in the midst of a hilly country with the swamp Nipsachick lying in a valley southward of the hill of that name. This was the first encounter upon the soil of Rhode Island.

[2] Nimrod, alias Woonashun, was a great captain and counselor. —Book of the Indians.

[3] Captain Andrew Edmonds of Providence commanded the Providence company which took part in the affair at Nipsachick. He was afterwards granted the privilege of operating a ferry where the red bridge crosses the Seekonk River, by the men whom, he said in his petition, "fought with me at Nipsatteke," as compensation for his valiant services in the war. In 1696 the ferry privilege was continued to his widow. —The State of Rhode Island and Providence Plantations (Edward Field), Vol. I, page 403.

[4] Lieutenant John Brown was the son of John of Wannamoiset. He was an early settler of Swansea of which town he was a leading citizen.

nihilating or turning Philip back toward Mount Hope, though even now the Nipmucks were rising and the unsuspecting settlers along the western frontier were in peril of massacre. Henchman continued his pursuit leisurely until his provisions were exhausted. Near Mendon the Mohegans left him and soon after, meeting Captain Moseley who was bringing up supplies, he gave over the pursuit.[1]

Philip's force nevertheless had been scattered. Weetamoo and her people turned again to their own territory. Many of the Wampanoags deserted, or, prevented from joining Philip through ignorance of his whereabouts, wandered around in small parties, falling upon the homes of solitary settlers and isolated hamlets.

Negotiations had already been commenced with the Indians left by Philip in the vicinity of Pocasset. By the persistence of Captain Benjamin Church and Captain Eels,[2] many were induced to surrender themselves and were taken to Plymouth, but, notwithstanding the terms on which they had submitted and the indignant remonstrances of Church and the other captains, the whole to the number of one hundred and sixty were ordered by the government to be sold into slavery.[3]

---

[1] Letter of Captain Nathaniel Thomas to Thomas Winslow.—Mather's History (Appendix), page 231.

[2] Samuel Eels of Milford, Conn., was a military officer in Philip's war and was afterwards at Fairfield, in 1687, but settled later in Hingham from which place he was representative in 1705. He died in 1709. —Savage.

[3] Church, page 13.

A letter written by the Rev. Mr. Fitch of Norwich to the Connecticut Council records the capture by Mohegans of 111 women and children about this time, who were afterwards sold into slavery.—Conn. Records, Vol. II, page 355.

F

Before we follow the developments which were rapidly unfolding during the month of July toward the western frontier of the Bay towns, let us turn for the moment to the state of affairs in the colony of Connecticut. Here we shall find a prompt realization of the dangers of the warfare which had broken out and an energy and decisiveness in marked contrast with the hesitation and blindness of both Massachusetts and Plymouth. That colony, though engaged in a fierce dispute with Governor Andros of New York, as soon as the first alarm of war was sounded took energetic measures, and, secure in the friendly disposition and active alliance of Uncas, was able not only to guard her eastern frontier but to lend valuable assistance to her neighbors.

The towns were ordered to set themselves in a position of defense, and on the first day of July, when Savage was marching into Mount Hope peninsula, Connecticut troops were being sent to New London, Stonington and Saybrook under Captains Waite Winthrop and Thomas Bull.[1] The Mohegans were encouraged to don their war paint by the promise of rewards for every scalp and prisoner taken, and scouting parties scoured the country from Norwich to the Narragansett frontiers. Winthrop, a few days after his arrival at New London, had invaded the Narra-

---

[1] Thomas Bull of Hartford came in the *Hopewell,* embarking at London in September, 1635. He was first of Boston or Cambridge, but accompanied Hooker to Hartford. He served in the Pequot war in 1637, and in 1675 was in command of the fort at Saybrook when Sir Edmond Andros attempted unsuccessfully to gain the place for the Duke of York. He was appointed lieutenant of a company raised in 1653, by order of the Commissioners of the United Colonies, to fight the Dutch. He died in 1684.—Memorial History of Hartford County, Vol. I, page 232.

gansett country and joined Hutchinson in forcing the Pettaquamscot treaty on the Narragansetts.

Uncas, though an old man, had not lost his cunning, and the suspicions in regard to the Narragansetts offered too valuable an opportunity for the sagacious sachem to overlook. The report that the Narragansetts were sheltering the women and children of the Wampanoags was certainly spread by him, and there is more than a suspicion that his warriors did not discriminate too carefully between the scalps of neutral Narragansetts and the hostile Wampanoags.

Connecticut realized to the full the value of the Indian auxiliaries as scouts and guides, while the Massachusetts authorities yielded to public clamor which held all the Indian race to be treacherous enemies. Connecticut, whose people tasted little of the bitterness of burned villages and slain settlers, associated the Mohegans with all their expeditions and by their assistance escaped those ambuscades so often fatal to the Massachusetts forces.

While desolation and terror prevailed in the isolated settlements towards Rhode Island and the Plymouth frontier, and Connecticut lay safe in the security of remoteness and the Mohegan alliance, the settlers to the west of the Bay towns and in the Connecticut Valley pursued their customary occupations, disturbed by occasional rumors, yet generally confident in the neutrality of the neighboring Nipmucks.

The Nipmuck and the valley tribes had planted their fields as usual and no unwonted movement had been noticed among them. Warnings, however, had come to the ears of the authorities early in June before Philip had plunged into the conflict.

CHAPTER VI

O NE Waban,[1] a Christian Natick, and several Christian Indians had early reported that the Nipmucks were disaffected. In fact all the Indian tribes seemed to have reached a state of excitement and concealed hostility which only needed such a spark as was furnished by Philip's example to break into flame, and there is considerable evidence that these tribes, formerly closely connected with the Wampanoags, had been visited by emissaries of Philip in the spring.

In accordance with their usual custom the Governor and Council of Massachusetts, though with no full realization of the great danger, sent Ephraim Curtis[2] of Worcester to the Nipmuck country on the 13th of July, in the dual capacity of negotiator and spy. Journeying through the country, particularly that part lying toward Brookfield, he visited many of the Nipmuck villages and

---

[1] Wauban, commonly written Waban, was supposed to be from Concord, and was an old man when Philip's war broke out. He was one of Eliot's converts; resided at Noantum (Newton), and later at Natick where he was "a ruler over fifty," and a justice of the peace. He was among those sent to Deer Island, October 30, 1675, and among the sick that returned in May, 1676, and it is particularly mentioned that he was one that recovered. The time of his death is unknown.—Drake's Book of the Indians, Vol. II, page 115.

[2] Ephraim Curtis was the son of Henry of Sudbury, and was 33 years of age at the breaking out of Philip's war. He was a notable scout and hunter, well versed in Indian ways and intimately acquainted with many of the tribes. He was also a trader and had a house at Quamsigamug (Worcester).

received promises of good behavior. Hardly had he reached Boston when the Council, now seriously alarmed by the conditions at Swansea, bade him return to the Nipmucks. On reaching Brookfleld,[1] Curtis was informed that Matoonas,[2] with Sagamore John and certain others, leaders of the party among the Nipmucks friendly to Philip, had robbed his house at Worcester and was given to understand by some Indians with whom he had traded for many years, that it would be dangerous for him to continue his journey. Securing two men and horses from Marlboro, however, with a friendly Indian for a guide, he set out for the Indian encampment at Quabaug, one of the Indian villages of which there were several near by.

On approaching the site of the village neither Indians nor wigwams were to be seen. He determined, however, to follow on toward one of the upper villages. A few miles to the west, coming upon an Indian path newly made he followed it for a considerable distance until they came by the abandoned lead mines on the old road to Springfield. A short distance farther on they came upon two Indians, one of whom they managed to overtake. He informed them that the others were encamped a short distance away, which led Curtis to send a Middleboro Indian to announce that he came as a messenger from the Governor of Massachusetts with peaceable word and no intention to hurt or fight them.

---

[1] The location of old Brookfleld was upon Foster Hill at a point about halfway between the present villages of Brookfield and West Brookfield. At present there are but few houses in this locality.

[2] Matoonas was a Nipmuck chief whom Hubbard calls "An old, malicious villian." His son had been executed for having murdered a young Englishman in Dedham.

The guide soon returned with the information that they would not believe the message sent them. Undeterred by their hostile attitude, which to an old trader acquainted with them conveyed its own warning, he went on towards their encampment and found the main body on an island of a few acres surrounded by a swamp and the river.[1] A party of warriors whom they found on the road cocked their guns at him. None who knew him would speak or return his salutation. Disturbed by these evidences of hostility his companions urged that it was too perilous to continue, but silencing them with the argument that their only safety lay in going boldly among them, he pushed on. On reaching the river bank he called out that he came peaceably to remind them of their engagements, at which a great uproar arose. Guns were aimed at him and many of the young men would have killed him had not the older men withheld them. Ordering the sachems to come over the river, they re-

---

[1] This was Menameset where the old turnpike road from Furnace village through Oakham crosses the Wenimisset Brook in New Braintree. The topography of the country has greatly changed and drainage and tillage has removed practically all traces of the swamp except immediately along the borders of the brook. The site of the encampment was about twenty rods from Ware River and may be reached by a walk of perhaps a third of a mile from the New Braintree station of the Massachusetts Central Division of the Boston and Maine R. R. This village was the most southerly of three, all known by the name of Menameset, and was perhaps a mere temporary lodging place. The other villages were located farther up the Ware River, the first about a mile from the former and the last two miles beyond the middle village. The two last were permanent abiding places, so far as any Indian dwelling could have that term applied, and evidence of this is still to be seen. The middle village has the distinction of having been the one to which Mrs. Rowlandson was brought after her capture at Lancaster.

MENAMESET LOWER VILLAGE

fused, and bade him come over to them. As he forded the river the Indians continued to threaten him and he requested them to lay down their arms. They demanded that he lay down his arms and that he and his companions come off their horses, a command with which he was compelled to comply. Many said they would not believe him or his masters unless two or three bushels of powder were sent them.[1] Among the chiefs were Muttaump,[2] chief of the Quabaugs, and Sagamore Sam[3] of the Nashaway Indians.

The feeling against him finally quieted down and they bade him stay with them over night saying that their hostile attitude had been due to the report that the English had killed a man of theirs on the Merrimac River a few days before and had an intention to destroy them all. Assuring them of the friendship of the authorities he left them apparently appeased. During his return to Boston news reached him that war had broken out along the Plymouth frontier.

The attack on Mendon again aroused the authorities to the threatening danger from the Nipmuck tribes, and, combined with the news which had reached them of the attitude of the eastern Indians, led them to consider the necessity of keeping the Nipmucks under control. In consequence Curtis was again dispatched from Boston to make a perfect discovery of the motions of the Nip-

---

[1] Massachusetts Archives, Vol. LXVII, page 215.—Curtis' Return and Relation.

[2] Muttaump or Mattawamppe, was the sachem of the Quabaugs. He was interested in the sale of Brookfield lands to the settlers.

[3] Sagamore Sam of the Nashaway tribe was one of the party which sacked Lancaster February 10, 1676. He was also known by the name of Uskatuhgun.—Drake's Book of the Indians.

mucks, and with a declaration under the public seal that the English had no intention to disturb them or any other Indians who remained peaceable.

After delivering a message to the constable at Marlboro to forward to Major Pynchon at Springfield, he followed his old trail and came upon the Indians at the place where he had found them encamped before. As he waved his hand to them across the stream they gave a great shout. Muttaump was away, but several minor chiefs spoke to him. The warriors seemed calmer and less sullen than before and listened to the Governor's letter quietly.

He told them if Muttaump and others would come to Boston they would be well treated, their bellies filled and their questions answered, and received their promise to send one or more of their chiefs to Boston within five days. Asked why they had been so abusive during his former visit they replied that Black James,[1] one of the leaders of the Quabaug Indians, had told them that the English would kill them all because they were not praying Indians.[2] They also informed him that one of Philip's men had been among them with plunder from Swansea at the time of his first visit.

The Council waited in vain for the embassy. None came, and, thoroughly alarmed, they determined to force matters to an issue. Captains Hutchinson and Wheeler,[3]

---

[1] Black James was a Quabaug, a dweller at Chabanakongkomun, near what is now Webster, Mass. He was constituted a constable of all the praying towns. "He is a person that hath approved himself dilligent and courageous, faithful and zealous to suppress sin."—Gookin.

[2] Massachusetts Archives, Vol. LXVII, page 223.

[3] Captain Thomas Wheeler was of Concord where he was admitted freeman May 18, 1642. He was early engaged in military affairs and

with twenty troopers, were accordingly sent from Boston, July 28th, to demand the reasons why the promised embassy had not been sent, and to warn them that unless they delivered up Matoonas, his accomplices and all hostile Indians who came among them, the Council would hold them as aids and abettors.

Marching leisurely by way of Cambridge and Sudbury the English came upon several Indian villages, but all were silent and deserted. Hearing on their arrival at Brookfield, August 1st, that the Indians were ten miles to the northwest, they sent Curtis with some other young men to inform them that they had not come to do them injury but to deliver a message. Curtis reported on his return that the chief sachems had promised to meet them at a place three miles from Brookfield on the morrow at eight o'clock, but that the younger warriors seemed surly and hostile.

On the next day they set out for the rendezvous, but no Indians came to meet them. Encouraged, however, by several Brookfield settlers who had accompanied them, and who relied upon the influence of one David,[1] a saga-

---

upon the organization of a troop of horse in Concord, became its captain. He was in this command when the company was called to active service in Philip's war, July, 1675. He died December 16, 1686.

[1] David was ruler of the Quabaug village in the southeasterly part of Brookfield, and was a trusted friend of the first Brookfield settlers. During the war he was charged with being privy to a murder committed at Lancaster and an attempt was made to wring confession from him through torture. In this situation, in order to avert immediate death, as well as to be avenged for the death of a brother captured by friendly Indians and by them delivered over to the English and shot, he accused eleven Indians of the act, which accusation he subsequently acknowledged to have been false, and in punishment for this treachery, as well as for shooting at a boy in Marlboro, he was condemned to slavery, and accordingly sold.—Book of the Indians, page 265.

more of the Quabaugs, who had long been a friend of the English and to whose tribe a majority of the Indians belonged, they determined to proceed despite the warning of their Indian guides. Riding in single file along the trail they entered a narrow path where a wooded hill rose abruptly from the edge of a swamp covered with thick brush and tall grass.[1] Here, when they had well entered, from all sides a murderous volley was poured in upon them and several fell. Unable to retreat by the way they had come or to enter the swamp, a few of the party, dismounting, held the savages from rushing and overpowering them, in a hand-to-hand conflict, until the rest had had time to rally. Wheeler's horse was shot and he himself wounded, but his son coming to the rescue placed him on his own horse and, though himself wounded in the abdomen, was able to catch a riderless horse and join the rest of the force.

Skillfully directed by their three Indian guides, the survivors fought their way step by step up the steep side of the hill and finally broke through, leaving eight of their number, including all the Brookfield men, dead on the field. The survivors, five of them badly wounded, Captain Hutchinson mortally, taking a circuitous route, reached Brookfield in safety. It is a sad commentary to add that the Indian guides, to whose skill and loyalty the survivors owed their lives, were soon afterwards driven by harsh treatment to join the hostiles. One Sampson is

_____

[1] The place of ambush in the Wenimisset fight was in the valley of that brook about a mile south of the lower Menameset village. The swamplike character of the ground has been reclaimed by drainage, but the steep and rocky hillside still remains. The old Indian path is supplanted by a traveled highway.

known to have been killed soon after while fighting against the English, and his brother Joseph taken prisoner and sold into slavery in Jamaica was to be released afterwards through the efforts of Eliot. From the other, Memecho, a Christian Natick, we obtain information of Philip's meeting with the Quabaugs.

The return of the defeated troopers made clear the deadly peril which now hovered over the little settlement of Brookfield. Abandoning their homes the people flocked to the house of Sergeant John Ayres,[1] the largest and strongest in the settlement, with such provisions and household goods as they were able to take with them.

Hardly had the necessary preparations been completed when the victorious Quabaugs poured into the village, plundering and burning the deserted houses and encompassing the garrison on all sides.

Curtis, and Henry Young of Concord, attempting to leave for the purpose of procuring aid from the other towns, after reaching the further end of the street were driven back, and the attack upon the garrison began in earnest. That evening Young, looking out of a loophole in the garret window, was shot and mortally wounded. A son of Sergeant Pritchard,[2] venturing out of the garri-

---

[1] John Ayres was of Haverhill in 1645, Ipswich, 1648, a petitioner for Quabaug in 1660, whither he removed with the first settlers and was a leading man in the new plantation. He was killed at Wenimisset August 2, 1675, and his sons received a grant of land on account of their father's services.—Temple's History of North Brookfield, page 65.

[2] Sergeant William Pritchard was of Lynn, 1645, and of Ipswich, 1648, He removed to Quabaug in 1667 where he was "clerk of the writs," and second sergeant in the Brookfield company. He was killed at Wenimisset fight August 2, 1675. His home lot in Brookfield was the one first east of Sergeant Ayres' tavern, and it was there that his son Samuel was killed during the siege.—History of North Brookfield.

son to his father's house near by, in order to bring in some valuables forgotten in the confusion of flight, was shot, his head cut off and set upon a pole. Fagots and hay were piled up at the corner of the house and fired, but the fire was put out and the garrison, standing to their posts, drove off the Indians with some loss. Curtis was again sent out but could not pass, but, going forth the third time, August 3rd, crept on his hands and knees through the lines of the besiegers and got safely away to Marlboro.

Through the third and fourth of August the siege continued. Blazing arrows were shot upon the roof of the house, but holes were cut through and water poured from buckets quenched the flames. Finally a wheeled contrivance loaded with hay and fagots was set on fire and pushed against the door while the warriors, sheltering themselves behind the trees and outhouses, fired at the settlers whenever they exposed themselves, but a downpour of rain quenched the fire and gave the defenders renewed hope. Thomas Wilson,[1] going out to fetch water, was shot through the jaw, and a woman killed by a bullet that entered through a loophole. But though the bullets occasionally pierced the walls they inflicted few casualties among the fifty women and children and the thirty-two men within.[2]

---

[1] Thomas Wilson was among the earlier settlers of Brookfield. In the division of lands he received lot No. 7, but a short distance west of the meeting-house lot, which was No. 10, that of Sergeant John Ayres upon which stood the tavern, being next east of the meeting-house.

[2] The best contemporary account of the ambuscade and the defense of Brookfield, is given in Captain Wheeler's "True Narrative of the Lord's Providences."

In the meanwhile, Judah Trumble[1] of Springfield, who had set out for Brookfield, saw the flames and, cautioned by the sound of guns and the shouts of the besiegers, crept up within forty rods of the burning houses. Immediately recognizing the desperate state of affairs he rode home in haste.

Preparations for the relief of the beleaguered town were at once made, couriers dispatched to Hartford and Boston asking for assistance, while warnings of the danger to which they were exposed were spread through the valley towns, and a force from Springfield under the command of Lieutenant Cooper,[2] reinforced by a company of troopers and Mohegans from Connecticut, Captain Thomas Watts[3] in command, was immediately sent forward. Major Simon Willard,[4] however, who had been dispatched

---

[1] Judah Trumble removed from Rowley to Suffield, now in Connecticut but then within the jurisdiction of Springfield, in 1676. At Suffield he was constable and held other town offices. He died April 1, 1692.

[2] Lieutenant Thomas Cooper came from England to Boston in 1635 when he was eighteen years of age. He settled in Windsor, Conn., in 1641, and two years later removed to Springfield. He was a man of varied accomplishments; practical carpenter and farmer, practicing attorney before the county court, bonesetter and surveyor. He built the first meetinghouse in Springfield in 1645, and was chosen on the first board of selectmen and served seventeen years, and was for one year deputy to the General Court. See First Century of Springfield, by H. M. Burt, Vol. II, page 553.

[3] Thomas Watts, son of Richard, was born about 1626. He lived in Hartford and was called sergeant in the list of freemen in 1669. He served as ensign, lieutenant, and captain of the Hartford trainband, and led his company in the desperate fight at Narragansett December 19, 1675. He also commanded the forces that went up the Connecticut River in 1676. He died in 1683.—Savage. Memorial History of Hartford County, Vol. I, page 266.

[4] Major Simon Willard was born in Hosmonden, Kent, England. He arrived in Boston in May, 1634, and soon settled in Cambridge. He

against some Indians near Groton, had fortunately been informed of the plight of the garrison by the Marlboro authorities as he was leaving Lancaster and immediately turned aside and marched toward Brookfield.

Soon after nightfall of the third, his company of forty-six men passed through the town and reached the garrison, now well-nigh worn out by loss of sleep and lack of provisions. His approach was known to the Indians, an outlying party of whom had allowed him to pass in the belief that the besiegers would ambuscade his force, but a large body of deserted cattle following his men misled the Indians as to the strength of the relieving force and caused them to draw off after setting fire to the remaining buildings. The anxious occupants of the Ayres house, hearing the confusion in the darkness, suspected it was another force of the enemy until English voices calling out in the night brought the welcome assurance that succor had come.[1] With the usual exaggeration the Indian losses were estimated at over eighty, a not unfamiliar measure of consolation.

Reinforcements were now pouring into Brookfield. Beers and Lathrop marched in from the east; on the same day, from Springfield and Hartford, came Cooper and

---

became one of the first settlers of Concord in 1637; entered into military affairs and in 1655 reached the rank of major, the highest at that time. He served as representative to the General Court for many sessions until 1654, and from 1657 until his death was an assistant of the colony. About 1659 he removed to Lancaster and to Groton in 1671. At the opening of King Philip's war he was the chief military officer of Middlesex County, and was then seventy years of age, and his services until the time of his death were full and efficient. He died at Charlestown, April 24, 1676.—Bodge, page 119.—Savage.

[1] Two pairs of twins were born in the Ayres tavern during the siege. —Old Indian Chronicle, page 145.

Watts with mounted men, and Mohegans under Uncas'
son Joshua, and the arrival of Captain Moseley with his
own and most of Henchman's company from Mendon,
on the 9th, brought the strength of the force under Major
Willard to about 350 men exclusive of Mohegans. Willard proceeded to patrol the country but with little success. Cooper then returned to Springfield but Moseley,
Lathrop, Watts, and Beers marched to the deserted village at Menameset and, having burnt its fifty wigwams,
separated, Watts marching to Springfield by way of Hadley, Beers and Lathrop scouring the country along the
Bay Path, while Moseley reconnoitered the country to the
north.[1] All alike failed to get in touch with the Indians
and none could tell where or when the next blow might
fall. The widely separated settlements throughout the
Connecticut Valley, it was evident, were in great danger,
and an immediate concentration in some stragetic position
in the valley was necessary.

Hadley, halfway up the valley, whose position in a
bend of the river afforded easy access to both banks,
was decided upon. There a stockade, having the river at
each end, was built, supplies were gathered and the
forces concentrated. Brookfield was soon abandoned by
all. Some months afterwards we hear that the abandoned cattle had returned to their old home and were
grazing among the ruined houses. The other settlements
up the river had, meanwhile, placed themselves in a state
of defense; stockades were built, the best situated and
strongest houses were fortified, and small garrisons were
left to assist the settlers in case of attack.

---

[1] Moseley to Governor Leverett, August 16th.—Massachusetts Archives, Vol. LXVII, page 239.

All knowledge of the Indians was lost, yet they were within easy striking distance. Their success at Wenimisset had drawn the waverers to arms and kindled the warlike temper of the tribes. Philip, too, was among them. He had met the Quabaugs retiring from the siege of Brookfield in a nearby swamp, on the 5th of August, and, giving them wampum as a pledge, praised their success. He told their chiefs how narrow had been his escape from capture or death in the fight at Nipsachick. Two hundred and fifty men had been with him including Weetamoo's force, besides women and children, but they had left him; some were killed and he was reduced to forty warriors and some women and children.[1] After this, save for vague rumors we hear little of Philip for some months. Tradition has named after him caves where he lived and mountains from which he watched the burning of the hamlets in the valley below, but his hand is hard to trace in the warfare of the valley.

Major Pynchon wrote to the Council of Connecticut, August 12th, that he was alone and wanted advice. Major Talcott was immediately sent to him with a recommendation to dispatch an agent to Albany to secure aid from the Mohawks.

The policy of the Iroquois did not favor the active alliance, however. The English were valuable allies against the French but the Iroquois were valuable to the English for much the same reasons. They had their own wars to wage without losing men for the English in a quarrel that did not concern them. It was no advantage to

---

[1] Testimony of George Memicho, a Christian Natick and one of Hutchinson's guides.—Hutchinson's History of Massachusetts, Vol. I, pages 293, 294.

OLD HADLEY STREET, LOOKING SOUTH.

them to help the English become too strong, and they disliked the English ally, Uncas, even more than the hostiles. They would be neutral, they informed Governor Andros of New York, and Pynchon in sending the news to Governor Leverett besought him to authorize the use of friendly Naticks as scouts.

On the 22nd Pynchon wrote to John Allyn[1] of Hartford, saying that the greater part of the forces had returned to Brookfield, Captain Watts was at Hadley, and a weak garrison had been established at Northfield. He was troubled at the thought of Watts being recalled and he suspected the Mohegan auxiliaries "to be fearful or false, or both."

While Captains Lathrop, Beers, and Watts were marching up the valley, and leaving men and supplies in the valley towns from Westfield to Northfield, Moseley, who had been sent to reconnoiter the country towards Lancaster, had been doing his best to turn the friendly Indians in that vicinity into enemies. News having reached him soon after his arrival at Chelmsford that seven people had been killed by Indians at Lancaster on the 22nd of August, he immediately marched to that place. On his arrival some of the townspeople actuated, as Gookin declares, by a desire for the land of the Christian Indians at Marlboro,

---

[1] John Allyn, son of Matthew, was born in England and married, November 19, 1651, Ann, daughter of Henry Smith of Springfield and granddaughter of William Pynchon. He resided in Hartford, was townsman 1655, town clerk 1659-96, deputy, many years magistrate, secretary of the colony 1663-65, again elected 1667, and held this office until 1695. He was of the committee of three chosen in 1662 to take the charter into their custody and safe keeping. In the military service he rose from cornet to rank of lieutenant-colonel. He died November 11, 1696. —Savage. Memorial History of Hartford County, Vol. I, page 228.

G

told him the attack had been made by them, a statement seemingly confirmed by an Indian named David, about to be executed. Moseley immediately raided this village of the Christian Indians, who had already been disarmed by Captain John Ruddock,[1] and, seizing eleven of their number tied them together by their necks and sent them to Boston for trial.[2] Continuing his march into the Pennacook country he burned the village and supplies of sachem Wannalancet,[3] near Concord, a friendly Indian who, fearing the same treatment that had been meted out to the Marlboro Indians, deserted his village at the approach of Moseley and withdrew into the woods.[4]

---

[1] Captain John Ruddock became freeman of the colony in 1640. He was actively engaged in forming the plantation of Marlboro. He built one of the first frame houses in the town, and was one of its first selectmen, first town clerk and deacon of the church. His second wife was the sister of Rev. William Brinsmead, the minister of Marlboro.—Hudson's History of Sudbury, page 40; also Hudson's History of Marlboro.

[2] Among these prisoners was old Jethro, who, confined at Deer Island, escaped, and, angered by his treatment, joined the hostiles.

[3] Wannalancet, in obedience to the advice of his father, always kept peace with the English. He resided at the ancient seat of the sagamores upon the Merrimac, called at that time Naamkeke, and his house stood near the Pawtucket Falls, but at the time of the war with Philip he took up his quarters among the Pennacooks, who were also his people. Wannalancet and his company were among those who came to Cochecho at the invitation of Major Walderne, September 6, 1676, were tricked, captured, some executed and others sold into slavery by the Massachusetts authorities. He was, however, among those that were set at liberty and returned to his home at Naamkeke to find his lands seized by the whites and he himself looked upon as an intruder, and, after an uncomfortable year among them, he accepted the invitation of a party of Indians from Canada who visited him, to accompany them home, and with all his people, reduced to less than fifty in number, went to that region and is not heard of after.—Book of the Indians, Vol. III, page 95.

[4] Gookin. Christian Indians. American Antiquarian Society Collections, Vol. II, page 463.

Moseley was censured for these acts but his course was approved by public opinion.

He then set out on his return to the valley. The prisoners sent down to Boston were acquitted with the exception of one, who was sold to appease public clamor, but was afterwards released, and the Governor and Council immediately sent Henchman to Wannalancet to make explanations.

During the summer the Nonatuck village on the bluff along the river above Northampton had become the rendezvous of a large number of Indians, and though they had committed as yet no overt act, and indeed had offered their services to the English, their temper was distrusted as it was reported they had celebrated the success of the Quabaugs at Wenimisett,[1] and the Mohegans' scouts declared they warned the hostiles to look out for themselves by shouts. It seemed probable that they were only awaiting a favorable opportunity to strike at one of the nearby settlements. Their arms had once been taken from them but afterwards returned, and a second demand put them on their guard. They had protested and the Council of Connecticut was even then drawing up a letter to Major Pynchon that the disarming of the Indians should be foreborne at the present.[2] Whether the Nonatucks were forced into hostilities at this time by fear is uncertain, but the advice in view of later events was bad, and, at any rate, in this case came too late.

At a council of war held at Hatfield on the 24th of August, it was determined to surprise and disarm them

---

[1] Letter of Rev. Solomon Stoddard to Increase Mather.—Mather's Brief History.

[2] Connecticut Records, Vol. II, page 356.

immediately, and a force of one hundred men, commanded by Captains Lathrop[1] and Beers who had come in from Brookfield two days before, was consequently dispatched late at night with instructions to co-operate with a force from Northampton going up on the other side of the river.

The dawn was upon the troops at they reached the Indian encampment. It was silent and deserted, but the fires were still smoldering and amid the embers lay the body of an old sachem, probably one of those appointed by the English, who was believed to have spoken too energetically for submission. A part of the force was sent back to protect the towns but the pursuit was vigorously taken up by the remainder, and the fugitives, encumbered with their women and children, were overtaken a mile south of the present village of South Deerfield and under the shadow of Mount Wequomps.[2] Finding flight no longer possible, the warriors, concealing themselves in what is now known as Hopewell Swamp, turned at bay and poured a volley into the pursuing English.[3] The

---

[1] Captain Thomas Lathrop was made freeman at Salem, May 14, 1634. He became captain of the Artillery Company in 1645 and served in the expedition against Acadia. He represented Salem and Beverly in the General Court for a number of sessions, and after that part of Salem in which he lived became Beverly he was a prominent actor in all its affairs. In August, 1675, he was given command of a company raised principally in Essex County. Bodge, page 133.—Savage.

[2] Wequomps was the Indian name of the sightly elevation near the banks of the Connecticut in South Deerfield, now known as Sugar Loaf Mountain. It rises abruptly from the plain to a height of about seven hundred feet. It looks down upon the Hopewell Swamp which lies to the southward, its northern boundary being perhaps a quarter of a mile distant from the mountain.

[3] A letter of Rev. Solomon Stoddard to Increase Mather gives what is probably the most reliable account.—Mather's Brief History.

HOPEWELL SWAMP

Now in Whateley, Massachusetts. The scene of the first fight of King Philip's War in the Connecticut Valley. Mount Wequomps in the distance.

troops kept their presence of mind, and rushing into the swamp sought cover behind the trees, and after three hours' fighting and the loss of nine of their number killed or fatally wounded, drove the Indians into flight. It was stated by an Indian squaw that the Nonotucks had lost twenty-six warriors, but all such tales of Indian losses are of little or no value, being generally invented to put the English in good humor and win their favor. The Indian losses in all cases where the English were ambushed were probably very much less than those they inflicted. It must be remembered that they not only enjoyed the advantage of surprise, but were sheltered and hidden.

Somewhat over halfway between Northampton and the frontier town of Northfield stands Deerfield, then a settlement of some one hundred and twenty-five souls, whose situation at the foot of Pocumtuck Mountain made it easily accessible to sudden attacks. Three of the houses had been fortified with palisades,[1] and ten men of Captain Watts' company were in garrison.

As after the siege at Brookfield, a strange calm seemed to have fallen upon the valley in the week following the fight at Wequomps, but it was a calm fraught with fear and anxiety and occupied with fruitless marches after a vanished foe; yet contempt of the Indians and careless confidence in their own power over those so long subservient and submissive, were in the ascendant; but what could be done against those who, like will-o'-the-wisps, could seldom be found or forced to stand, but struck at the settlers in the field, descended by night on the lonely hamlets and fought only at an advantage. It

---

[1] Sheldon's History of Deerfield, Vol. I, page 92.

was upon Deerfield that the next blow fell. For many years the Pocumtucks had found in the protection of the colonists, peace and safety from their old foes, the Mohawks, whose vengeance they had brought down upon themselves by the murder of Mohawk ambassadors some years previously; but here as elsewhere safety had been purchased at the loss of their independence. Drink had taken hold of them, and they saw themselves sinking in degradation and subservience before the rising power of their white neighbors, who with little sympathy and less suavity gave them the law. Wounded pride had rankled into hatred and the news of Indian successes enkindled in them the old passion for war, plunder and vengeance.

In August they had left their village on the mountain for the woods near the town, and were watching for a favorable opportunity. On the first day of September a Connecticut trooper[1] of the garrison, while looking for his horse which had strayed away, came by accident upon a body of some sixty warriors and paid for the discovery with his life.

The alarm, however, had been given and the people fled to the shelter of the garrisons. After a sharp fusilade the Pocumtucks drew off and turned their attention to the buildings and barns outside the range of the settlers' rifles, who, not daring to venture out, saw the labor of long years go up in smoke, and their cattle driven away.

---

[1] James Eggleston of Windsor, according to Savage and Sheldon, but this is denied by Miss Mary K. Talcott of Hartford. See Stiles' History of Ancient Windsor, Vol. II, page 199.

CHAPTER VII

THERE was consternation in the settlements down the valley at the news (which rumor did not fail to exaggerate) and Mather says that the people of Hadley were driven from a holy service by a most violent and sudden alarm.

It was this alarm which gave rise to one of those romantic legends with which history abounds for, in the midst of the panic-stricken people, a man, venerable and unknown, with long white beard, is said to have appeared and led them against the foe. It was the fugitive regicide, General Goffe.[1]

Historians have credited the legend because of the sanction it obtained from Governor Hutchinson,[2] on the strength of some papers that were destroyed by a Boston mob just before the Revolution. Romantic as the story is it is certainly a myth, and arose from the fact that Goffe was in the village at that time, hiding in the house

---

[1] Major-General William Goffe was the son of Rev. Stephen Goffe of Stanmer, County Sussex, England. He was a member of the pretended High Court of Justice selected by a minority of the Long Parliament to sentence Charles I to death. Compelled to flee for safety he arrived at Boston, July 27, 1660, and in February following went to New Haven in company with his fellow judge and father-in-law, Lieutenant-General Edward Whalley. They lived in concealment in and near New Haven for some time, but in October, 1664, they took up their residence with the Rev. Mr. Russell at Hadley; Goffe outlived Whalley a number of years and died probably in Hartford, Conn., about 1679.

[2] Hutchinson's History of Massachusetts, Vol. I, page 219.

of the Reverend Mr. Russell,[1] but no record of this dramatic appearance exists in any contemporary letters or narratives. The alleged furious attack on Hadley, which made it necessary for Goffe to take command of the panic-stricken settlers, never occurred.[2] No Indians were near, and when the town was actually attacked in the following spring it contained, unknown to the Indians, a force of nearly five hundred troops.

A few miles north of Deerfield, on the far frontier, lay the little settlement of Northfield.[3] Some seventeen thatched cabins, a palisade of rough logs eight feet high set upright in the ground and pierced with loopholes, and a log fort and church, composed this infant settlement born but three years before. A small garrison had been left here, but both settlers and troopers seem to have been careless of danger.

On the day following the attack on Deerfield, while the settlers and the troopers, ignorant of what had occurred down the valley, were working in the meadows, the Pocumtucks, reinforced by a band of Nashaways under Sagamore Sam and Monaco or "One-Eyed John," fell upon them. Some were killed in their houses, and a party

---

[1] Rev. John Russell graduated from Harvard College in 1645, and was ordained about 1649 as pastor of the church in Wethersfield, Conn., where he remained until the settlement of Hadley, 1659 or 1660, when he removed thither and was pastor of the church there until his death, December 10, 1692.—Judd's History of Hadley.

[2] New England Historical and Genealogical Register, Vol. XXVIII, page 379. Researches of the well-known antiquarian of the Connecticut Valley, Honorable George Sheldon.

[3] The original settlement of Northfield lay, as does the present village, on the plateau separated from the Connecticut River by a broad stretch of fertile meadow. The stockade and fort were at the south end of the village and their site is marked by a monument.

of men retreating at the alarm from the meadows, were shot down as they made their way toward the settlement. Women and children rushed to the stockaded inclosure and the surviving men held it safe against the rush of Indians, but the anxious people, more affected than those in Deerfield, had not only to contemplate the flames destroying their homes, but to mourn the loss of eight of their number.[1]

Even before this attack the commanders at Hadley, alarmed for the safety of the town, had determined to succor it and Captain Beers,[2] in ignorance of the condition of affairs, left Hadley on the third day with thirty-six mounted men and an ox-team loaded with supplies, intending to make a forced march and enter the town at night. Progress was, however, slow, and the night fell while the little force was struggling through the woods, some four miles from its destination. Vague rumors of the attack or of the presence of Indians must have reached them, for at dawn the main guard left the horses under a small guard and pushed on.

Their way lay for some distance along the plateau until they reached what is now known as Sawmill Brook. Disregarding the lesson of Wenimisset and Wequomps, carelessly, without flankers or scouts thrown out, they turned and followed it as it fell away toward the valley. The leaves were thick upon the trees, the ground was covered

---

[1] Rev. Solomon Stoddard to Rev. Increase Mather.—Mather's Brief History.

[2] Captain Richard Beers was made freeman at Watertown, March 9, 1637. He served in the Pequot war. He was representative to the General Court from Watertown from 1663 to 1675, and was for thirty-one years selectman of his town, holding both offices at the time of the breaking out of Philip's war.—Bodge, page 127. Savage.

with rank growth of grass and bush, while the trees shut
out the sunlight and cast the trail in deep shadow. Following the left bank of the brook they came finally to
where the path following a depression offered a fordable
crossing,

Here, concealed in front and along the steep bank above
the stream the Indians had laid their ambuscade, and
into it, unconscious of danger, marched Beers and his
men. They were in the act of crossing the brook when
a murderous volley smote them in van and rear. Thrown
at first into confusion they finally rallied and fought their
way out of the ravine and up to the high ground. The
Indians were pressing them hard and many of their number were down, but the rest fought desperately on, and,
after an ineffectual stand upon the plain, the remnant
finally gained a position in a small ravine three-quarters
of a mile away. Here, upon the southern spur of what
is now known as Beers' Mountain, fell Beers and most
of his men.[1] That evening, the guard left with the horses,
and the survivors of the main body, staggered wearily
into Hadley.[2] Hubbard gives the number of Indians in
the fight as many hundreds; Temple and Sheldon with
more accuracy place them at about one hundred and
forty.

The Indians, replenishing their ammunition from the
cart, got drunk from the keg of rum which was one of

---

[1] Sawmill Brook crossed the path or trail to the southward about a
mile from the stockade, while the level plain on which Beers made his
desperate stand, borders the brook on the south. The point at which
the stand was made is indicated by a suitable monument and is little
more than half a mile south of the brook, near the foot of what is now
known as Beer's Mountain.

[2] Temple and Sheldon's History of Northfield, pages 73-77.

the spoils of their victory. The ox-cart abandoned in the retreat is said to have remained upon the field for many years thereafter, and one hundred and fifty years later two Northfield men digging by a rough stone where Beers was said to have been buried came upon the crumbled remnants of his body.

Several of Beers' men were captured, one of whom, Robert Pepper[1] of Roxbury, was succored by Sagamore Sam and accompanied him on a visit to Philip near Albany in the winter. He fell in with Mrs. Rowlandson during her captivity and finally made his way home having been not unkindly treated.

Major Treat[2] with ninety mounted troopers marching up the valley by way of Westfield with instructions to use his own good judgment and to press forward to such towns where he might be directed to quarter,[3] had reached Northampton when the reports of the refugees from Beers' defeat and the dark fate which seemed about to threaten the frontier towns caused him to set out early the next morning, Sunday, September 6th, with one hundred men. Darkness fell upon them before they could reach their destination and they camped in the woods,

---

[1] James Quannapohit's Relation. A full copy may be found in the Connecticut Archives, War Doc. 35b.

[2] Major Robert Treat settled in Milford, Conn., when a young man, going thither from Wethersfield. He early became captain of the train-band of Milford. In 1672 he was placed in command of the New Haven colony forces. In September, after the outbreak of Philip's war, he was commissioned as commander-in-chief of the Connecticut military forces and served actively until after the death of Philip. On his return home he was elected Deputy Governor and afterwards Governor. He died in Milford, July 13, 1710.—Genealogy of the Treat Family. by J. Harvey Treat.

[3] Connecticut Records, Vol. II, page 357.

probably on the site of Beers' camp. The trail led them across the line of Beers' retreat and they saw with horror, stuck up on poles along the traveled path, the heads of many of the slain. Treat found the Northfield people safe within the stockade but worn out with constant anxiety. No Indians had been seen along the way, but as the settlers were burying the body of one of their number killed on the second, they were fired upon by lurking foes, and Treat himself was wounded.

The service of burying the dead was given over and it was determined to abandon Northfield immediately.[1] That night, accompanied by the settlers, the whole force marched away leaving the standing crops and all their belongings save horses and a few cattle, at the mercy of the Indians, and fire soon wiped out the once flourishing settlement. Treat's troopers, convoying the settlers, made their toilsome way down the valley, but though strongly reinforced on the march by Appleton, who urged Treat to return with him and make some spoil upon the enemy, the retreat was continued, the forces entering Hadley in a state of demoralization.[2] The fear of ambush, into which almost every force had walked and suffered, the constant strain of watching for lurking foes, the sight of those ghastly heads along the way and the decomposing bodies in the meadow, had completely unnerved them. Under these conditions a council of war held at Hadley on the 8th decided to give up operations in the field and garrison the towns. Treat also received orders from the

---

[1]Letter of Rev. Solomon Stoddard to Rev. Increase Mather.— Mather's Brief History.

[2]Hubbard says the majority of Treat's force decided against Appleton's proposal.—Vol. I, page 112.

PLACE OF BEER'S DEFEAT, NORTHFIELD, MASSACHUSETTS

Connecticut Council to return, scouring both banks of the river on his way down.[1]

With the abandonment of Northfield the plan of operations had fallen through and the fertile lands and fishing grounds in the upper valley came into possession of the Indians. The bad news made clear to the authorities both in Connecticut and Massachusetts that all the towns along the frontier were in serious danger. The settlers were ordered not to go into the fields to harvest except in companies. Patrols were sent out along the roads and all able-bodied men not in the field were organized into companies "to keep watch and ward by night and day." Henchman and Brattle were sent from Boston to protect the country around Chelmsford, Groton and Lancaster, and preparations were made to reorganize the forces in the valley and increase their numbers. Appleton was sent to garrison Deerfield, but the Connecticut Council, on the decision of the council of war to give up active operations in the field, recalled all the Connecticut contingent with the exception of small garrisons at Westfield and Springfield. They were urgent for active preparations and their views finally prevailed. The Commissioners of the United Colonies on the 16th of September recalled the former orders and ordered new forces to be levied.[2] Major Pynchon was appointed commander-in-chief and Connecticut named Treat for second in command. Bolder council had prevailed at Hadley in the meantime. Captain John Mason[3] of Connecticut with

---

[1] Connecticut Records, Vol. II, page 359.

[2] Connecticut Records, Vol. II, page 367. Letter from Commissioners of the United Colonies to Governor and Council of Connecticut.

[3] Captain John Mason of Norwich, son of the famous Major John,

a large body of Mohegans was already on the march, and Pynchon at Hadley was preparing to move when the Indians assumed the offensive.

Deerfield was greatly exposed and from the neighboring hills every movement in the village could be seen. On the 12th as some twenty men of the garrison were passing from one garrison house to another to attend meeting, they were attacked from ambuscade, but repelled the attack without loss. The north fort, however, was plundered and a sentinel, one Nathaniel Cornbury, on duty, was captured and never heard from. Two houses were burnt and a large quantity of pork and beef fell into the hands of the Pocumtucks.[1]

The next night volunteers from Northampton and Hadley reinforced Captain Appleton,[2] who was in command, and the whole force marched to the Indian encampment on Pine Hill but found it deserted. Reinforcements were marching into the valley in the meantime, for Captain Moseley had arrived at Deerfield on his return from the east, and on the same day Major Treat, with the Connecti-

---

was freeman 1671, representative 1672 and 1674. He was a merchant. Served as a captain in Philip's war and was severely wounded at the Narragansett Swamp fight, December 19, 1675. He was chosen an assistant in May, 1676, but the 18th of September following, died of his wounds.—Savage.

[1] Sheldon's History of Deerfield, Vol. I, page 99.

[2] Samuel Appleton was born in Waddingfield, England, in 1624. At eleven years of age he came with his father and settled in Ipswich. He was many times chosen representative to the General Court before and after the war. His commission as captain was issued September 24, 1675, although at that time he had been in active duty in the Connecticut Valley several weeks. Soon after the Narragansett fight he retired from the military service and assumed his duties as deputy until 1681, when he was chosen an assistant and remained in that office until the coming of Andros in 1686. He died May 15, 1696.—Bodge, page 142.

cut forces and a body of Mohegans, reached Northampton.

The ripened corn in the Deerfield north meadows had been stacked, but still offered as it stood in the field a tempting prize to the Indians, with whom winter was ever a season of more or less semi-starvation. The troops now pouring into Hadley from all directions would need a large supply of food, and Major Pynchon, September 15th, ordered Captain Lathrop, who was scouting around Deerfield in company with Moseley, to load the grain in sacks and convey it down the valley. Moseley had been beating the country for several days and had discovered no considerable force of Indians, and the road seemed clear when in the early morning of the 18th, Lathrop with his company of young men from Essex County, accompanied by seventeen Deerfield settlers as teamsters, set out for Hadley.

Down the street of the village, across the south meadows, up Bars' long hill and over the plain, they took their way, marching but slowly, for the heavy laden teams moved with difficulty over the rough road. The day was warm, and Lathrop without interference saw many of his men cast their arms upon the carts and stop to pluck the bunches of ripe wild grapes that grew abundantly along the way. No scouts marched in front of the force, no flankers searched the woods that lay on either side; careless of danger, unmindful of the lessons taught so constantly throughout the last two months, they marched at their ease. Little did they suspect that while they had slept the night before, a large body of warriors, Pocumtucks, Nonatucks, Nashaways and Squakheags, under Sagamore Sam, Monoco, Muttaump and possibly Philip, had crossed the river and now lay waiting for the careless English along the edge of a morass six miles south of Deerfield, where the road with a gentle fall passes over a marsh made by the waters of Muddy (ever since called Bloody) Brook.

Lathrop and the main body came carelessly on, straggled across the brook and halted on the farther side[1] to wait for the teams to drag their heavy loads through the mire. Then the bushes burst into flame and a volley smote them. Many fell, Lathrop probably among the first. Some of the survivors rushed back to the wagons for their arms, while others, paralyzed with fear and surprise, stood still and were immediately shot down. The whole force was deep in the toils and retreat or advance were alike impossible.

Henry Bodwell of Andover, a man of great strength and courage, clubbing his musket, fought his way out, and John Tappan of Newbury, wounded in the leg, threw himself into the bed of the brook and, pulling the bushes over him, escaped the notice of the savages, though more than one of them stepped upon him as he lay hid. For the greater number there was no escape. The seventeen teamsters died to a man among their sacks, and the whole escort, save for a few stragglers in the rear, was destroyed.[2]

It was the saddest day in the early history of New England. Fifty-four young men "the flower of Essex

---

[1] Hoyt's Indian Wars, page 106.

[2] A letter of the Massachusetts Council to Richard Smith gives the loss as, teamsters, 17, Lathrop's company, 41, and Moscley's men, 11. —Massachusetts Archives, Vol. LXVII, page 262.

The Rev. John Russell says 71.

DEERFIELD NORTH MEADOWS.

County," and nearly half of the male population of Deer-field, had been wiped out.

Moseley, with some sixty men, was scouting near Deer-field when the sound of the heavy firing fell upon his ear. He pushed on rapidly only to see the victorious warriors ripping open the grain sacks and plundering the dead. "Come on, Moseley, come on. You want Indians. Here are enough Indians for you," they shouted;[1] and it is said he recognized many Christian Indians among them. Keeping his force well together he charged through them, but several of his men fell and he could not drive them from their plunder. His force in turn would have fared ill had not Major Treat, with one hundred Connecticut men and sixty Mohegans, marching toward Northfield, been attracted by the firing and relieved him as evening fell.

The Indians were driven from the field, but darkness was now settling down, and Treat and Moseley, leaving the dead where they had fallen, took up their wounded and retired sadly to Deerfield. On the following day, Sunday, returning to the battlefield, they drove off the Indians, who had returned to strip the slain, and buried the bodies of the seventy-one victims of Lathrop's ill-fated force and Moseley's men who had fallen, in a common grave, now marked by a slab, to the south of the morass.

Hubbard eulogizes Moseley's course in keeping his men together instead of stationing them behind trees, and blames Lathrop for not having led his men in the same way. The real faults, however, of the English command-

---

[1] Drake's Book of the Indians, Vol. III, page 216.

H

ers lay in their continual neglect of the simplest precautions against surprise. It was not because of Moseley's dispositions that he escaped the fate of Lathrop but because circumstances rendered an ambuscade in his case impossible. With the natural exaggeration of a defeated party the loss of the Indians was placed at ninety. The figure is purely fanciful.

The defeat of the 18th sealed the fate of Deerfield. Amidst the anxiety and depression caused by the annihilation of Lathrop's command came the disheartening news that the northern tribes, provoked by harsh treatment and encouraged by the successes of the southern Indians, were harrying the remote settlements from the Merrimac to Pemaquid with fire and sword. On that remote frontier, where the enforcement of law was weakened by divided claims to ownership, and the rough character of many of the population, the Indians had much to complain of. Their people had been kidnapped and sold into slavery, they had been plundered and abused, while Moseley's conduct and the actions of the English settlers had convinced them that it was as dangerous to be a friend as a foe since the same punishment was meted out to both. Squando, sachem of the Saco Indians, had once been a friend of the English, but a brutal outrage committed against his wife and child had made him an implacable enemy who had long bided his time. It had come now, and the day that witnessed Lathrop's defeat saw also the murder of English settlers and the destruction of their homes at Casco.

At Deerfield, the victorious Indians flaunted from across the river, in the faces of the garrison, the garments of the slain at Bloody Brook, and soon its remaining in-

BLOODY BROOK, SOUTH DEERFIELD, MASSACHUSETTS

habitants were scattered in the towns to the south; the Indian's torch wiped out the empty dwellings and the fertile valley was left in desolation. The defeat meant more than the mere abandonment of a thriving hamlet; it brought the frontier down to Hatfield and Hadley and completely upset the plan to make Northfield the head-quarters of the Connecticut troops for active operations down the valley in co-operation with the force assembled at Hadley. The Indians, flushed with success, were threatening all the settlements in the valley with destruc-tion. Expedition after expedition had been lured into ambush and defeated with heavy loss, and no effective blow had been struck in return.

The commissioners of the colonies at Boston acted vigorously and a new levy of men was ordered. Major Pynchon[1] of Springfield, as commander-in-chief in the valley, wished to garrison the towns by a force sufficient to insure their safety, while a considerable force of mounted men and Indian scouts should strike at the hostiles wher-ever they could be found. "The English are awkward and fearful in scouting," he wrote to the Council, but "they would do the best they could. We have no Indian friends here to help us.[2]

---

[1] Major John Pynchon was born in England in 1621. He was the only son of William Pynchon, the founder of Springfield, and when the father returned to England in 1652, succeeded to his affairs and was elected in his place as magistrate. He was an officer of the trainband and later major of the local cavalry troop. He took an active part in King Philip's war, having the command of the entire army in the valley, until after the destruction of Springfield, when his request to be relieved of his command was granted. He died January 17, 1703.—First Cen-tury of the History of Springfield, by Henry M. Burt, page 625.

[2] Letter of Major Pynchon to Governor and Council.—Massachu-setts Archives (September 30), vol. 67, page 274.

The commissioners bade him denude the towns of their garrisons and send every available man to active service in the field. In issuing hampering orders to the captains in the field they bent to popular prejudice against the employment of friendly Indians. This was their fatal error; without Indian auxiliaries the troops were well-nigh helpless and no aggressive campaign possible.

No better opportunity could have been afforded the fast-moving tribesmen. Avoiding the columns in search of them and refusing all open conflict, they hovered near the settlements, shooting the unwary settlers who ventured out to till their fields, or lay in wait around the columns to cut off stragglers and scouts. A house and mill of Major Pynchon on the west side of the river[1] at Springfield, were burned on the 26th, and two days later two Northampton settlers were killed while cutting wood.[2] "The Indians cut off their scalps, took their arms, and were gone in a trice."

It was not until the 4th of October that Major Pynchon, having assembled a large force at Springfield, set out to join the troops already at Hadley. It was his intention, having collected the army at that point, to leave before daybreak on the following morning and attack a large force of Indians who were reported encamped about five miles to the north. The sachems, however, had their

---

[1] The house and mill of Major Pynchon "on the west side of the river," were located on Stony Brook in what is now Suffield, Conn., but then a part of Springfield territory, about half a mile above its entrance into the Connecticut River.

[2] Praisever Turner and Unzakaby Shakspere were cutting wood just back of Turner's house when attacked, near what is now the corner of Elm Street and Paradise Road.

SITE OF PYNCHON'S MILL AND HOUSE
On Stony Brook, Suffield, Connecticut

own plans and the fact that Springfield was denuded of troops was well known among them.

On Long Hill, just below the town, near the river bank, there had been for many years a village of the Agawams. It had existed when the first settlers of Springfield selected the site for their town, and its inhabitants had lived on friendly terms with the settlers for forty years. The disquiet and suspicions of the other tribes had, however, not failed of an effect upon these old neighbors, and Major Pynchon had informed the Connecticut Council that he intended to disarm them, but the Council suggested hostages,[1] whose delivery the Indians delayed. The departure of the troops from Springfield gave them an opportunity of which they were not slow to take advantage. They had been harboring now for some time wandering parties of hostiles, and a deadly blow might have been inflicted upon the unsuspicious settlement had not the plot been revealed by Toto, an Indian employed by an English settler at Windsor.[2] Noticing his uneasiness during the evening they pressed him for the cause and finally wrung the secret from him. The night was already far spent and the fate of Springfield hung on the minutes. Messengers riding in hot haste sped to Springfield, knocking fiercely in the darkness at the doors of the silent houses to awaken the sleeping inmates. The settlers at once took shelter in the three fortified houses,[3] and mes-

---

[1] Connecticut Records, Vol. II, page 356.

[2] Hutchinson's History of Massachusetts, Vol. I, page 295.

[3] It is generally thought that the well-known brick house of Major John Pynchon, which stood until 1831 on the corner of what is now known as Main and Fort Streets, was the principal fortified house of the town, but there is reason for doubting this. The common belief that the brick house was erected in 1661 appears to be based upon the record of an

sengers were sent in haste to the forces at Hadley for reinforcements.

The night passed without attack, confidence revived, and some of the people returned to their homes. Lieutenant Cooper, who was well known to the Indians, and put little faith in the reports of the hostile attitude of the Agawams, determined to go down to the Indian fort with constable Miller[1] and investigate. They had gone but a short distance toward their destination, however, when they were shot at from the woods near Mill River "by those bloody and deceitful monsters." Miller was instantly killed, but Cooper, shot through the body, managed to keep his saddle until he reached the nearest garrison house, where he fell from his horse dead. The In-

---

order from John Pynchon to Francis Hacklington of Northampton for 50,000 bricks, but what seems to be good proof of a later date for the building of the house appears in the records where, on June 3, 1678, a period of more than two years after the destruction of the town, Pynchon desires leave of the selectmen "to set up a flanker in the street at the east end of his new house *now building,* on the north side of his home lot." As it is known that Pynchon built no house subsequent to the erection of the brick edifice, it leaves little room for doubt that the fortified house used as a refuge during the war, was the frame dwelling built in the earliest days by William Pynchon, inherited and occupied by his son, Major John. See Selectmen's Records (MSS.), Vol. II, page 131.

Of the other fortified houses one was the house of Jonathan Burt which stood near the southwest corner of the present Main and Broad Streets, and the third was the well-known "Ely Tavern," built about 1665 and then located on Main a little south of Bliss Street. This was removed about 1843 to Dwight Street a few rods west of State, where it remained until 1900 when it was pulled down on account of its unsafe condition. See Bi-Centennial Address by Hon. Oliver B. Morris, 1836.

[1] Thomas Miller was constable and surveyor of highways. His son Thomas took part in the Falls fight the next spring, May 19th, and the John Miller who was killed in the same fight was probably his son.

dians following closely behind, tried to rush the garrisons. One savage advanced, sheltering himself behind a large pewter plate, but two bullets pierced it and he fell.[1] Several others were shot, and, finding their attempt at a surprise a failure, the rest withdrew. A woman and two settlers had been killed,[2] and thirty-two houses (including "saddest to behold the house of Rev. Peletiah Glover furnished with a brave library newly brought back from the garrison and now made fit for a bonfire for the proud insulting enemy") and "not even a bible saved," these and twenty-five barns were in flames by the time Major Treat, marching from Westfield, reached the west bank of the river which he was prevented from crossing by the fierce fire of the Indians.

Late in the afternoon came Major Pynchon and the companies of Captains Sill[3] and Appleton, who, hearing in the early morning that an attack was contemplated, had ridden furiously from Hadley to the relief with two hundred men. The enemy, however, had retired to Indian Orchard [4] and escaped punishment, all save an old

[1] Hoyt's Indian Wars, page 110.

[2] Pentecost Matthews, the wife of John, was killed at her home a quarter of a mile north of the Burt garrison. Edmund Pryngrydays and Nathaniel Brown were severely wounded and both died soon afterwards.

[3] Captain Joseph Sill was born in Cambridge about 1639. He was called into military life early in King Philip's war and served almost continually in important times and places, in the campaign of 1675 in the Connecticut Valley. He was removed by the General Court of Massachussetts from his command, in October, for offensive conduct; later he was conspicuous in the eastern towns. Some time after the close of the war he removed to Lyme, Conn., where he died August 6, 1696.

[4] A locality on the Chicopee River six miles east of Springfield. Now a busy manufacturing village in the Eighth Ward of Springfield.

squaw taken prisoner, who, if we are to believe Moseley,
"was ordered to be torn in pieces by doggs and was so
dealt withall." The number of Indians concerned in the
attack was variously estimated at from 100 to 500. Rev.
John Russell of Hadley gives the former figure which,
if correct, is evidence that few beside the Agawam or
Springfield Indians were concerned.

Discouragement and gloom settled heavily upon men's
minds when the news from Springfield became known.
Large quantities of provisions had been destroyed; a
town, the most important and the most removed from
danger in the upper valley had been devastated, and its
inhabitants, but for a warning at the eleventh hour, had
been massacred. "The Lord will have us in the dust
before him," wrote Pynchon sadly to Rev. John Russell.
Months of warfare, the sacrifice of valuable lives, the
levying of large bodies of troops, and the expenditure of
considerable sums of money, all seemed to have been in
vain. The field of operations was spreading over a wider
area, while the Indians, their numbers augmented by
wandering bands from the northern tribes and from villages formerly neutral, were encouraged by their successes to fiercer aggressions.

Men sought to evade military service and it was becoming increasingly difficult to keep up the companies in
the field to their full complement,[1] and the reports sent
to the Connecticut Council of the captures of old men,
women and children by the Mohegans operating from
Norwich, offered but little compensation for the disasters
elsewhere.

---

[1] Secretary Rawson to Major Pynchon, September 30.

Major Pynchon had, as before noticed, taken issue with the plan of campaign worked out by the commissioners at Boston. He had repeatedly urged upon them the danger of leaving the towns ungarrisoned while the troops followed the fast-moving warriors into the thickets. "To speak my thoughts all these ought to be garrisoned. To go out after the Indians unless we know where they keep is to hazazd our men," he wrote.[1] He urgently asked again to be relieved of his command, which he had never desired. "I would not" he had written some time before, "willingly sin against God nor offend you, and I entreat you to ease me of my (trust)." "Pursue and destroy," they had replied, expressing their confidence in him.

The attack on Springfield strengthened Pynchon's dissatisfaction with the plan of the commissioners. An estimable man and magistrate he was fitted neither by nature nor training for a military command. He felt helpless and worried over the conduct of the campaign, the loss inflicted upon Springfield and the care of its destitute people weighed heavily upon his mind; and now,

---

[1] Letter of Pynchon to Governor and Council October 8.—Massachusetts Archives, Vol. LXVII, page 287.

NOTE.—The correspondence in regard to the attack on Springfield and events in the valley during the last of September and early October will be found in the Massachusetts Archives:

Maj. Pynchon to Gov. and Council, Sept. 30, Vol. 67, page 274.
Gov. and Council to Maj. Pynchon, Sept. 30, Vol. 67, page 270.
Gov. and Council to Maj. Pynchon, Oct. 4, Vol. 67, page 280.
Maj. Pynchon to Rev. John Russell, Oct. 5, Vol. 67, page 283.
Rev. John Russell to Gov. Leverett, Oct. 6, Vol. 67, page 289.
Letters of Maj. Pynchon to Gov." Oct. 8-12, Vol. 67, page 287-290.
Capt. Moseley to Gov. Leverett, Oct. 5, Vol. 68, page 17.

for the third time, he requested that he be relieved from command. He wrote that he was still opposed to the policy of the commissioners, felt his own unfitness for command and must devolve the command to Appleton unless Treat, who had been summoned away to Connecticut by the report of a body of Indians having been seen near Wethersfield, returned.

The request conveyed in his former letter had already been granted and Captain Appleton had been appointed October 4th to succeed him. He, too, shared Pynchon's view as to the need of garrisoning the towns and urged upon the Council the advisability of leaving the question discretionary with the commander, and complained of Treat's long absence,[1] but the Council held firm to their original plan and Appleton reached Hadley on the night of the 12th to begin operations in the field, having left small garrisons in certain of the towns despite the orders of the Council. A few days later he again writes to the Massachusetts authorities. He knows not when Treat will return, the scouts are timorous and accomplish little and he finds it difficult to know what to do. He realizes, too, both the strength and weakness of the commissioners' position in regard to active operations. "To leave no garrisons and concentrate all for active service in the field, is to expose the towns to manifest hazard. To sit still and do nothing is to tire us and spoil our soldiers and ruin the country by the unsupportable burden and charge."[2]

---

[1]   Appleton   to   Governor   Leverett,   October   12.—Massachusetts Archives, Vol. LXVIII, page 3.

[2]   Appleton   to   Governor   Leverett,   October   17.—Massachusetts Archives, Vol. LXVIII, page 23.

Dissatisfaction and dissension made his task difficult from the start, for a conflict of opinions had existed for some time between the Massachusetts and Connecticut officers. Summoning Moseley and Seeley from their posts at Hartford and Northampton, October 15th, in order to concentrate his troops for the offensive, the latter came tardily and alone and, pleading lack of orders, was with difficulty persuaded to bring in his troops. On his return to Northampton, finding orders from Treat not to leave the town, he notified Appleton, who felt himself powerless to enforce his commands, for, though the commissioners of the United Colonies had made the Connecticut force part of the confederate army and taken it out of the control of the Connecticut authorities, the commissioners were not present and Appleton lacked the strength of character to arbitrarily enforce their decrees.

Alarmed by the report of Indians having been seen near Glastonbury, the Connecticut Council had recalled Treat and the greater part of the Connecticut forces to Hartford, and information from Governor Andros of New York that an Indian, pretending to be friendly, had warned him that the hostiles intended to attack Hartford "this light moon,"[1] caused them to retain the troops until the middle of the month. "We have news of the recalling of Major Treat from you with a great part of the Connecticut men, and the disobedience of those who were left behind," wrote the Council of Massachusetts to Appleton, and they bade him organize garrisons and security for the towns and prepare the force for return,

---

[1] Connecticut Records, Vol. II, page 377.—Governor Andros to Connecticut Council.

for the burden of providing for so many men, lack of provisions and the need of men elsewhere were heavy upon
them[1]

---

[1] Massachusetts Colony Records, Vol. V, page 53.

CHAPTER VIII

THE enforced withdrawal of the Connecticut troops was a blow to the new commander. They alone were accompanied by a band of Mohegans, whose presence had saved them repeatedly from running into ambuscades, and Appleton had depended upon these Mohegans for his guides and scouts in the coming campaign. Notwithstanding the refusal of Seeley[1] to join him, Appleton, having concentrated the bulk of his command, set out for Northfield on the 15th of October. He had but started, however, when information reached him that a large force of Indians was encamped on the west bank of the river. He hastened back to Hadley, and, crossing the river to Hatfield in the evening, struck the Deerfield trail and pushed forward in the hope of effecting a surprise, but the flash of a gun and the shouts of the Indians soon made clear that his movement had been discovered. A tempestuous night was setting in, and, fearful for the unguarded towns of Hadley and Hatfield in his rear, he turned back.

Hardly had he arrived at Hadley than Seeley at Northampton asked for reinforcements, as the Indians were near by. The air was full of rumors. Indians were here, there, everywhere, but Appleton, marching from one place

[1] Lieutenant Nathaniel Seeley, son of Robert of Wethersfield, was of New Haven in 1646 and later removed to Fairfield. He early entered upon military duty in the service of Connecticut, and fell in the Narragansett Swamp fight at the head of his company, December 19, 1675. —Savage.

to another, could not get in touch with them. Vague unrest prevailed throughout the towns and insubordination grew more rife among the troops as their long and hurried marches proved ever fruitless. The Connecticut troops were unwilling to remain in garrison at Westfield and among the captains jealousies and misunderstandings were frequent.

Across the river, a mile through the meadows from its north bank, and opposite Hadley, stands the little village of Hatfield. Here, on the 19th of October, Captains Poole[1] and Moseley were resting their companies, when, about noon, several large fires were observed to the north of the village. Moseley immediately sent out a party of men to reconnoiter. The building of these fires was a trap such as the Indians delighted to set and in which the colonial forces were only too prone to be caught. There is little doubt but that the ambuscade was laid with full expectation that the whole garrison would march out and fall into it, for the scouting party had progressed but a short two miles beyond the stockade when a fierce volley fired from the brush practically exterminated them. Six were killed, three captured, and a lone survivor found his way back.[2]

---

[1] Captain Jonathan Poole was of Reading. In October, 1671, he was appointed quartermaster, and in May, 1674, cornet of the "Three County Troop," and held that office when the war broke out in 1675. He served at Quabaug and Hadley and when Major Appleton was given command of the army of the west he appointed Poole to a captaincy. The Council refused for a time to confirm the appointment, but, later, when the main army was withdrawn for the Narragansett campaign Captain Poole was placed in command of the garrison forces in the valley towns. He served as representative to the General Court in 1677, and died December 24, 1678.—Bodge, page 258. Savage.

[2] Drake's "Old Indian Chronicle," page 166.

Moseley was too well acquainted with the Indian character to believe this ambuscade the work of any but a large and aggressive force, who meant to attack the village. Sending word to Appleton who soon joined him, having left only twenty men at garrison at Hadley, the arrangements for defense were quickly completed. Several hours passed and no Indian had yet appeared, when suddenly, about four o'clock, a large body of warriors made their appearance at the edge of the meadows, rushing toward the stockade. Several heavy volleys, however, told them that the force on guard was large and well prepared, and after killing Freegrace Norton,[1] a sergeant of Appleton's company, and sending a bullet through Appleton's hat, "by that whisper telling him that death was very near,"[2] hey retired, as Treat, who had at last returned to Northampton, appeared upon the scene. Hatfield had escaped the intended stroke, but no safety existed outside the stockade. The crops, ungathered in the fields, afforded subsistence to the Indians, and the scattered farms throughout the valley and to the eastward lay in ruins or deserted.

From Springfield northward the warriors lay in wait for any too venturesome settler or small body of troops and watched patiently for any opportunity to surprise the towns themselves.

The mill at Springfield had been destroyed and the people found it necessary to carry their corn to the mill at Westfield.[3] On the 27th Major Pynchon and a small

---

[1] Freegrace Norton was the son of George of Salem. He was first of Saco but removed to Ipswich.

[2] Hubbard, Vol. I, page 125.

[3] The original location of Westfield was at the junction of the West-

force, having ground the corn they were escorting, were fired upon from ambush and three of the party were killed.[1]

The previous day a party of seven or eight Northampton settlers, gathering their crops from the Pynchon meadow,[2] had been surprised by a small force of Indians. No sentinels had been posted; their arms were deposited under the carts, but, cutting the traces, they mounted their horses and fled, followed almost up to the stockade by the Indians, who retired only after having burned four or five houses and several barns. The next day the same band surprised and killed two men and a boy in the meadows in Northampton opposite the town mill,[3]

---

field and Little Rivers. Here was the log fort, under which a cellar had been provided for the retreat of the women and children in case of an attack. The ground on which this stood has disappeared through the encroachment of the river. Close upon the present highway stood the church, built of logs, "barn fation with a bell coney." The settlement was surrounded by a stout palisade. The original saw and gristmill was built upon the brook in the easterly part of the town, probably near the present village of "Little River," two and a half miles east of the center of the present Westfield.

[1] These were John Dumbleton, and William and John Brooks.

[2] Pynchon's meadow was a tract of 120 acres of ground granted to Major John Pynchon, situated at the most northerly turn of the "Ox Bow," and bounded on the south by Hurlburt's Pond, into and through which the Mill River at that time flowed. The Indians followed the fleeing settlers along what is now South Street, and the houses and barns destroyed by them were located not far from the present iron bridge over Mill River, and were at that time the most southerly buildings of the town.—See Trumbull's History of Northampton.

[3] Northampton Town Mill, built in 1671 at "Red Rocks," was located on the bend of Mill River between what is now College Lane and Paradise Road, and upon the land of Praisever Turner, who had been murdered and scalped on the 28th of the previous month (September) while cutting wood on the hill just above the mill. Opposite the mill

but in an attempt to destroy the mill were driven off.[1]

Operations conducted in other parts of the field in a more or less perfunctory manner had brought but little result and the end of the war seemed farther off than ever and the Council found fault with Appleton for his failure. "I am not without feeling some smart in your lines, though I would not be over tender," he wrote them in reply, and the fault was as much theirs as his.[2]

Captain Henchman, marching from Boston, November 1st, to reconnoiter the country around Hassamenesit, came, November 3d, on some fires recently kindled by the Indians and, urged by his officers, continued on to the Indian encampment. No Indians were found, but the scouts, under Captain Sill, early in the morning discovered a miller's lad who, recently captured near Marlboro, had been abandoned on their approach.

A few days later Henchman, drawing near to Mendon, received information of Indian wigwams about ten miles off. Mounting twenty-two of the company, Henchman and Philip Courtice,[3] his lieutenant, set out in the hope of surprising them. Having come within a short distance

---

on the west side of the river was the meadow, now known as Paradise meadow, where the Indians had killed two men and a boy just before the attack on the mill.

[1] Appleton to Governor Leverett, November 10th.—Massachusetts Archives, Vol. LXVIII, page 52.

[2] Appleton to Governor Leverett, November 17th.—Massachusetts Archives, Vol. LXVIII, page 63.

[3] Philip Curtis, born in England, was of Roxbury.

NOTE.—Other correspondence of Governor Leverett and Council,

I

of the Indian encampment they tied their horses and divided, Henchman taking one-half the company and Courtice the remainder. Henchmen's men were closing in upon the village when the Indian dogs began to bark. All halted, then slowly moved forward; but "the captain's foot slipping, he could hardly recover himself and suddenly looking behind him he saw no man following him."

Courtice, however, had pushed on and coming upon the wigwams was met by a sharp and sudden fire. Courtice himself was shot as he reached the door of a wigwam, one of his men also fell dead, while the remainder took to flight. Henchman called upon them to shoot into the wigwams and "they replied that they only went back to fall on and charge, yet left the field entirely."[1]

Winter was near at hand, the trees were shedding their foliage, the naked forests no longer offered opportunities for ambuscades, and as November progressed hostilities ceased and the Indians vanished.

In the valley operations also had come to a close. Treat, who had maintained a friendly attitude toward Appleton during the campaign at the instance of the Connecticut Council, finally returned to Connecticut, and Appleton, having destroyed the Indian crops wherever he could find them in the valley, left small garrisons in Had-

and of Major Appleton, with each other, during October and November 17, will be found in the Massachusetts Archives:

    Oct. 4th, Vol. 67, page 245.
    Oct. 15th, Vol. 68, page 14.
    Oct. 16th, Vol. 68, page 19.
    Oct. 17th, Vol. 68, page 23.
    Nov. 16th, Vol. 68, page 58.

[1] This account is taken from Henchman's letter in Massachusetts Archives, Vol. LXVIII, page 80, and Hubbard.

ley, Northampton and Springfield, and departed with most of the troops for Boston, where plans were already prepared for a blow at the Narragansetts in their winter quarters.

The campaign in the Connecticut Valley had been a disastrous failure through lack of harmony, hampering commands from the Council and commissioners, and the absence of a definite plan of operations. The anxious inhabitants settled down with meager supplies to face the hard winter, while houses were strengthened against attack, and the burned out settlers of Springfield crowded the houses of their friends or covered over their cellars for a winter refuge. The Indians, their crops destroyed, their powder scarce, and without their winter supply of dried fish, faced winter in the recesses of the swamps or wandered to remote parts in search of sustenance. The constant defeats, the wiping out of settlements where destruction and death struck so near and poignantly to all, aroused the stern but latently emotional New Englanders to vengeance. With the spread of the war from one end of the land to the other, the conflict assumed a religious and racial character that could have no other outcome than the extermination of one or the other of the combatants. The fury of fire and sword, without mercy, was to sweep alike over cabin and Indian village. Suspicion and hatred of all Indians became intense throughout Massachusetts. Though many of the Christian Indians remained faithful, there were others who joined the hostiles and distinguished themselves by their cruelty. It was but natural that the settlers, knowing not whom to trust and suspicious of all, should include innocent and guilty in the same condemnation. It is unnecessary to enumerate the results born of this attitude. Even a year later when peace had come in the south, the women of Marblehead, coming from church, massacred Indian prisoners from Maine who were being convoyed through the town.[1] The rough element of the community plundered the wigwams of the neighboring friendly Indians and in several cases wounded and murdered the women and children.[2] Indian prisoners were tortured for the purpose of eliciting information and women, children and old men were sold into slavery. Christian Indians who had served successfully as scouts were driven to join the hostiles. The Indians in the stockaded towns near Boston were ordered by the General Court not to be received in any town except in the prison, and were finally removed to Deer Island where, ill supplied with the necessaries of life, they suffered great hardships during the winter.[3] A mob called upon Captain Oliver [4] to lead them in an attack on the jail where Indians were confined, but Oliver, though an exponent of the harsh policy, belabored the

---

[1] Letter of Increase Mather, May 23, 1677.

[2] Gookin's Christian Indians.—American Soc. Coll., Antiquarian Vol. II, page 482.

[3] *Ibid.* page 485.

[4] Captain James Oliver came to New England from the mother country with his parents, March 9, 1632. He was admitted freeman of Boston, October 12, 1640; became a merchant; was of the Artillery Company, ensign 1651, lieutenant 1653, captain 1656 and again in 1666. He was of the First Military Company of Boston and elected captain about 1763. His appointment to the command of a company for the Narragansett campaign was dated November 17, 1675. He was one of the few officers commanding companies that came out from the Swamp Fight unscathed. After this campaign his company returned to Boston where it was dismissed February 5, 1675, 1676. He died in 1682.—Bodge.

ringleaders with a stick.[1] It became necessary for the time being for the authorities to bend to the popular tempest and disband the companies of Indians organized by Gookin,[2] and the courts appeased popular clamor by convicting prisoners whom they afterwards released. "O come, let us go down to Deer Island and let us kill all these praying Indians," was the cry of the irresponsible. But the Council, informed of the plot of about thirty men to pull out to the Island from Pullings Point to kill the Indians, sent for two or three of the ringleaders and warned them to attempt it at their peril.[3]

Whoever adopted most repressive measures won popular approval, and the appeals of men like Major Gookin and Rev. John Eliot for humane treatment, and their representations as to the folly of estranging the friendly Indian, alike fell upon deaf ears. "The error of selling away such Indians unto the islands for perpetual slaves" wrote Eliot to the commissioners, "may produce we know not what evil consequences upon all the land, . . . this usage of them is worse than death. Christ hath said, Blessed be the merciful. . . . All men (of reading) condemn the Spaniards for cruelty . . . in destroying men and depopulating the land. Here is land enough for them and us too." [4]

Gookin and Eliot were threatened by angry mobs, and the former was defeated at the election for magistrate.

---

[1] Old Indian Chronicle, page 152.

[2] Order dated August 30th.

[3] American Antiquarian Soc. Coll., Vol. II, page 494. Gookin's Christian Indians.

[4] Letter from Rev. John Eliot to Commissioners of the United Colonies. Acts of Commissioners, Vol. II, page 451. Plymouth Colony Records, Vol. X.

Several curious depositions show the feelings of the baser element toward him. One Rie Scott called him an "Irish dog, never faithful to his king or his country, . . . a rogue, God confound him, he is the devil's interpreter. I and a few more designed to cut off all Gookin's brethren on the island and some English dog discovered it."[1]

Warnings were sent both to Gookin and Eliot purporting to be from a secret society, calling them traitors and warning them to prepare for death.[2] The men of Captain Henchman refused to serve under him on account of his moderate views, and even Major Savage and Captain Prentice were held up to popular hatred as friends of the "incarnate devils."

These measures cost Massachusetts dear; it left her forces helpless to carry on a successful campaign. Many a company was ambushed because of the lack of Indian scouts, and many a town was burned because of the refusal to credit the reports of friendly Indians and their own Indian spies. Connecticut, comparatively free from Indian attacks, was naturally able to take a broader view, and, by employing the Mohegans, did not suffer a reverse or surprise in the whole campaign.

For some time the mutual suspicion between the Narragansetts and the settlers had been drawing to a head. It was believed that numerous women and children of the Wampanoags had taken refuge in Canonchet's domains, and Uncas had spread the story that many young warriors were to be found in the Narragansett villages re-

---

[1] Massachusetts Archives, Vol. XXX, pages 192-193.
[2] *Ibid.*

covering from wounds received in the conflicts in the valley.

The unprovoked invasion of the Narragansett country at the beginning of the campaign had added fresh fuel to the bitter remembrance of Miantonomah's fate and the harsh and arbitrary acts of Massachusetts constantly repeated in the intervening years; nor can Canonchet have been blind to the fact that, whatever Philip's failings might be, every hope of Narragansett independence would fall with him.

The treaty, wrung by Captains Moseley and Savage at the sword's point from the old men, requiring the surrender of all Philip's subjects, even women and children who should take refuge with the Narragansetts, was for a long time openly flouted by Canonchet, yet on the demand of the commissioners of the United Colonies he confirmed, on the 18th of October, the terms of the treaty of July to deliver all the men, women and children to the Governor or Council at Boston before October 28th and was presented with a coat trimmed with silver, and dismissed.[1]

The sachems would have remained neutral if possible. They had kept aloof from any alliance with Philip and were held by both Philip and his allies to be friendly to the English. Such was the testimony of James Quanapohit, an Indian spy in the service of the English among the Quabaugs and Nashaways, who, questioned by Cap-

---

[1] The signers on behalf of the English include no members of the Massachusetts Council, but Samuel Gorton, James Brown and Richard Smith, all neighbors of the Narragansetts.

Acts of the Commissioners of the United Colonies, Vol. II, page 361. Plymouth Records, Vol. X.

tain Nathaniel Davenport as to "whether the Narragansetts had aided or assisted Philip and his company in the
summer, against the English," replied that they had not
and that the hostiles "regarded them as friends of the
English all along, and their enemies." This view of the
Narragansetts was also held by the Indians around Plymouth, for when Peter, Awashonk's son, who had warned
Church of Philip's designs just previous to the outbreak
of hostilities, was examined at Plymouth in June, 1676,
he testified that the Saconet Indians when the English
had fired their houses, "understanding that the Narragansetts were friends to the English, we went to them."
No hostile actions marked their course, but in the excited
state of mind that existed among both magistrate and
people of New England at the time, neutrality was impossible.

If the friendly Indians were objects of keen distrust
and suspicion, a neutral tribe could only be regarded as
hostile, harboring evil intention and waiting only a favorable opportunity for war and massacre.

The policy of peace at any price among the Narragansetts, so diligently pursued by Canonicus and Pesascus,
had broken down. Submission and subserviency had
neither mitigated the white man's suspicions nor made
the English less diligent in furthering their own interests
and those of Uncas. The lesson taught by the Pequot
war had grown dim in memory, and the young warriors
found in Canonchet a leader who represented far more
than his father or uncles, the warlike spirit of their tra-
ditionary leaders.

Swayed by such influence the Narragansetts were in no
mood to commit so great an outrage against the traditions

of Indian hospitality as to surrender the women and children who sought their protection, among them, no doubt, many from the sub-tribes of the Wampanoags who feared the resentment both of the English and their own kindred.

The attitude of reserve and suspicion assumed by the Narragansetts and the sullen temper of the young warriors had not passed unnoticed by those who knew them best. Pessacus, soon after the signing of the Pettaquamscat treaty in July had told several of the Rhode Islanders that the young warriors would not listen to his words of peace, and were desirous of war. Roger Williams had warned the authorities late in July that their words of peace were treacherous. He knew only too well the humiliations to which the whole tribe had been subjected, and weighed the desire for vengeance which burned in their hearts.

Immediately after the signing of the October treaty, Williams, while carrying one of the sachems (probably Canonochet, returning from Boston) in his canoe to Smith's Landing, took the opportunity to warn him against breaking the treaty.

"I told him and his men that Philip was his looking-glass, and how Philip was dead to all advice and now was over set.

"He asked me in a consenting, considering kind of a way 'Philip over set?' . . . and I told him that if they were false to his engagements we would pursue them with a winter's war when they should not, as mosquitoes and rattlesnakes in warm weather, bite us. They gave me leave to say anything, acknowledging loudly your great kindness in Boston, and mine, and yet Captain

Fenner[1] told me yesterday he thinks they will prove our worst enemies at last."[2]

The warning did not fall upon deaf ears. The 28th of October came and the anxious but resolute commissioners knew that the treaty had been in vain.

It was believed at the time that Philip was Canonchet's evil counselor, but there exists no doubt that the Narragansett had himself determined to submit no more to every demand and threat Massachusetts might see fit to make, for his was a nature imbued with a strength and temper more certain to act on its own initiative than on the persuasion of others.

One more attempt at persuasion the English are reported by a popular tradition of the time to have made, only to meet in the stern, inclusive reply, "No, not a Wampanoag nor the paring of a Wampanoag's nail,"[3] a refusal that bade them do their worst.

The commissioners, as well as public opinion, racked with the anxiety and depression over the disasters in the valley and the failure of the plan of campaign, felt it was safer to strike at the Narragansetts immediately, while concentrated in winter quarters, than to be hampered by fear of their rising in the spring.

On the refusal of Canonchet to keep the terms of the treaty, the commissioners of the United Colonies assembled at Boston, November 2d, and, without further

[1] Captain Arthur Fenner of Providence was born in England in 1622. He was made freeman in 1655. He was commissioned captain of the trainband in 1672 and when a garrison was established at Providence he was appointed commander, and is sometimes called "the Captain of Providence."

[2] Roger Williams to Gov. Leverett, Mass. Archives, Vol. 67, 296.

[3] See Hubbard's account of Canonchet's Trial, Vol. 2, page 60.

negotiations, practically declared war in the following proclamation:

"For as much as the Narragansett Indians are deeply accessory in the present bloody outrages of the barbarous Indians that are in open hostilities with the English, this appearing by their harboring the actors thereof, relieving and succoring their women and children and wounded men, and detaining them in their custody notwithstanding the covenant made by their sachems to deliver them to the English, and as is creditably reported, have killed and taken away many cattle from the English, their neighbors, and did for some days seize and keep under a strong guard Mr. Smith's house and family, and at the news of the said lamentable mischief that the Indians did at or near Hatfield, did in a most reproachful and blasphemous manner triumph and rejoice. . . . The commissioners do agree to raise one thousand men beside the number of soldiers formerly agreed upon, and the commander-in-chief shall with the said soldiers march into the Narragansett country, and in case they be not permitted by the Narragansett sachems the actual performance of their covenant made with the commissioners, by delivering up those of our enemies that are in their custody, as also making reparation for all damages sustained by their neglect hitherto, together with security for their further conduct, then to compel them thereunto by the best means they may."[1]

The commissioners appointed Governor Josiah Winslow of Plymouth commander-in-chief, referred the appointment of a second in command to the Council or

---

[1] Acts of the Commissioners of the United Colonies, Vol. II, page 357. (Not literal). Plymouth Colony Records, Vol. X.

General Court of Connecticut, fixed the allotment of men to be furnished by each of the colonies and advised that all troops be picked men, well equipped, warmly clothed, and supplied with a week's provisions in knapsacks and a supply in reserve. The 2d of December was named as a day of humiliation and prayer.

The fact that the Rhode Islanders, within whose boundaries the Narragansett country lay, were opposed to hostilities, and the contemplated invasion was in defiance of the royal charter of that colony was entirely ignored.

The hierarchy of the other colonies seldom wasted courtesy upon the authorities of heretical Rhode Island, and in this case, when they deemed time all important, they can hardly be blamed for considering that the safety of their people must not be endangered by the attitude of a weak government and the terms of a general charter.

CHAPTER IX

SUCH a situation as obtained throughout the colonies during the year 1675 could not exist in the New England of the period without a serious searching of heart and conscience. In the public mind such trials and tribulations were the punishment inflicted for the wickedness and sins of the whole people, and the General Court of Massachusetts in setting apart the second day of December as a day of humiliation and public prayer, gives voice to the orthodox conscience.

"Whereas God has not only warned us by his word but chastized us with his rods . . . and given permission to the barbarous heathen to rise up against and become a smart rod, a severe scourge to us, burning and depopulating several hopeful plantations . . . hereby speaking aloud to us to search and try our ways and turn again unto the Lord our God, from whom we have departed with a great backsliding. "

The court enumerates a few of the offenses that have incurred the divine displeasure: The great neglect of discipline in the churches as regards the spiritual estate and instruction of the children. The sin of manifest pride made apparent by the wearing by the women of their hair long, "either their own or others hair," and by some women "wearing borders of hair, and their cutting, curling and immodest laying out of their hair, especially among the younger sort." A feeling of pride in apparel, "strange fashions in both rich and poor, with naked breasts and

arms and superfluous ribbons." Shameful and scandal-
ous sin of excessive drinkings and company keeping both
of men and women, in taverns and ordinaries. "The
sin of idleness, which is the sin of Sodom." And the
court orders that better order be kept in the churches,
that profanity and idleness and attendance at Quaker
meetings be punished, that measures be taken to restrict
the licenses of public houses and that the magistrates be
more active in the discharge of their duties.[1]

This careful scrutiny of public morals, with its attendant measures of reformation, was accompanied by vigorous action looking to the security of the colonies and the
organization of the forces for the winter campaign. The
neutral Indians were ordered confined to the islands in
Boston Harbor, the exportation of all provisions except
fish was prohibited, and captains were appointed to
the command of the various companies ordered for
service.

Following the lead of Massachusetts, the Council of
Connecticut issued orders for the levying of three hundred and fifteen men and the accumulation of food, powder, lead and flints, at Norwich, Stonington and New
London.

Major Treat was named second in command of the
united forces, the various companies were placed under
the command of Captain Samuel Marshall,[2] Captain

---

[1] Massachusetts Records, Vol. V, page 59.

[2] Captain Samuel Marshall of Windsor, 1637, was a tanner. Free-
man, 1654. He had a short but honorable service in the war against
Philip, and November 30, 1675, was made captain in the place of
Benjamin Newbury who was disabled.—Stiles' History of Windsor,
Vol. II, page 466.

Mason, Captain Watts and Lieutenants Avery, Seeley and Miles,[1] and instructions were sent to the Reverend Mr. Fitch [2] of Norwich, to organize a body of Pequots and Mohegans as auxiliaries.[3]

By the 8th of December the Massachusetts and Plymouth forces were fully organized and Winslow, after a conference at Boston with Governor Leverett, proceeded with his staff, which included Benjamin Church, Joseph Dudley and a number of ministers, surgeons and volunteers, to Dedham, the rendezvous of the Massachusetts contingent, where were concentrated the forces called in from the valley, and the new levies. Here were Major Appleton and Captain Moseley with their veterans, Captain Isaac Johnson with the levies of Roxbury, Dorchester, Weymouth, Hull; and adjacent towns; Davenport [4] with the men of Cambridge and Watertown; Oliver with the men from Boston; Gardiner with the Essex County levies, and Thomas Prentice with a troop of horse, a total of

---

[1] Lieutenant John Miles was born October, 1644, and lived in New Haven. He was admitted freeman in 1669, made lieutenant 1675, and later captain. He died November 7, 1704.—Savage.

[2] Rev. James Fitch of Saybrook was born December 24, 1622, at Bocking, County Essex, England. He was ordained in the ministry in 1646. His wife died in 1659 and he removed the next year with a large part of his Saybrook church to the settlement of Norwich. He gave up his office in 1696 and removed to Lebanon where he died November 18, 1702.—Savage.

[3] Connecticut Records, Vol. II, pages 383-387. Allotment 110 men to Hartford County; New Haven, 63; Fairfield, 72; New London, 70.

[4] Captain Nathaniel Davenport was a native of Salem. His father was for many years commander of the Castle at Boston, and the son naturally acquired experience in military matters, and at the time of the fitting out of the Narragansett expedition in Philip's war, he was summoned to take command of the 5th company in the Massachusetts regiment.

465 foot, 275 horse, besides volunteers, teamsters and servants.[1]

Early on the morning of the 9th, Winslow took over the command from Major-General Denison[2] and, having promised the troops a gratuity in land, besides their pay, if they should drive out the enemy from the Narragansett country, gave orders for the advance.

The evening camp was pitched at Woodcock's garrison, Attelboro,[3] and by the evening of the next day they reached Seekonk,[4] where Richard Smith's sloop which had sailed from Smith's Landing to meet them, lay at anchor in the stream. Captain Moseley's command, Benjamin Church, Joseph Dudley and a few others, immediately embarked, while the remainder of the force, ferrying around to the head of the bay, joined Major William Bradford and Captain Gorham, with the one hundred and fifty-eight men of the Plymouth contingent, at Providence.

The united force now pushed into Pumham's country, marching by night in the hope of surprising and capturing the sachem Pumham, formerly a most submissive and servile friend but now a stout-hearted ally of Philip. But the night was bitter cold, the guides lost their way in the darkness and the troops, worn out with floundering

---

[1]Hubbard, Vol. I, page 139.

[2]Daniel Denison, Cambridge, 1633, born in England about 1612, was freeman April 1, 1634. Removed to Ipswich with the early planters; its representative 1635 and seven years after; speaker several years. Artillery Company, 1680, and every rank in the militia to the highest. Assistant from 1654 till his death September 19, 1682.—Savage.

[3]Located at the north end of the present village of North Attleboro, and its foundation stones and cellar hole may still be seen.

[4]Seekonk was upon the river of that name in what is now the town of East Providence, about a mile or a little more below its northern limit. It was practically identical with old Rehoboth.

through the deep snow, gave over the quest and, turning southward with the thirty-five prisoners they had captured, reached the appointed rendezvous, Smith's Landing at Wickford, on the 13th.

Here they found Moseley and Church who, having established the camp, had already begun an aggressive campaign on their own initiative. Nearly two score prisoners, men, women and children (many of whom they subsequently sold to Captain Davenport for the sum of eighty pounds), had been taken and a number of the Narragansetts slain.

During Winslow's march there had come to him a Narragansett Indian named Peter Freeman, who having "received some disgust among his countrymen" now revenged himself by playing the traitor, acting as a guide to the English on several occasions and giving them full information of the Narragansett stronghold.

Nearly ten years later a reward which had been promised him was paid and the General Court of Massachusetts ordered that his daughter be sought and redeemed from slavery.[1]

The Connecticut contingent had not yet arrived, but on the following day Winslow led out his force to the nearby village of the squaw-sachem, Matantuck,[2] or the

---

[1]Mass. Col. Records, Vol. V, page 477.

[2]Queen Magnus was the widow of Mexanno, who was the eldest son of Canonicus. She was sister to Ninigret the great Niantic chieftain. This squaw sachem had several successive names, thus, Quaiapen, Magnus, Matantuck, the Saunk Squaw (meaning the wife of a sachem), and the "Old Queen" of the Narragansetts. She was the mother of Quequaganet, the sachem who sold the Pettaquamscot lands to the English. She was related by marriage with the most distinguished sachems of the Niantic and Narragansett tribes, and succeeding Canon-

Saunk Squaw, burnt over one hundred and fifty wigwams, and, having killed seven Indians, returned with nine prisoners; at the same time a scouting party of thirty men sent out by Oliver, who had been left behind to guard the stores, killed an Indian warrior and squaw and took several prisoners.

At dawn on the 15th, came an Indian known to the whites as Stonewall or Stonelayer John,[1] professing authority to enter into negotiations. He was, however, a

---

chet, became the great squaw sachem of the Narragansetts, and her last stronghold was the "Queen's Fort." She was killed and her band destroyed, July 2, 1676, near Nachek on the Patuxet River, by Major Talcott and his forces. William Harris of Providence wrote of her personal character: "A great woman; yea, ye greatest yt ther was; ye sd woman, called ye old Queene."—The Lands of Rhode Island, by Sidney S. Rider, pages 240, 241.

The Queen's Fort.—This rude fortification stands upon an elevation exactly on the line separating North Kingston from Exeter. It is two miles in a northwest direction from Wickford Junction station on the N. Y., N. H. & H. R. R., and about three and one-half miles from the Smith garrison house. It occupies the top of the elevation, the hill falling away from the walls on all sides. The builders taking advantage of huge bowlders, laid rough stone walls between them, making a continuous line. "There is a round bastion or half moon on the northeast corner of the fort, and a salient or V-shaped point, or flanker, on the west side." It was in this neighborhood, a little to the southeast of the fort, near the headwaters of the little river Showatucquere, that the Narragansetts had a considerable village, undoubtedly the deserted village destroyed by the army on the 14th of December, 1675. (See Bodge, Soldiers in King Philip's War, page 180.) The Lands of Rhode Island, by Sidney S. Rider, page 236.

[1] Stonewall John is said by Sidney S. Rider to have been the builder of the ancient stone fort known as the "Queen's Fort." He quotes Mr. Samuel G. Drake (Book of the Indians, Vol. III, page 77): "One writer of his time observes that he was called the stone layer, for that, being an active, ingenious fellow, he had learned the masons' trade and was of great use to the Indians *in building their forts,* and" Mr. Rider adds that "he and he alone of the Indians could do such things." Stone-

GLIMPSE OF THE OLD QUEEN'S FORT

Near Wickford, Rhode Island. While the wall of the fort may be traced in its entirety, the dense growth of trees and brush, together with the innumberable boulders scattered over the surface of the ground, make a picture of more than a small portion impossible

chief of minor importance, and Winslow, believing that he came only to gain time and spy out the numbers of the English, dismissed him with the brief reply, "We might speak with the sachems."

During his visit the Narragansetts were hovering around in considerable numbers, and on the departure of the ambassador began to pick off the troops, shooting down from behind a hill three men of Gardiner's company on the outskirts of the camp, and even firing from the shelter of a stone wall[1] upon a considerable force which had been sent out under Captains Moseley, Oliver and Gardiner to bring in Appleton's company from outpost duty; but repulsed here with the loss of one of their leaders they drew off towards evening.[2]

Some eight miles from Winthrop's camp, in a clearing on Tower Hill, lay the large stone house of Jirah Bull,[3]

---

wall John's Indian name has been lost to us. He was killed in Talcott's attack on the encampment of Queen Magnus, at Nachek, July 2, 1676. —Lands of Rhode Island.

[1] Sidney S. Rider says the stone wall here mentioned was probably the wall of the Queen's Fort. "It may be stated, with a reasonable degree of historical accuracy, that the Queen's Fort was the spot around which lay the great 'town' of the Narragansetts in 1675, and from behind the stone walls of which the Indians fired thirty shots upon the advance post of the English army on the 15th of December of that year."

The fort was just three and a half miles from Smith's garrison, the distance at which Appleton's company lay, and it appears to be the only place that can be made to fit the description.—Lands of Rhode Island, page 240.

[2] Hutchinson's History of Massachusetts, Vol. I, page 301. Captain Oliver's Letter.

[3] Jirah Bull, son of Governor Henry, born at Portsmouth, R. I., September, 1638. Kept a garrison house on Tower Hill at Pettaquamscut. This was about two and a half miles northwest from the present village of Narragansett Pier, and perhaps a mile and a half east from the village of Wakefield.

"a convenient large stone house with a good stone wall yard before it which is a kind of fortification to it,"[1] and which had been selected as the rendezvous of the army on the arrival of the Connecticut troops. Here, on the night of the 15th, had assembled some seventeen people; careless in the face of danger, and relying on the near presence of the troops, no watch was probably set, when, in the darkness, the Indians repulsed at Smith's Landing in the afternoon stole upon it, broke in the doors and massacred all but two of the inmates.

Captain Prentice, following the trail of the Indians the next day, saw smoke rising among the trees in the still winter air and the silent smoldering ruins told the tale of surprise and massacre.

Discouragement and humiliation fell heavily on the minds of Winthrop's men on the return of Prentice, but with the morrow came the welcome news that the Connecticut force, three hundred and fifteen troops and one hundred and fifty Mohegans and Pequots, had arrived and were encamped at Pettaquamscut.

On the 18th, as the short winter day was drawing to its close, Winthrop joined Treat at Pettaquamscut and assumed command over the largest army ever assembled up to that time in New England. As the weather was becoming unsettled and provisions were running low it was decided to make the attack on the Narragansett stronghold the next day. Fires were built and by this light the troops cleaned their guns and completed their preparations. The night was cold, the sky overcast, and

---

[1] Letter of Waite Winthrop to his father, Governor John Winthrop, of Connecticut, July, 1675.—Connecticut Colony Records, Vol. II, page 338.

the troops, unprovided with tents, lay out under the open sky. Clustered for warmth around the camp fires, whose flickering lights in the clearing cast the woods in deeper shadow, they heard the trees crackling in the frost and the long-drawn sough of the night wind. Sleep was almost impossible and before the gray dawn had come the camp was astir.

Sixteen miles to the west, by a circuitous route, lay the objective point of the expedition, a fortified winter village of the Narragansetts[1] situated on a hillock of some five or six acres, in the midst of a cedar swamp, which presents to-day much the aspect it then wore. Here were collected many warriors and a large number of women and children. Their bark wigwams were lined with skins and well stored with their winter supplies of corn and dried fish. Joseph Dudley states, on the authority of a squaw, that there were assembled here, in addition to a thousand in the woods in reserve, 3,500 warriors and their women and children, which would have made a total of about 14,000 souls; a ridiculous estimate. Five or six acres would not have accommodated 2,000, and the Narragansetts could not assemble 1,000 to 1,200 fighting men all told.

Strong as the position was by nature—for the only ap-

---

[1]The great Narragansett Swamp is located in the town of North Kingston, R. I., and is crossed by the line of the N. Y., N. H. & H. R. R. between the stations of Kingston and Kenyon. The island upon which the fort was located lies between Usquapaug River and Shickasheen Brook, now known as Queen's River and Muddy Brook, and may be reached by a drive of two and a half miles from Kingston station. A causeway has been constructed between a point of elevated land reaching out in near proximity to the "island," to the island itself, enabling one to reach this point of interest dry-shod.

proach was over a fallen tree, save when the severest weather froze the surface of the swamp—it had been fortified in a manner seldom employed by the Indians. They had often fenced in their villages with a stockade of logs set on end, but here a stockade more than usually stout and strong was reinforced with a hedge and inner rampart of rocks and clay, while numerous blockhouses and flankers commanded every approach with a cross fire.[1] The Narragansetts, according to Hubbard, were advised in the erection of their fortifications by a settler named Tiffe (or Teft[2]).

It was five o'clock Sunday morning, December 19th, when the army began its march along the uplands, a circuitous route but one less exposed to the possibilities of an ambuscade; the Massachusetts division in advance, the companies of Moseley and Davenport leading, Plymouth men in the center and the Connecticut contingent bringing up the rear, while the Mohegans and Pequot auxiliaries covered the flanks of the army or scouted ahead.

Keen eyes were watching them as they pushed on, guided by Peter, and as they neared the edge of the swamp shortly after the noon hour, scattering shots were fired upon them by warriors who fled ostentatiously toward the log which led to the principal entrance. It has been generally believed that the English forced their way in at this point. Such was not the case, for, either by chance or directed by their guide, the Massachusetts men in the

---

[1] Old Indian Chronicle, page 181.

[2] Captain Oliver's Letter. Rider thinks that Stonewall John may have been the engineer of the Narragansett fort, and says, "We may hazard but little in his conjecture."—Lands of Rhode Island, page 242.

van inclined their march a little to the right and came upon the one weak point in the defenses, where an unfinished portion of the stockade commanded by a blockhouse, but unprotected by abattis, had been filled in with a large tree. "Wherefor the providence of Almighty God" says Hubbard, "is the more to be acknowledged, who, as he led Israel by the pillar of fire and the cloud of his presence to light a way through the wilderness, so it now directs our forces upon that side of the fort where they might only enter."

With a rush, the Massachusetts men, running over the frozen swamp, charged this entrance, but a deadly fire smote them in front and flank. Captain Johnson fell dead, with many of his men, at the entrance, while Captain Davenport, distinguished by a handsome buff coat, gained the fort only to face a volley that killed him and decimated his company.

The survivors of the three companies drew back in confusion to the edge of the swamp and threw themselves on their faces. Moseley and Gardiner reinforced them, but Gardiner himself was shot dead near the entrance and the men could make no headway until Major Appleton, with the remainder of the Massachusetts men, dashing forward with the cry "they run, they run," gathered them in the rush and the whole mass, storming over the tree together, drove the Indians out of the flanker on the left.

They were now somewhat protected from the sharpshooters in the nearby blockhouses, but many of them continued to fall, and the Narragansetts, rallying again, began to press them fiercely, when the Connecticut troops, suffering fearfully from the fire directed upon them, made their way in through the breach, though Gallop,[1] Marshall, and Seeley, among their leaders, fell dead and Mason was mortally wounded.

A short time later the Plymouth men also made their entrance. Little by little the stern and determined attack of the English told, and the Narragansetts fell back, foot by foot, though the warriors fought desperately from the shelter of the bags and the baskets of grain in the wigwams.

Even yet the issue might have been doubtful, but, either through chance or deliberately fired by some English hand, the Indian wigwams caught fire and the wind swept the fire in a mighty wave of flame through the crowded fort. An indiscriminate massacre must have followed "for the shrieks and cries of the women and children, the yelling of the warriors, exhibited a most horrible and appalling scene, so that it greatly moved some of the soldiers. They were in much doubt and they afterwards seriously inquired whether burning their enemies alive could be consistent with humanity and the benevolent principle of the gospel."[2]

But though the Narragansetts had been driven out of

---

[1] Captain John Gallop, Boston, 1637. He served in the Pequot war, for which Connecticut made him a grant of one hundred acres of land. He removed to New London in 1651, but had been in Taunton for a short time in 1643. He finally settled in Stonington and was representative from that town in 1665 and 1667.—Savage.

[2] Manuscript of the Rev. W. Ruggles.

NOTE.—Details of this campaign are to be found at considerable length in the letters of Captain Oliver given in Hutchinson's History of Massachusetts, Vol. I, page 300; the letters of Joseph Dudley to Governor Leverett, December 15th, Massachusetts Archives, Vol. LXVIII, page 101; and December 21st, Hutchinson's History of Massachusetts, Vol. I, page 302.

the village they still hung on the outskirts of the swamp, firing continuously at the English from the shelter of the woods, and Captain Church, who had had little share in the storm, sallying out, beat them back but was himself wounded. The victory had been won, but the price paid had been heavy.

The short day was fast drawing into a wild winter's night when the surviving commanders gathered around Winslow in the glare of the blazing wigwams. Their figures, turning white in the swift-falling snow, were silhouetted against the flames, and among the dead and wounded English and warriors around them, lay many an Indian woman and child.

The debate was long and earnest. Church vehemently urged that they should camp where they stood, collect the wounded in the shelter of the blockhouses and give the weary troops needed rest and food.[1] An eighteen-mile march through a broken trail, encumbered with the wounded and exposed to the fierce blast of the storm, was folly. Others saw more clearly than he. Their position was at the best precarious. They had, it was true, inflicted heavy loss on the Narragansetts and destroyed their winter shelter and supplies, but their own losses had been very heavy. Six captains and over twenty men were already dead. One hundred and fifty wounded were upon their hands. The blazing village offered little shelter or provision, the food and ammunition were well-nigh exhausted and the base of communication lay eighteen miles away, and who knew but the Narragansetts, rallying on the morrow, might be upon them. Better to

---

[1] Church's Entertaining History, page 16.

expose the wounded to the storm than risk a siege or ambuscade in the morning. Now, when the foes were dispirited and their plans unformed, was the time to return. Such was the deciding opinion and the tired and weary troops, leaving twenty of the dead in the fort to deceive the Indians as to their loss, and carrying the wounded on litters made of muskets and saplings, filed out of the smoldering ruins into the woods and storm, lighted for three miles of their journey, as the author of the old Indian chronicle assures us, by the flames of the burning wigwams.

It was a terrible march. The fierce blast blew the snow in their faces; sometimes they stumbled over the logs and trees that lay across their path and heard the agonized groans of their wounded comrades brought to ground, twenty-two of them dying on the march. The trail was indistinct and often they sank to their knees in the drifted snow, while the heavily-laden boughs slashed them in the face. Faint from hunger and fatigue, weighed down with their wounded, and blinded by the storm, well it was for them that the older chiefs turned a deaf ear to the appeals of the young warriors that they should be followed and attacked on the march.

It was two o'clock in the morning before the main body struggled into Wickford. Many lost their way and wandered amid the storm all night. Winslow with forty men did not reach the camp until seven the next morning. Seven of their captains and about seventy-five of the men were dead or died during the next few days.

The number of the Indians killed has been greatly exaggerated by the historians. Mather says there were

one thousand killed;[1] Hubbard, seven hundred fighting
men killed, three hundred more died of wounds, besides
women, old men and children beyond count. No effort
was made after the fight to count the Indian dead. Tifft,
on his capture, stated it to have been ninety-eight killed
and forty-eight wounded, besides women and children.
The Narragansetts told the Indians at Quabaug that
they had lost "forty fighting men and a sachem killed,
and some three hundred old men, women and children
burnt in the wigwams, which were mostly destroyed.[2]
Considering the fact that the Indians fought from shelter
and that though there was, according to Hubbard, "but
one entrance into the fort, the enemy found many ways
to come out," their own statement seems the most reliable. The desire of the young men to pursue the English is very good proof that their losses in men were not
as great as reported by the English.

The provisions of the Indians for the winter had been
destroyed, their shelter burnt and themselves driven out
into the woods in the dead of winter to face famine. The
hornet's nest had indeed been scorched, but the hornets
were loose and the plight of the troops, without shelter
or provisions, exhausted and exposed to the fury of the
elements, was little better than that of the Indians, and
only the fortunate arrival of Captain Richard Goodale[3]

---

[1] "We have heard of two and twenty Indian captains slain, all of them,
and brought down to hell in one day."—Mather's Prevalency of Prayer,
page 265.

[2] James Quanapohit's Relation.—Conn. War, 1 Doc. 35b.

[3] A letter from Joseph Dudley to Governor Leverett, written from
Smith's garrison, December 21, 1675, credits Captain Goodale with
bringing the needed relief, though Church in his Entertaining History
(page 62) states that it was Captain Andrew Belcher whose vessel

of Boston with a sloop load of provisions, at Smith's Landing the same night, saved them from terrible suffering.

---

arrived at that time. It is more than probable, however, that Dudley's statement, written at the very time of the event, is more reliable than that of Church written forty years later. Both Goodale and Belcher were contemporary merchants and vessel owners.

CHAPTER X

T HE wounded of the Massachusetts and Plymouth contingent were sent over to Rhode Island, and the Connecticut wounded to Stonington and New London, but the Connecticut force was so disabled that Major Treat was obliged to withdraw from further operations December 28th, despite the protest of the other officers. Joseph Dudley had already written to Governor Leverett, requesting two or three hundred more men and captains, "blunderbusses, hand grenadoes and armours if it may be, and at least two armourers," and until the arrival of these reinforcements and other supplies the army was tied to its base and incapable of assuming the offensive.[1] The Narragansetts had, in the meantime, returned to their ruined fort without molestation and probably secured considerable supplies of corn and fish which had escaped the conflagration.

Four days after the battle the Narragansetts, probably fencing for time, sent ambassadors to ask for terms, a report on the condition of the white forces probably being not the least of their duties. The deep snow and the intense cold following a sudden thaw, held the main body of the army in camp, but scouting parties who were sent out almost daily secured from time to time corn from the Indian barns, and some prisoners. Supplies of

---

[1] Dudley's letter to the Governor and Council. Hutchinson's History of Massachusetts, Vol. I, page 302.

food, ammunition and clothing were slowly being brought in from Connecticut and Boston by vessels, and the commissioners were organizing reinforcements and urging Connecticut to hurry forward their reorganized companies. On December 27th the ground was again frozen and Captain Prentice marched upon Pumham's village[1] (near Warwick) and destroyed one hundred wigwams, but "found never an Indian in any one of them."

Through a captive squaw taken the following day, the Narragansetts were informed that the door to peace would be opened by the surrender of all the Wampanoags who had taken refuge with the Narragansetts, and compliance with such conditions as the authorities deemed necessary to impose. The squaw did not return but there came a messenger returning thanks for the offer of peace and a reply, "It was not we who made war upon the English, but the English upon us without notice."

The return of Canonchet in the spring for the purpose of procuring corn for the spring planting affords strong evidence that the destitution of the Narragansetts at this time was less severe than the English believed, and the

---

[1] The Massachusetts colony, claiming the lands of Shawomet (Warwick), had forbidden their occupation by any person without the permission of the colony, and in order to aid their ally, Pumham, in holding them, built an earthwork or fort, which they garrisoned with an officer and ten soldiers. Tradition locates this fort on the east bank of Warwick Cove and what very plainly indicate its remains may still be seen there. It commanded the entrance to the cove, while in the rear was said to have been an impenetrable marshy thicket to protect it in that direction. This feature has now disappeared and the old earthwork may be reached dry-shod from the track of the electric railway on the east. Pumham's village, it is most likely, was at this point. His domain covered the territory now occupied largely by the town of Warwick, R. I.

thaw that allowed Prentice to make his expedition afforded
the Indians an opportunity of securing food by raiding
the settlers' cattle and reaching their stores of buried
corn.

Negotiations continued but each party was suspicious
of the good faith of the other. On the fourth of January,
1676, two messengers came to Winslow "to make way,
as they declared, for a treaty of peace." They laid the
blame of hostilities upon Canonchet, who, they said, had
misinformed them as to the terms of the treaty, having
told them that the Wampanoags were not to be surrendered until Canonchet's brother, held as a hostage at
Hartford, had been delivered up. On the following day
a little child, three years old, who had been captured near
Warwick was sent in as a peace offering and a few days
thereafter a messenger came from the old sachem Ninigret, recalling his friendship for the English and informing them that provisions in the Narragansett camp were
scarce; but whatever the wishes of the old man, the power
had passed into younger and bolder hands "for that young
and insolent Canonchet and Panoquin[1] said they would
fight it out to the last man rather than they would become
the slaves of the English."[2]

In the meantime the reinforcements raised by the commissioners at Boston had been equipped and the first
company under command of Captain Samuel Brocklebank[3] set out on the sixth of January, but again the

---

[1] Panoquin, usually called Quinapin, was at one time the husband of
Weetamoo, Queen of the Pocassets.

[2] Hubbard, Vol. I, page 161.

[3] Captain Samuel Brockelbank was of Rowley. He was a native of
England and born about 1630. He was elected captain of the first

winter storms and cold set in, and before they reached
Wickford, four days later, sick and disheartened, several
of their number had perished from exposure.[1]

Several scouts going out on the 11th, next day came
upon an Indian hiding in one of the Indian corn pits
under the leaves, and brought him into camp, "but he
would own nothing but what was forced out of his mouth
by the twisting of a cord around his head; he was therefore adjudged to die as a Wampanoag," says Hubbard,
a naive confession of torture which he or Mather would
have embellished with a page of scriptural quotations if
committed by the Indians.

Early the next day (the 12th of January) Canonchet
and the sachems sent a request to Winslow for a month's
truce for the discussion of a treaty. This request aroused
Winslow's indignation and caused him to press more energetically than ever for the return of the reorganized
Connecticut forces. It is difficult to agree with Winslow
in the matter of these negotiations. He seems throughout
obstinate and hot-tempered and unable to make use of
his opportunities. It was well known that there existed
among the Narragansetts a considerable party, neither
uninfluential nor few in numbers, anxious for peace,
among them Pessacus and Ninigret, sachem of the Niantics, yet no effort was made to strengthen their influence
and divide the enemy, which a little diplomacy could
have advanced. Winslow was still to wait two weeks

---

company at Rowley, in 1673, and was active in recruiting for the Narragansett campaign. He was killed at Sudbury, April 21, 1676.—Bodge,
page 206.

[1] Old Indian Chronicle (Present State of New England), page 195.

before making any forward movement, and when made it was to prove worse than abortive, spreading the war over a larger area.

Four days later a party of Providence settlers under Captain Fenner, pursuing some Indians who had seized their cattle, wounded and brought in Joshua Tift, the renegade Englishman who had joined the Narragansetts.[1]

Roger Williams, who acted as clerk at Tift's court-martial, records, in a letter to Governor Leverett, Tift's defense.[2] He said that twenty-seven days before the battle at the Narragansett fort, the Narragansetts had burned his house, seized his cattle and that he himself had only escaped death by agreeing to become Canonchet's slave. He had been taken to the fort and there held. The Narragansetts had made terms with the Mohegans and Pequots before the battle, and after the capture of the fort the sachem had retired to a swamp not far away. On the departure of the English they sent to ascertain their losses and found ninety-eight dead and forty-eight wounded, and five or six bodies of the English. Their powder was nearly gone. Pessacus was for peace, but Canonchet was determined on war. The sachems were now about ten miles from Smith's and believed the English proposal of a truce a trap to catch them. Philip, he said, had been at Quabaug in December whither the Narragansetts were now retiring, leaving foraging parties and a strong rear guard.

His defense was of no avail, and the judgment of the court soon received vindication from the report of James

---

[1] Hubbard, Vol. I, page 162.

[2] Winthrop Papers. Massachusetts Historical Society Collections, Vol. XXXVI, page 307.

K

Quanapohit,[1] who was told by the Narragansetts that he had killed and wounded several of the English both before and during the battle at the fort. He was hanged and quartered. "A sad wretch, he never heard a sermon but once these fourteen years," wrote Captain Oliver.

While the English were making final preparations for an offensive movement, Canonchet was not idle; houses and barns were burnt and cattle captured and, as late as the 27th when the English were about to march upon him in force, he raided Warwick and despoiled William Carpenter of that place of 200 sheep, 50 cattle and 15 horses.

On January 28th the Connecticut troops to the number of about three hundred, marching from New London by way of Westerly, reached the rendezvous, and reinforcements from Plymouth and Massachusetts brought the strength of the army to over 1,400. Then began what was known as the "hungry march." Winslow moved forward through the Narragansett country burning the wigwams and seizing supplies wherever they were to be found, capturing here and there a few Indian stragglers, the sick and the old, women and children, whose strength had failed them.

---

[1] "Of the aboriginal possessors of Nashaway (Lancaster), none, unless Sholan, better deserves to be honored among us than that Indian scout, whose courage, skill and fidelity, should have saved the town from the massacre of 1676, James Quanapaug, alias James Wiser, alias Quenepenett, or Quanapohit. This Christian Indian was so well known for his bravery, capacity and friendship for the English that Philip had marked him for martyrdom, and given orders accordingly to some of his lieutenants."—Early Records of Lancaster, by Hon. Henry S. Nourse, pages 99, 100.

See, also, James Quanapohit's Relation. Conn. Archives, War Doc. *35b.*

At times they came upon the still smoking embers of the Narragansett camp-fires, and twenty-five miles from Warwick found the skeleton heads of sixty horses that had been butchered for food.

Northward through Rhode Island, through Warwick, whose inhabitants abandoned it as the army passed on, through Woodstock in Connecticut into Massachusetts, they pushed their way over frozen streams and swamps or along the exposed uplands, foraging for whatever they could procure. Their camps were pitched in the snow under the shelter of a hill or in the woods, and they warmed their numbed bodies over the open fires. Still they pressed on, footsore, wet and hungry, in pursuit of the Narragansetts ever retreating before them and out of reach until, worn out by the dreary march, reduced to eating their horses and ground nuts for food, Winslow reached Marlboro and there disbanded his forces on the 3d of February, leaving Captain Wadsworth and a company of foot in garrison, whom, soon afterwards, Captain Brocklebank reinforced.

Marlboro was a position of considerable strategic value. It lay on what was called the Connecticut or Bay path, and was the last town of importance until the Connecticut Valley was reached. It served as a base of operations and a rendezvous of the troops from the Bay towns in the movements to and from the valley. A small garrison had been stationed here. Already it had been threatened in the summer and fall of the previous year, and it was believed that it would be the first town to be attacked in the coming spring.

The disbandment of the army which sent the Connecticut troops homeward and most of the Massachusetts contingent to Boston, was a blunder of the first magnitude, and, in view of the events of the past few months, astonishing in its disregard of the principles of Indian warfare as taught by events in the valley. The whole frontier toward the east was left at the mercy of the Indians. It was no doubt difficult to procure provisions for so large a force, but the need of a large body to defend the frontier was an imperative necessity which should have been met.

The Indians to the north, informed by a runner of the attack on the Narragansett village, had received the news with suspicion, a messenger bringing in the heads of two Englishmen was shot at and was informed that the Narragansetts had been the friends of the English all summer and they did not trust him. They even debated putting the messenger to death as a spy, but, day by day, fugitives and messengers bearing the heads and hands of slaughtered Englishmen came thronging into their camps.[1] The Narragansett nation were now among them as allies, and their leaders must have had their hopes raised high by a reinforcement that more than made up the losses of the previous year.

Around Quabaug, in numerous small colonies, were Sagamore Sam, One-Eyed John,[2] Matoonas, Mautaump,

---

[1] James Quanapohit's Relation.

[2] Monoco, or "One-Eyed John," as he was called by the English because of a defect in his vision, lived near Lancaster. He was active in the attack on that town, principal in the assault on Groton, and on his own word, the destroyer of Medfield. At the close of Philip's war he gave himself up, with others, to Major Walderne at Cochecho (Dover), and was sent to Boston and, with Sagamore Sam, Old Jethro and Mautaump, was executed upon the gallows at "the town's end," September 26, 1676. He is known to have had a magnanimous disposition and perhaps no charge can be brought against him that would not comport

and two or three hundred Quabaugs and Nashaways. Further north, at Wachusett, a favorite camping ground of the Nashaways, was another small settlement, while the main body of the valley tribes, Nonotucks, Pocumtucks, Agawams and Squakheags, had established winter quarters in the vicinity of Northfield and Peskeompscut.

The wanderings of Philip, that will-o'-the-wisp of contemporary chroniclers, are now well known. Roger Williams believed he had made a visit to the Narragansetts during the fall, and Joseph Dudley, in a letter to Governor Leverett, stated that he had been seen by many in the thick of the battle at the swamp, but both were mistaken. Philip, with the remnant of his Wampanoags and Pocassets, had spent the late fall and early winter at Quabaug, but late in December, attended by his own followers and a considerable following from the valley tribes, went west toward the Hudson and established winter quarters at Schaghticoke in Van Rensselaer County, some twenty miles northeast of Albany where he was joined by several bands of roving adventurers.

On January 6th Governor Andros wrote to the Governor and Council of Connecticut, "This is to acquaint you that late last night I had intelligence that Philip and four hundred or five hundred fighting men were come within forty or fifty miles of Albany, northeasterly, where they talk of continuing the winter. Philip is sick."[1]

The report of Andros is confirmed by other testimony, for to Schaghticoke also came Robert Pepper[2] and

---

with his character as an Indian warrior.—Book of the Indians. Old Indian Chronicle.

[1] Connecticut Records, Vol. II, page 397.

[2] Mrs. Rowlandson's Removes.

James Quanapohit. It is also supported by the less reliable evidence of Thomas Warren[1] captured in October and taken to the Indian encampment who, on his return, declared the assembled force, including some 500 French Indians, to have exceeded 2,100 men and that Philip himself with 400 others was then absent; most certainly an exaggeration leading to the belief that he was either ingeniously permitted to see the same warriors several times, or possessed a wild imagination.

This far removal of Philip from the scenes of operations possessed several advantages. It was safe under all ordinary circumstances from attack. It afforded communication with both French and Mohawks and convenient means of access to the Dutch traders from whom he desired to procure supplies of powder, of which the Indians stood in pressing want.

It was openly declared by the New England authorities at the time that the Dutch traders were actively engaged in selling arms and ammunition to Philip, and an acrimonious correspondence took place in respect to the matter between Governor Andros and the Governor and Council of Connecticut, the irascible Governor replying to their reiterated charge January 31st, "I do now plainly see that you look upon it as a signal favor that that bloody war is removed toward us. I cannot omit your great reflection on the Dutch in which you seem to make me an accomplice, for which I pray an explanation, and to name the guilty, there being

---

[1] Probably Thomas Warren, a soldier in Captain Moseley's company. See also The Old Indian Chronicle (Present State of New England), page 226.

none in this government but his Majesty's subjects which obey all his laws."[1]

The traders indeed, warned by Andros, refused to sell direct, but the Mohawks, acting as intermediaries, took the furs from Philip's warriors and traded them off as their own, for powder, lead and guns.[2] Philip was also busily engaged in intrigues with both Mohawks and the French, guarding negotiations with the latter carefully from the former.

The Mohawks, it is said, told Philip that they would gladly strike at the Mohegans but would not take up arms against the English. At the same time, according to Andros' letters to the Connecticut Council, they were holding out hopes to the English of an offensive alliance against Philip, a species of double dealing negotiations in which the Iroquois were perfectly at home.

A strange story comes down to us to the effect that Philip sought to inflame the rage of the Mohawks against the settlers by himself destroying a party of Mohawk warriors and imputing the outrage to the whites, but that the Mohawks, discovering his treachery, fell upon his force and drove it to the east.[3]

The most careful research yields no satisfactory evidence of such treachery on Philip's part. It seems, like many other tales, to have been used to color Philip's character. The belief, widespread in New England, that Philip made a visit to Canada during the winter in person, is also unlikely, for a journey to the French and their Indian allies, which could not have been disguised from

---

[1] Connecticut Records, Vol. II, page 404.
[2] James Quanapohit's Relation. Conn. War, Vol. I, Doc. 35*b*.
[3] Increase Mather's Brief History, page 168.

the Mohawks, would have turned them into deadly enemies. There is no doubt however but that Philip sought
French aid indirectly. In the fall of the previous year
he had met Monsieur Normanville who had been at
Boston, and the Frenchman had aroused his hopes by
telling him not to burn the best houses as the French
would come in the spring with three hundred men and
ammunition.[1] The promise of the boastful Frenchman
was valueless, but Philip's position at Schaghticoke offered exceptional facilities for procuring the aid they were
willing to give in supplies of arms and powder.

Throughout the tribes disease had been rife and had
cost them more in lives than the warfare of the preceding
months,[2] but they asked no peace. The old men desired
it, but Philip and the young leaders and warriors would
not hear of it. The severity of the whites, the numerous
executions, the selling of all captives into slavery had
had their effect. Peace offered nothing better than punishment, slavery, or complete and humiliating submission
to every caprice and pleasure of the English. Rather,
said they, "Let us live as long as we can and die like
men and not live to be enslaved."

The winter was one of great suffering among all the
Indians; the war had prevented the Connecticut Valley
tribes from reaping their crops which were even at the
best seldom sufficient to supply their wants, and the Wampanoags, driven from their fishing grounds into the Nipmuck country, and bringing few supplies of their own,
had added but so many more mouths to feed.

---

[1] James Quanapohit's Relation. Conn. War, Vol. I, Doc. 35b.

[2] Testimony of James the Printer. Increase Mather's Brief History,
page 173.

Such was the condition of the hostiles when, in the dead of winter, several thousand Narragansetts, destitute of supplies, poured in upon them. The already slender resources of the Nipmuck tribes were immediately exhausted, and though the trees were bare and the ground deep with snow, raids upon the English villages for the purpose of securing food became imperative.

The garrisons at Chelmsford, Billerica, Groton, Lancaster and Sudbury had all been withdrawn as early as January 11th, and, with the exception of the small garrison at Marlboro under Captain Wadsworth, the whole frontier lay open to attack.

Already on the first of February, a small party of Nipmucks, under Netus, had fallen upon the house of Thomas Eames on the outskirts of Sudbury, and, after burning it, led his family and that of his son into captivity,[1] Eames himself being absent in Boston.

The commissioners of the United Colonies were not unmindful of the danger that threatened the western towns, and within a week of the disbanding of Winslow's army, determined to raise a force of six hundred men for an offensive campaign against the Indians at Quabaug and Wachusett. To that end, February 8th, they called upon Massachusetts to fill out her quota and bade the Governor and Council of Connecticut send Major Treat and a body of Pequots and Mohegans,[2] but before the force could be raised the blow fell upon Lancaster.

On the evening of the 9th of February, the people at

---

[1] A boy of the family escaped in May and after long wanderings reached the English town. All of the family were subsequently ransomed or found except a little girl.

[2] Connecticut Records, Vol. II, page 409.

Lancaster, with some fourteen soldiers who had been stationed in the town, as usual assembled in the fortified houses of which there were five in widely separated localities.[1] The principal one, that of the Reverend Mr. Rowlandson,[2] who was himself absent in Boston for the purpose of securing from the Governor and Council an adequate garrison for the defense of the town, stood in the center.

Warning of the attack had not been wanting. James Quanapohit had informed the Governor and Council as early as January 24th that the Indians at Quabaug intended to attack the town, and at midnight, February 9th, another Indian spy, Job Kattenait, a Christian Natick, knocking at Major Gookin's door in Cambridge, in an exhausted condition, having traveled over eighty miles through the wilderness on snowshoes, told him the blow

---

[1] See Marvin's History of Lancaster.

In the History of Worcester County, Vol. I, page 600, it is stated that the first garrison was that of Rev. Mr. Rowlandson, located in the center of the town. The next was probably that of John White, situated about twenty rods north of the present railroad station. Then came that of Thomas Sawyer, half a mile south of the Rowlandson garrison, in the center of the settlement of South Lancaster. Then that of John Prescott in Clinton, while the fifth (Wheeler's) was probably in the southwest part of Bolton.

[2] The Rowland garrison house was located on the western slope of the hill, on the top of which, now occupied by the cemetery, stood the meetinghouse. The road from Lancaster to the south village passes between these two sites about fifty rods southerly of the iron bridge over the west branch of the Nashaway River. The settlement of Lancaster consisted of farms spread out over a considerable territory, there being nothing in the semblance of a village; but the meetinghouse and the minister's dwelling may be considered the nucleus of the settlement. The exact site of the Rowlandson house is marked by a prominent pine tree, planted there as a means of identification.

SITE OF THE ROWLANDSON GARRISON

The tree stands upon the spot.

was about to fall.[1] Gookin immediately sent messengers to Captain Wadsworth at Marlboro, but it was too late.

In the Rowlandson garrison were gathered forty-two, possibly fifty, men and women, who, awakened by the firing of guns and the Indian war cry, rushed to the windows and looked out. The sight that met their eyes was terrifying. Several houses were in flames and the Indians, whose forms could be dimly seen in the gray of the morning, were massacring the inmates with rifles and tomahawks.

Three in one house were knocked on the head, a young man falling on his knees begged for mercy "but they would not hearken to him." Three others trying to reach the garrison were shot down by Indians posted on the roof of a barn, and the sound of other and more distant shots told that the whole settlement was being assaulted.

The inmates of the Rowlandson garrison, barricading the doors and windows, repulsed the first attack;[2] the house, however, stood on the slope of a hill and the Indians lying along the crest poured a continuous fire upon it. First one and then others of the defenders were shot down. For two hours they held their own, but the fatal weakness of the house, the covering of the loopholes in the rear by firewood laid up for winter fuel, soon attracted the keen eyes of the Indian warriors. A cart filled with flax, hemp and hay seized from the barn was wheeled to the side and fired. One daring soul sallied out and quenched the flames, but the pile was immediately re-

---

[1] Gookin's Christian Indians. American Antiquarian Soc. Coll., Vol. II, page 489.

[2] This account is taken from Mrs. Rowlandson's Narrative.

kindled. The roofs and sides caught fire, the house was enveloped in flames and soon the blazing roof threatened to fall in. Then men, women and children, Mrs. Rowlandson and her children among them, rushed out in the desperate hope of reaching the next garrison, but in vain. A shot passing through Mrs. Rowlandson's side pierced the hand and bowels of the child she carried in her arms.

Thomas Rowlandson,[1] her husband's nephew, aged seventeen, was killed, her sister's son was struck down, and Mrs. Henry Kerley,[2] wringing her hands in the doorway of the blazing house at the news of her son's death, was instantly killed.

Of the ten or twelve men, only one, Ephraim Roper,[3] leaving his wife dead behind him, escaped. The rest were killed and the women and children were seized.

---

[1] "Thomas Rowlandson," says Joseph Willard, on page 39 of his History of Lancaster, "was *brother* to the clergyman," and Mr. Marvin perpetuates this error on pages 96 and 106 of his history of the town. Rev. Joseph Rowlandson had a brother Thomas who lived in Salisbury, and died there in July, 1682. It was his son, Thomas Jr., who perished at Lancaster. Even the careful John Langdon Sibley adopts Willard's error on page 319, Vol. I, of his Harvard Graduates.—Supplement to Early Records of Lancaster, by Hon. Henry S. Nourse, page 17.

[2] Henry Kerley married Elizabeth, daughter of John White and sister of Mrs. Rowlandson, as above related. His wife, his sons, William, aged 17, and Joseph, aged 7, were killed at the attack on the garrison, and a son and three daughters carried into captivity. He was probably in Boston at the time with Rev. Mr. Rowlandson.—Early Records of Lancaster.

[3] Ephraim Roper was, in King William's war, the owner of a garrison house situated on the George Hill road. His father, John Roper, was killed by the Indians March 26, 1676, the day Lancaster was finally abandoned by its inhabitants. Ephraim Roper served as a soldier under Captain William Turner and took part in the Fall Fight, May 18, 1676. He was killed at Lancaster during King William's war, in the massacre of September 11, 1697.—Early Records of Lancaster.

So in midwinter were carried off the survivors of the Rowlandson blockhouse and several other of the townspeople, accompanied by the captured cattle, while Captain Wadsworth with forty men, hurrying along the further bank found the river swollen in flood and the floor of the bridge torn up. He arrived in time to save the other garrisons, the Indians drawing off at his approach, but too late to rescue the captives.

A few days later the town was abandoned, its surviving inhabitants taking refuge in the settlements to the east, and its houses, with the exception of the meetinghouse and a garrison, soon fell a prey to the flames.

The diary kept by Mrs. Rowlandson[1] in the midst of her wanderings affords us an intimate knowledge of the movements of Philip and of life among the Indians during the winter. It is exceedingly touching in its simplicity and pathos.

Encamped in a deserted house on the hill[2] above the town that night, she heard the Indians, glutted with the flesh of the captured cattle, dancing and singing around their camp fires. "My children gone," she wrote, "my relatives and friends gone, there remained to me but one poor wounded babe." The next day they set out. One

---

[1] Mrs. Mary Rowlandson was the wife of the Rev. Joseph Rowlandson of Lancaster, the first minister there, and daughter of John White of that place. Mrs. Rowlandson is well known to the student of King Philip's war by the diary she kept through the captivity following the destruction of her home February 10, 1676. This she published after her return from captivity and the work has passed through many editions. Rev. Mr. Rowlandson became settled in Wethersfield, Conn., in April, 1677, and died there November 23, 1678. Mrs. Rowlandson was living at that time but the time and place of her death are unknown.

[2] George Hill, an elevation about one mile from the Rowlandson house.

of the Indians carried her wounded child upon a horse, "it went moaning all along." At length she took it in her arms and carried it until her strength failed and she fell. They mounted her upon a horse and at night built a fire and a lean-to for her. At Menameset village she met her daughter and also Robert Pepper, who had been captured at Beer's defeat, and who told her that he had been carried to Albany and had seen Philip.

Her child, badly wounded and lacking medical care, was dying, and "a few days afterwards, about two hours in the night, my sweet babe like a lamb departed this life." The Indians buried it on a hilltop and in the morning showed her the newly-made grave.

She accompanied her masters in their wanderings, sharing their scanty food and at times suffering keen privation. They were often destitute of food and driven to boil the hoofs of the dead horses or procure the marrow from old bones, eking out their fare with ground nuts, the tender buds of trees or a little meal. At times a deer or a bear was killed and the long fast gave place to a gluttonous feast. But the sight of her children, a girl and a lad of sixteen, safe and well treated, consoled her for much misery.

They were constantly moving and covered extensively the country east of the Connecticut. She was sold to Quinnapin[1] and his wife Weetamoo, who seem to have

---

[1] Quinnapin was a noble Narragansett by birth, being the son of Coginaquan who was nephew to Canonicus. He was one of the chiefs who directed the attack on Lancaster, February 10, 1676, and he purchased Mrs. Rowlandson from a Narragansett Indian who had seized her as she came out of the garrison. At this time he was the husband of Weetamoo, the widow of Alexander and Queen of the Pocassets.

treated her kindly. She mended the worn clothes of the Indian children and made a shirt for her master's son.

Once, invited to eat with Philip because she made a shirt for his son, she was given a small cake of corn cooked in bear's fat; probably all he had to offer. She offered him her money but he bade her keep it and she bought some horseflesh therewith.

A Mrs. Joslyn,[1] with a small child, and who was about to become a mother, was killed by her captors, but Mrs. Rowlandson and her son and daughter were, in general, treated with kindness, as were most of the other captives.

In connection with the captivity of Mrs. Rowlandson it may be said that one party was as forward in the exercise of cruelty as the other. The torture of Englishmen by the Indians was the exception rather than the rule. The women and children were not tortured and were generally spared if the pursuit pressed not too fast upon their captor's heels. The Indian conqueror never lowered himself to the level of the European soldiery of the time in the sack of captured towns and villages with their carnival of rape and murder.

In all the chronicles of the time the reader finds no recorded instance of outrage upon a woman captive or the useless torture of children. "And such was the goodness of God to those poor captive women and children

---

At the Narragansett Swamp fight he was next in command to Canonchet. He is described as "a young, lusty sachem and a very rogue."—Old Indian Chronicle; also Book of the Indians.

[1] Mrs. Ann Joslyn was the wife of Abraham Joslyn, Jr. Her husband was killed at the Rowlandson garrison fight and her daughter, Beatrice, aged twenty-one months, was killed in captivity.—Early Records of Lancaster.

that several found so much favor in the sight of their
enemies that they were offered no wrong to any of their
persons save what they could not help, being in many
wants themselves, neither did they offer any uncivil carriage to any of the females, or any attempt the chastity
of any of them, either being restricted of God as was
Abimeleck of old, or by some other external cause
which withheld them from doing any wrong of that
kind."[1]

The settlers slew without discrimination as to age or
sex, and inflicted torture with a stern self-righteousness.
The former generation had set an example in the destruction of the women and children in the Pequot fort: the
present followed it closely; the next was to burn the
Salem witches.

The temper of the age and their belief that they were
the people of the new Israel, their foes the old Canaanites
and Philistines with new faces, hardened them to mercy.
In the books of the Old Testament they sought and found
precedents and divine commands in plenty that spoke
with the same authority and inspiration for the guidance
of their Israel of the new dispensation as to the fate to
be meted out to hostile people, as it had for the old.
Hence arose more than one instance of bad faith. Hence
men, women and children were slaughtered or sold into
slavery in the West Indies; Rhode Island alone, to her
credit, prohibiting the practice by statute. Hence the ex-
clusion from mercy of the captured sachems at the close
of the war and the refusal to recognize in the manly character of men like Canonchet aught but "the obstinate

---

[1] Hubbard, Vol. I, page 167.

and perverse spirit of the heathenish and bloodthirsty blasphemers who made war on God's people."

The same day as the attack on Lancaster a small party of Indians made an attack on Concord,[1] in which Abraham and Isaac Shepherd were killed near Nashobah in Concord village while threshing grain in their barn. Apprehensive of danger, says tradition, they placed their sister Mary, a girl about fifteen years old, on a hill a little distance off to watch and forewarn them of the approach of an enemy. She was, however, suddenly surprised and carried captive into the Indian settlements, but, with great heroism, while the Indians were asleep in the night, seized a horse and, taking a saddle from under the head of her Indian keeper, mounted and rode through the forest to her home.

The attacks on Lancaster and Concord were but the beginning of the storm. All was movement among the tribes, and attacks fell thick and fast on towns and solitary farms alike. The course of one particular party, under One-Eyed John, could be clearly traced by a trail of blood southward toward Plymouth colony.

The alarm occasioned by the attack on Lancaster had aroused the authorities to the necessity of dispatching troops to the outlying settlements. Captain Jacob[2] and

---

[1] Hubbard Vol. I, page 223.

[2] Captain John Jacob was born in England about 1630. He resided in South Hingham, and his house was fortified as a garrison by order of the General Court. He served in King Philip's war as a captain and at the Narragansett Swamp fight succeeded Captain Isaac Johnson, who was killed, as commander of the company. He died September 18, 1693, aged about 63 years. His son John, slain by the Indians just back of his father's house near "Glad Tidings Rock," April 19, 1676, was the only person slain by the enemy in Hingham. See History of

Lieutenant Oakes who had been scouring the country between Lancaster and Medfield, were now at the latter place, but their commands, instead of being kept in their entirety, had unwisely been scattered among the different houses. In Medfield, as in many of the small towns, the settlers in their greed for land had taken more than they could possibly cultivate, and large tracts from which the timber had been cut had been allowed to grow up so the houses seemed "as if they were seated in the midst of a heap of bushes."[1]

During the night of February 21st, the Indians, under One-Eyed John, stealing upon the town, hid themselves in this brush, behind the orchard walls, under the sides of barns and outhouses, in the midst of the settlement itself. Samuel Morse,[2] going out to his barn early in the morning to feed his cattle, saw an Indian hiding in the hay. With rare presence of mind he affected ignorance of the intruder's presence, but left the barn immediately, and gathering his family fled to the garrison, beholding on the way his house and barn bursting into flames behind him. Then from all sides came the shots, the yelling of Indians, and the cries of the alarmed settlers. Many of the houses were burning, and soldiers and settlers coming to their doors were shot down on the threshold; eighteen persons in all were killed, others were taken away alive,[3] and an old man of near one hundred was

---

Hingham, Vol. II, page 372. Soldiers in King Philip's War, by Geo. N. Bodge, page 283.

[1] Hubbard, Vol. I, page 169.

[2] Samuel Morse of Medfield, the son of Joseph, was born January 10, 1640. Died February 28, 1718.—Savage.

[3] John Wilson to Governor Leverett. Massachusetts Archives, Vol. LXVIII, page 134.

burned to death in his home. Lieutenant Adams[1] of the town was among the slain, and his wife was accidentally killed by the discharge of Captain Jacob's gun, the bullet piercing the floor and passing through her body as she lay sick in bed.[2]

Soon forty or fifty houses were in flames, but the greater part of the troops and settlers had now reached the garrison house and the cannon of the garrison was roaring the signal of the attack to the people of Dedham.

Before the soldiers in the town could rally the Indians had drawn off across the river to a neighboring hill, burning the bridge behind them, and were roasting an ox in full view of the smoking ruins. The soldiers halted at the bridge where the following notice met their eyes:

"Know by this paper, that the Indians thou hast provoked to wrath and anger will war this 21 years if you will. There are many Indians yet. We come 300 at this time. You must consider the Indians lose nothing but their life. You must lose your fair houses and cattle."[3]

On the same day as the attack on Medfield, nearly two weeks after the call of the commissioners, the Council of Massachusetts voted to raise one hundred foot and

---

[1] Lieutenant Henry Adams was born in England about 1604. He lived first at Braintree in New England, then removed to that part of Dedham which became Medfield, of which place he was the first town clerk. He was of the Artillery Company in 1652, representative in 1659, 1665 and 1764, 1765. He was a lieutenant in the militia.

[2] Drake's Book of the Indians, Book III, page 37.

[3] Written, it is said, by an Indian apprentice of Samuel Green of Cambridge, known as James the printer, seventeen years old. He afterwards surrendered under the terms of the proclamation of July 8th, and was pardoned.—Gookin's Christian Indians. American Antiquarian Society Collections, Vol. II, page 494.

seventy-two troopers to fill the quota levied by the commissioners. Major Savage was placed in command.
John Whipple[1] was made captain of the horse and Captain William Turner of the foot. To this force was added
two companies of foot under Captains Moseley and Benjamin Gillam,[2] and at Savage's request John Curtice and
six friendly Indians as guides,[3] among them James Quanapohit and Job Kattananit.

The rendezvous had been fixed by the commissioners
for Quabaug some days before, but it was the first of
March before the forces of Connecticut and Massachusetts assembled at Brookfield, Major General Daniel
Denison organizing the force, the command of which fell
to Savage as ranking officer of the contingent in whose
territory operations were to be conducted.[4]

When the troops reached Quabaug the Indians had
withdrawn to a swamp some seventeen miles away.

---

[1] Captain John Whipple was born in Essex, England, about 1626.
He came with his father to Ipswich before 1638. He was appointed
cornet of the Ipswich troop before 1675, and captain in 1683 in place of
Captain John Appleton. He was lieutenant in Captain Paige's troop
at Mount Hope, June, 1675, and was appointed captain of a troop raised
for service under Major Savage in March, 1676. He was representative to the General Court in 1674, 1679 and 1683, in which year he died,
August 10th.

[2] Captain Benjamin Gillam, born in England in 1634, was of Boston.
Savage says, "He was probably master of that ship in which Colonel
Cartwright, one of the royal commissioners, was going home in the
autumn of 1665, taken by the Dutch, was related by Morton, Mem. 315:
Hutchinson, I, 250, and Hubbard, 585." He had command of a com-
pany in Philip's war and served under his father-in-law, Major Thomas
Savage. His will, dated March 28, 1681, was probated June 17, 1686.
He was buried, says Sewall, June 13, 1685.

[3] Massachusetts Records, Vol. V, page 74.

[4] Hazard, Vol. II, pages 538, 539 (Records of Commanders).

"There were" says Mrs. Rowlandson, "many hundred, old and young, some sick and some lame, and many had pappooses on their backs." As Savage pushed on, this camp too was broken up. "They went as if they had gone for their lives, and then made a stop and chose out some of the strongest men and sent them back 'to hold the English in play. Then, like Jehu, they marched on furiously to the river near Athol." Reaching the river they made rafts of trees, and finally all went over, while the party sent back had played with Savage for two days and led him on a false scent. When he finally struck the trail of the main body they had crossed Miller's River in safety, and the English, standing on the banks, beheld only the smoking ruins of their deserted wigwams.[1]

It had been the intention of Savage and his commanders to strike at the Indian encampment at Wachusett but, fearful for the towns on the Connecticut, now that the Quabaug Indians had effected a juncture with those who had wintered at Northfield, he turned against the advice of his guides and marched to Hadley.[2] He had been completely outmaneuvered.

Even as he left Quabaug, the Indians who had wintered at Wachusett had stolen upon Groton (March 2d), rifling eight or ten houses and carrying away many cattle and hogs. Major Willard and Captain Sill, coming up the next day, saw nothing of them, but on the 9th, freed from the fear of any attack by Savage, they again appeared, and, lurking in the outhouses during the night waited for the settlers to appear in the morning.

---

[1] Mrs. Rowlandson's Narrative.

[2] The guides were so maltreated and insulted by Moseley and his men that they returned to Deer Island.—Gookin's Christian Indians.

They were not disappointed, for at dawn four settlers, escorting two carts, appeared going out to the meadows. Two of the settlers, spying the Indians, made a difficult escape. One of the others was immediately shot down and one taken, and the Indians, setting fire to several houses and barns, apparently withdrew as suddenly as they had come. But on the 13th the lookouts at one of the garrisons[1] saw two Indians against the sky line of one of the hills close to the town. Immediately a considerable number of soldiers of Captain Parker's[2] company who had been sent to protect the town, sallied out to capture them. It was the old story of an ambush for, as they reached the top of the hill, behind which the Indians had disappeared, a volley was poured into them. One was killed and several wounded, while at the same time another party of Indians was seen making its way into the town from the rear. The ambushed pursuers turned and ran for the shelter of a nearby garrison, which they reached in safety, and where, in helplessness, they saw the town burn before their eyes.

A few days later, a wagon train laden with household belongings, women and children, and guarded by all the men and by a company of troops under Lieutenant Oakes,

---

[1] The village of Groton was protected by four garrison houses, while a fifth is said to have been a mile distant, and its site is at present unknown. A view up the main street of the village covers the location of the four. The first stood near the present high school, the next just north of the townhall, the third on the farther side of James Brook, and the fourth at some little distance beyond.

[2] Captain James Parker was of Woburn in 1640; freeman in 1644. He first removed to Chelmsford and later to Groton. He held the rank of captain and accompanied Major Willard in his relief and reinforcement of the beleagured garrison at Brookfield. He died in 1701 in his eighty-fourth year.—Savage.

who had been sent to bring them off, might have been
seen toiling over the roads to the east. It was the Groton
settlers abandoning their homes. Even on the march
their enemies struck at them, shooting down two of their
number from ambush, but the troops and settlers held
fast against the attack and, driving them back, passed
on in safety.

CHAPTER XI

IN the early morning of March 14th, a large force of the valley Indians fell upon Northampton, but fortunately, in addition to Captain Turner and seventy-eight men of the original garrison, Major Treat with two hundred of the Connecticut troops, without their knowledge, were quartered in the town. Breaking through the stockade at the lower end of Pleasant Street, the Indians found themselves, in the first flush of triumph, in a trap, and were glad to withdraw after losing one of their number killed and four wounded. Four men and one woman were killed, and several houses and barns, all with one exception outside the stockade, were burned.[1] Yet, despite this repulse the Indians still hung around waiting for opportunity to strike, and the garrisons at Hatfield and Hadley slept on their arms.

The spring was opening with terror. No man dared go out to his fields unless guarded by his neighbors and soldiers. Food was scarce. No husbandman stirred from his door save with arms in hand, and at night the town guards watched upon the stockade. Families on the outskirts dared not occupy their houses, and even in the villages people left their homes at night for the protection of the garrison.

Savage, his pursuit of the Quabaugs having failed as

---

[1] Rev. John Russell to Governor Leverett. Massachusetts Archives, Vol. LXVIII, page 163.

we have seen, marched over to Hadley where Turner, who had been left at Quabaug, joined him, and was promptly sent over to garrison Northampton.

Moseley took up his station at Hatfield, while Major Treat came back to his old territory—the west bank of the Connecticut from Westfield to Northampton. In the meanwhile and unknown to the English commanders, an event of great importance had taken place near Northfield. There, on the 9th of March, Canonchet and Philip met for the first time during the war and a great council of war was held. Besides the two sachems were Pumham, Quinnapin, Pessacus, Sancumachu of the Pocumtucks, Annawan, several other chiefs of the Wampanoags, Queen Weetamoo and representatives of the various tribes of the Nipmucks, dressed in all the glory of wampum and deerskin.

Now full of hope, yet within six months the bullet, the gallows, or slavery were to claim them all, and Increase Mather should write of them, "Where are the six Narragansett sachems and all their captains and councillors? Where are the Nipmuck sachems with their captains and councillors? Where is Philip and the squaw-sachem of Pocasset with all their captains and councillors? God do so to all the implacable enemies of Christ and of his people of New England."[1]

No record of their plans has come down in history, but the knowledge of the conditions that confronted them and the operations that followed the council furnish considerable evidence of its general scope.

The question of supplies was all important, seed must

---

[1] Mather's Prevalency of Prayer, page 265.

be secured for the spring sowing and the planted lands made secure from attack.

Above Deerfield, to the north, for miles, lay a safe refuge for the women and children if need came. Spring was coming and with it the game and fish would be abundant. Between Northfield and Deerfield lay fertile fields where corn and maize and beans could be cultivated in abundance, while the reaches of the river at Peskeompskut afforded a rare fishing ground.

If war could be carried fiercely to the east they believed the colonists would concentrate their force in that direction, and the valley, denuded of troops and held by the valley tribes would be left unmolested. If the English would only commit the follies that had marked the last year's campaign, there was hope. Alas for Indian hopes; the plan had not foreseen the employment of the friendly Indians by the whites. It underrated the force and character of the colonists and it was to receive at the beginning a disastrous blow.

How nearly the plan succeeded, however, and how clearly they gauged the measure of the authorities and the panic of the eastern communities will soon be made evident.

By Savage's march to the valley, the eastern frontier of the Bay settlements and the countries south of Plymouth and Narragansett Bay were again left open to attack, and here the blows fell thick and fast and the war parties roamed at will.

A short time after the breaking up of the Indian council at Northfield, Canonchet set out with a small or picked body of warriors to his own territory to procure seed corn from the supplies hidden in the Indian pits and tree trunks. Monoco, or One-Eyed John, had preceded him and the cowed bands of the Wampanoags, left behind on Philip's retreat, again arose to arms at their approach, while Philip and the gathering forces of the valley tribes struck at the valley settlements.

All the winter the settlers had been fortifying their houses and stockading their towns. Now the storm burst upon them. No man dared pass alone from one village to another, and there were nights when the sentinels saw on the outskirts the light of burning farms and houses.

Throughout the Connecticut Valley eastward, even to Plymouth and Providence, the war parties of the tribes were spreading death and desolation. On the evening of February 25th several dwellings and other buildings in Weymouth[1] were destroyed, and on March 12th the garrison house of William Clark,[2] near Plymouth, was attacked by Totoson; an Indian who had enjoyed the hospitality of the Clarks a few days before having notified him of the careless guard maintained. Totoson and his band, coming early in the morning, lay in hiding until most of the men had marched forth to church, then they fell furiously upon it.[3] Eleven persons were killed and the Indians, after plundering the house of provisions, eight guns, and thirty pounds of powder, set it on fire and retired.[4]

Everywhere there was terror and fear and every day

---

[1] This was the nearest approach to Boston made by the Indians; a distance of eleven miles.

[2] This garrison was at Eel River, a half mile to the eastward of the present village of Chiltonville. Its site is occupied by the house erected for the Rev. Benjamin Whitmore, perhaps eighty years ago.

[3] Plymouth Records, Vol. V, page 205.

[4] Old Indian Chronicle (Present State of New England), page 220.

brought news of buildings burnt and settlers killed. The towns around Narragansett Bay were abandoned save by the soldiers and the most resolute, who took refuge in the garrisons, and even Providence could count but fifty of its five hundred inhabitants.

"Brother Williams," said one of a band of Narragansett warriors, replying to Roger Williams who, going out to parley, leant upon his staff and bade them make peace, for their doom was certain in the end if they fought on, "Brother Williams, you are a good man, you have been kind to us many years, not a hair of your head shall be touched." They told him he must venture no further among them for there were strange Indians about, but they did not cease to devastate the settlement of which he was the founder, and the people of Providence, who had taken refuge on the island of Rhode Island, heard, before the month was out, of the destruction of their homes and belongings left behind, the garrison being unable to protect them. "And one Wright was killed, that was neither a Quaker nor Anabaptist, but opinionated."[1] The author of the Old Indian Chronicle relates that he had a strange conceit that while he held a Bible in his hands he was "secure from all kinds of violence, but the Indians finding him in that posture, deriding his groundless apprehension or folly, ripped him open and put his Bible in his belly."

On the 17th the flames wiped out deserted Warwick, down the bay, with the exception of a stone house known as Green's stone castle, and a band of straggling Indians from the valley tribes, marching down past Pine Meadow

[1] Connecticut Records (Letter from Governor and Council of Massachusetts, quoted), Vol. II, page 433.

(now Windsor Locks, Conn.), where they killed Henry Denslow, plundered the deserted houses of Simsbury,[1] across the mountains from Hartford, and gave them over to the flames on March 26th. A cave in the hills above the town, from which Philip, according to local tradition, watched the burning of Simsbury, is known as Philip's (Phelps) cave, though Philip was never there.[2]

On that most gloomy day of the year, the 26th of March, the people of Marlboro[3] were at church; the hymn had

---

[1] The plantation of Simsbury was spread out over a distance of about seven miles in length, and lay on both sides of the Tunxis (Farmington) River, an unfordable stream of considerable width, and contained about forty houses.

[2] An Indian named Menowniet was taken near Farmington about the 12th of August, 1676. He said he was "halfe a Moheag and halfe a Narragansett." That he was engaged in hunting, but had taken part in the several engagements in the Connecticut Valley. He was examined by the Council. In reply to the question, "Who killed Henry Denslow?" he said, "Wequash, Weawwosse, Whowassamoh, Pawwawwoise and Mawcahwat, Sanchamoise and Wesoncketichen, and these were those that burnt Simsbury."—Connecticut Records, Vol. II, page 472. Three of these were Springfield Indians, the rest were of other tribes. Philip's cave and Philip's mountain is undoubtedly a corruption of the name of the contemporary owner, "Phelps."

[3] Marlboro was built very "scatteringly," and the original town covered a wide territory. By separating into small companies it was possible for the enemy to compass and destroy the town dwellings without much hindrance from the garrisons. The meetinghouse stood near the center of the present city on what are now the high-school grounds and immediately in front of that building. The town held a prominent place in Philip's war by reason of its being used almost constantly as a military garrison. There were at least four garrison houses in the town, two of them within the limits of what is now the town of Westboro, one situated about two miles west from the center, on the present boundary line separating Marlboro from Northboro, and the remaining one was located on what is now Hayden Avenue, on land known as "the Daniel Hayden farm," scarcely more than a quarter of a mile from the site of

just been sung when the Reverend Mr. Brinsmead,[1] who had been compelled to come down from his pulpit and seek relief from the extremity of the toothache by walking to the door, discovered the Indians and, rushing back to the church with the cry, "the Indians are upon us," drove the congregation to the garrison. Only one of their number was cut off, but eleven barns and thirteen dwellings were burned and the cattle driven away.[2]

The evening brought some satisfaction, for Lieutenant Jacob, setting out in pursuit, fell upon a part of the marauders in the woods that night as they slept around their camp-fire and claimed to have killed and wounded nearly forty of their number, among the slain, according to Hubbard, being Netus, leader of the Indians who had attacked the Eames house in Sudbury.

It was a day, however, fated with misfortunes, for Canonchet, returning homeward with a large band of warriors, had near Seekonk, on the 25th fallen in with Captain Michael Peirse[3] of Scituate, who had been sent from Plymouth with some fifty soldiers and a score of friendly Indians under Captain Amos.

That night Peirse and his men slept at the garrison

---

the old meetinghouse. It was probably to this that the people fled when driven from the meetinghouse by the attack of March 26, 1676.

[1] Rev. William Brinsmead was bred at Harvard College but left before graduation. He preached 1660–65, at Plymouth, and thence went to the new town of Marlboro, where he was ordained October 3, 1666. He never married and died July 3, 1701.—Savage.

[2] Massachusetts Council to Major Savage, April 1. Massachusetts Archives, Vol. LXVIII, page 191.

[3] Captain Michael Peirse was of Scituate and has a record of usefulness in public affairs. He served in the Narragansett fight in December, 1675, and fell in the fierce battle on the Pawtuckot River, March 26, 1676. See Deane's History of Scituate, page 325.

house at Seekonk, setting out in pursuit early the next morning; they soon encountered the Indians who, leading them on, fell slowly back.

Canonchet had divided his force into two parties, one circling around the flanks to a selected position while the other, some of them "limping along to make believe they were lame" or had been wounded, lured the impetuous captain over the Pawtucket into a position unfavorable for defense.

In vain Peirse, realizing too late the numbers confronting him, fell back to the river bank.[1] Unable to draw off across the river, and galled by the fire from the opposite side, he formed his men in a circle, according to some chroniclers, or in two lines, back to back, and fought on[2] in the vain hope that Captain Edmunds, whose co-operation he had requested that morning, would come up from Providence, only eight miles distant, and relieve him. But it was Sunday, and while the messenger waited for Edmunds at the church door, not wishing to disturb the meeting,[3] Pierse, cut off from all retreat, fell, and almost the whole of his command were killed or captured,[4] nine of the latter, it is said, being led by a cir-

---

[1] Mr. Welcome Arnold Greene of Providence, has located the scene of Peirse's fight at a point a few rods west of the railroad bridge across the Pawtucket River, just north of Central Falls, R. I. Peirse proceeding from Seekonk marched a few miles in a northwesterly direction, and crossed the river at a wading place diagonally under the present bridge. His stand was made on the west bank of the river within a few rods of the water. This spot is now in the street between two manufacturing buildings. Mr. Greene remembers the spot before it had been touched by the hand of improvement.

[2] Deane's History of Scituate, page 121.

[3] Backus Hist. New Eng., Vol. I, page 423.

[4] Letter of Rev. Mr. Newman to Rev. John Cotton. Deane's Scituate,

cuitous route to a swamp ever since known as "Nine Men's Misery," some miles to the north, where they were tortured and killed. Only eight whites and a few friendly Indians survived to tell the fate of the party and relate their own marvelous achievements.

The loss of the Indians, set by both Hubbard and Mather at one hundred and forty slain, is palpably an exaggeration, for, taking the wounded at the conservative figure of two wounded to one killed, the Indian casualties would have reached four hundred and twenty, or six times the total number of Peirse's party, who, drawn into an ambuscade and exposed to a flanking fire, were at a most fatal disadvantage. Their losses were probably considerable, however, as Tom Nepanet, a Christian Indian, employed by Massachusetts in negotiations with the Indians, in April, reported that in the fight they had lost many score. The high figures claimed must be regarded merely as a customary measure of consolation. Two days after the destruction of Captain Peirse the victorious Indians descended upon and burned Seekonk.[1]

On the same day, a party of settlers and soldiers under Captain Whipple, sixteen or eighteen men, and a number of women and children from Longmeadow, journeying to Springfield on their way to church, were at-

---

page 122. The original is in possession of the Antiquarian Society of Worcester, Mass. Council to Major Savage, April 1. Massachusetts Archives, Vol. LXVIII, page 192.

[1] This town was built in a semi-circular form around what is now Seekonk Common, with the meetinghouse in the center. This circle is alluded to in the records as "The Ring of the Town." The garrison house which stood on the southerly side of the Common, and one other, were the only dwellings not destroyed.

tacked.[1] John Keep[2] and a maid, riding in the rear, were killed, and Sarah Keep with another woman and two children captured. Thrown into a panic the settlers and their guard, who far outnumbered their assailants, fled with the other women and children to Springfield, "a matter of great shame and humbling to us," wrote the Council on receipt of the news.

Soldiers and settlers, under Major Pynchon, hurried to the scene of the attack and the next day overtook the Indians who struck down the women and children and escaped into a swamp where the miry ground forbade pursuit. Sarah Keep died from her injuries, but the other woman survived and gave considerable information. Their captors, she said, were Springfield Indians, who, until their pursuers came up had treated them kindly. They told her two Dutch traders, named Jacob and Jarrard, had supplied them with four bushels of powder; that there were three hundred Indians at Deerfield, three hundred above that place (probably at Turners Falls), and three hundred at Northfield; that Frenchmen had been among them and there had been a quarrel with the Mohawks, but peace was now made again.[3]

As early as the 14th of March, the Council of Massachusetts, alarmed by the activity of the Indians in the east, had set out to do the very thing the Indians ex-

---

[1] It is commonly believed that the attack on the Longmeadow people was made at the point where the path crossed Pecowsic Brook, now in Forest Park at the southern end of Springfield.

[2] John Keep was of Springfield, 1660, living in that part of the town now Longmeadow. He was freeman 1669. His wife Sarah, was the daughter of John Leonard.—Keep Genealogy.

[3] Major Savage to the Governor and Council of Massachusetts, March 28. Massachusetts Archives, Vol. LXVIII, page 189.

M

pected of them, writing Savage that they deemed it wise, on account of the appearance of the Indians on the frontier towns the day before, to retain one hundred and fifty men whom they had intended to send him.[1] A few days later they advised him to withdraw his command from the valley, abandoning all the towns but Hadley and Springfield. "The lesser towns must gather to the greater," they wrote, "for unless they come together and well fortify the large towns all will be lost, the enemy being so many in these parts (the eastern townships) that the army must remove from the (valley)."[2]

Both these letters reached Savage on the same day, March 26th, but the settlers refused to abandon their goods and houses to destruction and Savage did not accept the advice proffered him.

Compelled to break up his force in order to guard the towns, deprived of expected reinforcements, and weakened by the withdrawal of Major Treat, who, recalled by Connecticut to co-operate with the forces operating in the Narragansett country,[3] had been retained at Hartford on the burning of Simsbury, Savage felt himself powerless to assume the offensive. A more resolute and capable commander would have marched with the greater part of his troops against their villages, but Savage was cautious and held his men to the towns, while war parties roamed at will throughout the length of the valley, watch-

---

[1] Council of Massachusetts to Major Savage, March 14. Massachusetts Archives, Vol. LXVIII, page 166.

[2] Council of Massachusetts to Major Savage, March 20. Massachusetts Archives, Vol. LXVIII, page 166.

[3] Connecticut Records (Journal of the Council of War), Vol. II, page 423.

ing their opportunities to surprise and attack the settlers who should attempt to break ground for the spring sowing, and constantly seizing cattle and sheep to supply their wants, which, Mrs. Rowlandson records, were so pressing that "many times they would eat that that a hog or dog would hardly touch."

In the meantime, the Connecticut Council was engaged in a spirited correspondence, far from creditable to either party, with Governor Andros of New York, for the purpose of securing the co-operation of the Mohawks. They owed him more than they ever gave him credit for, but the art of conciliatory expression and tactfulness was as wanting in one as in the other, and the pious expressions and constant accusations and advice of the Council kept the irascible soldier in constant ill-temper.

In reply to their request that he should induce the Mohawks to help them by attacking the valley tribes, he asked whether they would provide these savage allies with food and receive them in their own towns. Their reply implied a suspicion that the Mohawks, if once in the field, would strike at the Mohegans as readily as at the hostiles, and their request for permission to send their own representatives to confer with the Mohawks aroused Andros' wrath as an impertinent interference in the affairs of his governorship. He did not intend to have the war spread in his own province if he could help it, and told them that they seemed as ignorant in respect to the Mohawks as they did in regard to their own Indians.[1]

The Mohawks were of considerable assistance to them, however, for the fear of their hostility hung heavily upon

---

[1] Connecticut Records (Journal of the Council of War, February to August, 1676), Vol. II, page 404.

the valley tribes, and in March or April their war parties attacked the New England Indians who were encamped near the Hudson, and drove them westward.

The Connecticut Council entered into negotiations with the Indians above Deerfield, declaring in a letter to Pessacus, the Narragansett, and the chiefs of the valley tribes, that they had done them no injury but had been obliged, by treaty, to succor Massachusetts and Plymouth, and if the Indians could show that any of them had been wronged they would endeavor to have that wrong righted. They had some Indian captives and were willing to exchange prisoners, and if the sachems desired to negotiate a treaty they should have liberty to come and go without molestation.[1]

The Narragansett sachems, Pessacus and Pumham, were among the valley Indians exhorting the young men to defiance, and even those most inclined to peace were probably suspicious that the object of the negotiations was not so much to establish peace as to secure the release of the captives. Their answers were, therefore, unsatisfactory; they accepted nothing; they proposed nothing.

The expectations of the war party, from the plans formed early in March, seemed near to fulfillment, and, in connection with the belief that these negotiations had been opened for the purpose of securing the release of the English captives, and that the English were discouraged, utterly discredited the little influence possessed by the older sachems who hoped for peace. Among the Wampanoags and the Narragansetts there was no desire for

---

[1] Connecticut Records (Journal of the Council of War), Vol. II, pages 425, 439.

peace. Philip had never wavered from his determination of war to the death. He knew, that for him at least, there was no mercy. Canonchet, too, was firm, and would have no peace such as the English would give.

CHAPTER XII

IMMEDIATELY after the attack on Northampton, a considerable force of Narragansetts had left the valley for the Indian rendezvous at Wachusett Hill, from whence Canonchet almost immediately set forth with a picked band of warriors, toward his own territory.

Here, in the midst of the unknown land, was a secure base of operations within easy distance of both the valley towns and frontier of the Bay settlements. Here, if the worst came to the worst, they could seek a refuge among the Pennacooks and Tarratines in the wilderness to the north.

The attack on Northampton had failed, yet the whites were idle in the valley; along the eastern frontier the tribes had left a swath of blood and fire from Groton to Warwick. They derided the slowness and dullness of the English, and asked Mrs. Rowlandson when they should come after them. "I could not tell," said she. "It may be they will come in May,"[1] they said with fine irony.

But if the English in the valley could not move they would, and, April 1st, a party of them, encompassing a small body of Hadley settlers as they made their way under escort to the meadows at Hockanum, three miles south of Hadley, killed Deacon Goodman[2] as he was

---

[1] Mrs. Rowlandson's Narrative.

[2] Deacon Richard Goodman was of Cambridge in 1632. He removed early to Hartford, and went with others to the founding of Hadley.

MOUNT WACHUSET

examining his boundary fence, and two guards who had set out to make an ascent of Mount Holyoke; a third, Thomas Reed[1] (of whom we shall hear more hereafter), was captured.

The burning of Providence, Rehoboth (Seekonk), Marlboro and Simsbury, the practical annihilation of Peirse's force, and the serious condition of affairs in Maine, had so intensified the alarm and terror in the eastern towns that the Council of Massachusetts wrote to Major Savage, April 1st, ordering his immediate return. They noted his advice as to the unwillingness of the settlers to concentrate for defense, and the peril to which the towns would be exposed by the withdrawal of the army. They would allow him to leave one hundred and fifty men, all single, under Captain Turner, to protect the valley, "but we explicitly command you to draw homeward with the remainder and endeavor on your return to visit the enemy about Wachusett and be careful not to be deceived by their lapwing strategems by drawing you off from the nest to follow some men."[2] He was at liberty before his return, however, to attack the Indians at Deerfield if Major Treat returned in time.

Treat did not return, and on the 7th of April, despite the protests of the valley towns, leaving Captain Turner with a nondescript force of one hundred and fifty men, with headquarters at Hadley, he started homeward. On reach-

---

[1] The writer believes this Thomas Reed to have been the son of Thomas of Sudbury, and that one who married, May 30, 1677, Mary, daughter of John Goodrich of Wethersfield. Both families came from Levenham in England. Thomas Reed served under the immediate command of Captain Gillam.

[2] Council of Massachusetts to Major Savage.—Massachusetts Archives, Vol. LXVIII, page 192.

ing Quabaug, a council of war was held as to the advisability of a dash and attack on Wachusett as ordered by
the Council, but though the chaplain, the Reverend Samuel Nowell,[1] voted in the affirmative, Captains Moseley,
Gillam, Whipple, and Lieutenant Drinker[2] decided
against the plan on account of the scarcity of provisions,[3]
and Savage continued his journey homeward.

With the departure of Major Savage and his army
vanished every prospect for the negotiation of a peace
opened by the overtures of Connecticut. The Indians
up the valley saw with delight the opportunity for planting their crops and catching fish without molestation.
Their joy was short-lived, for Savage had not reached
Boston when there came the news that Canonchet had
fallen into the hands of the English and was dead.

On the 30th of March, Major Palmes [4] of Connecticut,

---

[1] Rev. Samuel Nowell of Charlestown was a chaplain in Philip's war,
both on Connecticut River and in the Narragansett campaign. He was
freeman 1677; assistant 1680, and October, 1685, was chosen treasurer
of the colony, but was relieved the next year. He died in London in
September, 1688. Mather says of him, "At this fight (Narragansett)
there was no person more like a true son of 'Abraham in Arms,' or
that with more courage and hazard fought in the midst of a shower
of bullets from the surrounding savages."—Mather's Magnalia, Book
VII, chapter 6.

[2] Lieutenant Edward Drinker of Charlestown was a potter, and constable in 1652. He removed to Boston and was one of the founders of
the first Baptist church. A lieutenant in Captain Turner's company,
though at first refused a command by the bigoted government of the
day. He preached in 1678 in Boston, and died in 1700.—Savage.

[3] Massachusetts Archives, Vol. LXVIII, page 235.

[4] Major Edward Palmes was of New Haven in 1659. A merchant.
He removed in 1660 to New London and married Lucy, daughter of
Governor John Winthrop. He was representative 1671 and 1674 and
1677, and major in Philip's war. He was named in the royal commis-

in charge of the forces operating toward the Narragansett country, had sent from Norwich some seventy-nine soldiers, under the command of Captains George Denison,[1] James Avery[2] and John Stanton,[3] accompanied by a mixed force of Niantics, Pequots and Mohegans, the latter under Uncas' son, Oneko. Passing through the Narragansett country they reached the Pawtucket on the 3d

---

sion, 1683, to adjust claims in the King's Province, or Narragansett country. He died March 21, 1715.—Savage.

[1] Captain George Denison came from England in the *Lion* at thirteen years of age. Lived with his father at Roxbury, and in 1649 moved with his family to the Pequot settlement, now New London, Conn., but in 1654 settled at Stonington. He was early a military leader and from 1671 to 1694 represented Stonington. He held a commission as captain and participated in the Narragansett Swamp fight, and later was associated with Captain James Avery in a series of forays against the Indians in Philip's war. He also served under Major Talcott in the expedition up the Connecticut Valley at the time of the termination of the troubles in that section. He died at Hartford, October 23, 1694. See Descendants of George Denison, by John D. Baldwin and William Clift, page 297.

[2] Captain James Avery, born in England about 1620, came to America with his father and lived at Gloucester, but removed to New London in 1651. In 1656 he built a house at the head of Poquonnock Plain in Groton, where he passed the remainder of his life. This house remained standing until within a few years, when it was destroyed by fire caused by a spark from a passing locomotive. Its site is commemorated by a handsome monument. He was much interested in military affairs and became a captain in the militia. At the Narragansett Swamp fight the Pequot allies were commanded by Captain Avery, and he was prominent in the subsequent forays into the Indian territory which occurred in the latter part of Philip's war. In civil life he served many years as representative to the General Court and as a judge upon the bench. He died April 18, 1700. See The Averys of Groton, by H. D. L. Sweet.

[3] Captain John Stanton of Stonington was sent to Harvard College at the desire of the Connecticut authorities, that he might be educated for an Indian teacher and interpreter. He was made freeman in 1666.

of April, and fell in with a fat Indian, whom they slew, and two squaws, one of whom informed them that Canonchet was encamped near by. Pushing forward with all speed they came upon two Narragansett sentinels, on the crest of a small hill,[1] who fled in panic down the further slope, past the place where Canonchet and a few of his men, were lying at ease. The English, following close at their heels, were almost upon the camp when another sentinel, rushing among the startled Narragansetts, called out that the English were upon them. In a moment the warriors were flying in all directions. Canonchet himself ran swiftly around the back of the hill to get out of sight on the opposite side, but, seeing the Niantics and Mohegans in close pursuit, he threw off his blanket, then his silver trimmed coat and the royal belt of wampum. Recognizing immediately from these articles that the fugitive "was the right bird" the friendly Indians and a few of the English followed with renewed zeal.

Forced by his pursuers toward the river, through which his only way to safety lay, he rushed into the stream, but his foot slipped, and falling heavily into the water he wet the priming of his gun. His pursuers were upon him before he could recover himself, and Monopoide, a Mohegan Pequot, seized him "within thirty rods of the river side."

Defenseless, and finding escape impossible, he faced

A captain in Philip's war and much employed in everything relating to the Indians.—Savage.

[1] This hill is recognized by some as the "Study Hill" of William Blackstone in Lonsdale, R. I. There is no vestige of it now remaining, it having been leveled for the purpose of filling and grading the railroad yards.

his foes and yielded himself with dignity. A young man, Robert Stanton,[1] the first of the whites to reach him, ventured to ask him a question. "Looking with a little neglect upon his youthful face" the sachem answered: "You much child, no understand matters of war. Let your brother or chief come, him I will answer."

Having put to the sword all the stoutest of their prisoners to the number of forty-three, the English set out with their prize for Stonington. Offering him his life if he could persuade his people to make peace, he indignantly refused and told them his death would not end the war.[2]

"The heir of all his father's pride and insolence and also of his malice toward the English." "A most perfidious villian," says Hubbard, "for he was as good as his word, acting herein as by a Pythagorean metamorphosis, some old Roman ghost had possessed the body of this western pagan, and like Attilius Regulus he would not accept his own life when it was tendered to him upon that (in his account) low compliance with the English, refusing to send an old councillor of his to make any motion that way, saying he knew they would not yield."

Charged, as the Old Chronicle tells us, with his breach of faith in making war, and twitted with his boast that he would "not give up a Wampanoag nor the paring of a Wampanoag's nail, but would burn the English alive in their houses," he replied that "Others were as forward

---

[1] Robert Stanton, son of Thomas of Stonington, "was" says Savage, "that youthful soldier, 1676, to which the Indian captive, Prince Nauunteno made reproachful answer, as Hubbard tells." He died October 25, 1724, aged seventy.

[2] Hubbard, Vol. II, page 59.

for the war as himself and that he desired to hear no more thereof."[1]

Asked "why he did foment that war," he would make no other reply than this, "That he was born a prince, and if princes came to speak with him he would answer, but none present being such, he thought himself obliged in honor to hold his tongue."[2] He told them he would rather die than remain a prisoner and requested that Oneko might put him to death as he was of equal rank.

The author of the Old Indian Chronicle tells us that the Mohegans "and most of the English soldiers, declaring to the commanders their fear that the English should, upon conditions, release him, and that then he would (though the English might have peace with him) be very pernicious to those Indians that now assisted us;" it was determined to put him to death.

When told his sentence was to die, he "liked it well that he should die before his heart was soft or he had spoken words unworthy of himself."[3]

They carried out the sentence at Anguilla, near Stonington, all the Indians being encouraged to inculpate themselves equally in his death and mutilation "the more firmly to engage the said Indians against the treacherous Narragansetts, whereby they are become most abominable to all the other Indians." The Pequots shot him; the Mohegans cut off his head and quartered his body, and the Niantics built a fire, burned his quarters and sent his head to the Council at Hartford as a token of love and fidelity (acknowledged April 8th). "This was the

---

[1] Hubbard, Vol. II, page 60.
[2] Old Indian Chronicle (Present State of New England), page 231.
[3] Hubbard, Vol. II, page 60.

confusion of a damned wretch that had often opened his mouth to blaspheme the name of the living God, and those that made profession thereof."[1]

So perished Canonchet, the most romantic figure that we know among the New England Indians; the unfortunate son of a most unfortunate father, both worthy of a kinder fate. Young and impetuous, he lacked the farsighted craft and subtilty that distinguished Philip, but as a leader of men and a warrior, the younger man was the superior, and his death was a terrible blow to the Indian cause. His death was as honorable to him as its infliction and the shameful mutilation of his body was disgraceful to his enemies. Something of his lofty and dignified character seems to have impressed itself upon the grudging minds of his foes, but it called up no corresponding chivalry of action.

Before the middle of the month, Philip, after a month spent with the valley tribes, left his quarters near Northfield, with his Wampanoags, and joined the bands of the Narragansetts and Nipmucks assembled at Wachusett Hill.

The death of Canonchet had left him, through the support of the Narragansetts, the chief figure of the war, and his removal to Wachusett was more for the purpose of directing operations against the Bay towns than through fear for his personal safety from the disaffection of the valley tribes, among whom Pessacus and Pumham, Narragansett sachems, friendly to his interests, still remained.

Like all leaders of a confederation ill organized and ill equipped among people so susceptible to sudden ex-

---

[1] Hubbard Vol. II, page 60.

tremes, Philip's influence no doubt had its ups and downs, but it should be borne in mind that neither Hubbard nor Mather, who were the principal contemporary historians of the war, are safe guides either to Philip's character or his standing among the tribes.

Canonchet's death, as he had warned his captors, brought no overtures of peace from the Narragansetts. The blow they had suffered was not fully realized, nor was its effect immediately felt.

April 9th, a small party of the Wampanoags, probably under Tuspaquin,[1] came upon Bridgewater, destroying a few houses and barns before they were driven off. The same day the Indians at Wachusett fell upon Billerica. On the 15th, fourteen houses were burnt at Chelmsford, where, on the 18th of the previous month, the two sons of Samuel Varnham had been killed and several houses destroyed. Two days later the remaining houses at Marlboro were given over to the flames. The next day but one the Indians applied the torch to Weymouth, and in Hingham,[2] young John Jacob, who had served against the Indians in the Narragansett Swamp fight, on going into the field back of his father's house to shoot deer that had been disturbing the crops, was shot and killed. Wrentham was raided the same month, its deserted houses were fired and only two dwellings, which sheltered victims of the smallpox, a disease greatly feared by the Indians, were left unmolested.

---

[1] Tuspaquin, sachem of Assowamset, was one of Philip's most faithful captains and very active in the war, doing much mischief in the Plymouth colony.

[2] An old fort on Cemetery Hill in Hingham, built for defense in those days, is still preserved.

From Casco Bay to Stonington the flames of burning buildings lit the sky; death lay in every bush. So great was the alarm that even towns as near to Boston as Cambridge applied and received permission from the court to erect stockades.

Philip's appearance at Wachusett was soon followed by one of the fiercest conflicts of the war. By the abandonment of Groton, Billerica, Lancaster and Marlboro, Sudbury had become the frontier town of the Bay settlements. Situated, with the exception of a few houses, on the east bank of the Sudbury River it was a point of considerable importance, since from it as a center, the roads radiated to the settlements, east, south and west.[1]

Small parties of soldiers with supplies were continually passing through it on the way to and from the valley, finding shelter along the way at night in the military garrisons maintained at Marlboro and Quabaug.

The concentration of the Indians at Wachusett was known early in the month, and among the forces ordered out was that of Captain Wadsworth, who was dispatched by the Council with a company of foot to relieve the garrison at Marlboro. As was the case too often in the latter part of the conflict, the full force assigned to him could not be collected.[2] Many of those impressed failed to appear and he began his march with only seventy troops, many of them boys.

The advance parties of the warriors were already in the woods about Sudbury when Wadsworth, in the evening of the 20th of April, passed through the town un-

---

[1] The eastern part of Sudbury, now the town of Wayland, was originally known as "The five paths."

[2] Massachusetts Colony Records, Vol. V, page 78.

mindful of the large number of Indians near by, for during the day, some of the Sudbury settlers had been fired upon and a house or two upon the distant outskirts had been burned, a warning sufficient to drive the settlers into the garrison. It was believed, however, that this was the work of only a small party, and Wadsworth, ignorant that over five hundred warriors, Philip probably among them, were lying in wait to fall upon the town, continued on to Marlboro, his destination, which he reached about midnight.

Knowing well the layout of the town the Indians crept upon it before the dawn of the 21st and many of the houses, whose occupants had sought refuge in the garrisons, were in flames before the settlers knew the town was in danger.

Near the west bank of the Sudbury River was a small isolated garrison, known as the Deacon Haynes house,[1] well fortified but badly situated. It was at this point that their first efforts, continuing from dawn to noon, were directed. The attack, however, was not vigorously pressed, being probably in the nature of a feint, and the garrison even made several successful sallies.

Captain Edward Cowell[2] marching by the north road from Quabaug to Boston, with eighteen troopers, had reached the outskirts of the town early in the morning,

---

[1]The Haynes garrison stood on the "Water-Row Road" by the margin of the river meadow. It was about one-eighth of a mile northerly from the Wayland and Sudbury Center highway, two or three rods from the road, and fronted south. It was standing in 1876 but has since been demolished.

[2]Captain Edward Cowell was of Boston in 1645, and was a cordwainer. He served as captain in King Philip's war, and died September 12, 1691.—Savage.

when the sound of intermittent firing and the appearance
of small bodies of Indians at different points warned him
of the danger. Keeping his men well in hand he abandoned the main road and set out by a circuitous route to
approach it from another direction.

An ambush had evidently been prepared for him and
the Indians hung upon his flanks and rear, firing on his
men and endeavoring to bring on a decisive action. Cowell wisely refused to commit himself to battle, but ordered
his men to hold their fire and keep the Indians at a distance by constantly raising their guns as if about to shoot.
By skillful maneuvering he was able to reach Sudbury
with the loss of only four men who, lagging behind, had
been cut off.

The news of the attack on Sudbury was soon known
in Boston, Watertown and Concord. A small party of
eleven men from the latter town, coming down the west
bank of the river, were the first to arrive, and the occupants of Haynes' garrison saw them lured into an ambuscade in the river meadows where a large body of the
enemy lying hidden in the grass rose up and closed in
upon them, massacring all but one of their number.

Soon after, Captain Hugh Mason,[1] with a company
from Watertown, reached the east bank of the river, then
in flood, drove the Indians out of the village and passed
over the bridge to the west bank, attracted by the sound

---

[1]Captain Hugh Mason was one of the first settlers of Watertown.
He was admitted freeman March 4, 1634–35. He was a tanner by trade,
selectman of the town twenty-nine years, representative to the court ten
years. He was a commissioner to determine small causes, or what
would now be a justice of the peace. He was commissioned as captain
May 5, 1652, and died October 10, 1678, aged 73. See Bond's Genealogies and History of Watertown, page 356.

N

of heavy firing from Green Hill. In vain Mason and his men endeavored to force their way toward the hill which lay not far away, but the Indians held them sternly at bay, and, beginning to circle around their flanks, compelled them to retreat to Captain Goodnow's garrison.[1] All the afternoon the sound of firing at Green Hill continued, gradually growing fainter and dying down with the sun, and there was foreboding among all that some great disaster had taken place.

In the evening the worst was confirmed. Captain Wadsworth had learned, soon after his arrival at Marlboro, of the storm gathering in the rear. Leaving the least efficient of his command in garrison, and taking with him Captain Brocklebank and the troops who had been relieved, he marched back without delay. He was expected. As he neared Sudbury by the south road, a few warriors appearing across the path ahead amid the trees, fled before him toward Green Hill. Experienced soldier though he was he believed that the main body of the foe had been seized with a panic on his approach, and, leaving the road, in eager pursuit rushed into the woods. The flitting of dusky forms and the roar of musketry from all sides soon undeceived him. The troops rallied and fought their way to the crest of the hill and, sheltering themselves behind the trees and rocks, held their own until the evening fell. Then the Indians fired the bushes and grass to windward, and as Wadsworth's weary men fell back in the dusk, blinded by the smoke, and their

---

[1] The Goodnow garrison stood a few rods northeast of the East Sudbury R. R. station, and perhaps twenty or thirty rods from the South Sudbury and Wayland highway. This house was standing about ninety years ago.

SCENE OF THE SUDBURY FIGHT

The monument in memory of Wadsworth and his men

nerves shaken by the loss of many of their comrades, a panic seized them, the Indians closed in, there was a brief hand to hand conflict, and all was over.

Few details of the death struggle of Wadsworth[1] and his men have come down to us, but, wrote the author of the Old Indian Chronicle, I am creditably informed, that in that Fight an elderly Englishman endeavoring an escape from the Indians by running into a swamp, was overtaken by an Indian, and, being destitute of weapons to defend himself, the Indian insulted over him with the Blasphemous Expression, "Come, Lord Jesus, save this poor Englishman if thou canst, whom I am about to kill." This (I even tremble to relate it) was heard by another Englishman hiding in a bush close by. Our Patient, Long-suffering Lord permitted that Bloody Wretch to knock him down and leave him dead.

Thirteen or fourteen of the fifty escaped to Noyes' stone mill,[2] a quarter of a mile away, barricaded the doors and windows and waited with anxious hearts for attack or rescue.

----

[1] Captain Samuel Wadsworth came with his father to Duxbury and about 1656 removed to Milton. In December, 1675, Captain Wadsworth, with his company, took part in the "hungry march" from Narragansett to Marlboro. He was of service in dispersing the enemy at Lancaster, but is better known by his brave but fruitless efforts at defense at Sudbury, where, with the greater part of his command, he was killed April 21, 1676. A monument erected by the State of Massachusetts and the town of Sudbury, stands upon the burial place of Wadsworth and his men at the foot of the battlefield. See Bodge, page 218.

[2] The stone mill was located at what is now South Sudbury village, on the site of the present Parmenter mill. The distance from the top of Green Hill is from a quarter to half a mile. This mill was erected in 1659 by Thomas and Peter Noyes. In 1699 the mill property was given to the town by Mr. Peter Noyes for the benefit of the poor.

Captain Mason, reinforced in the meantime, by Cowell
and small parties from the nearby towns had repelled
successfully and with some loss the Indians opposed to
him. The night was coming on, the firing from Green
Hill had died away, and as the Indians withdrew in the
gathering darkness, Mason assumed the offensive and
set out to Noyes' mill.

No people were dwelling there but the mill was known
to be easy of defense, and, lying as it did, in the near
vicinity of Green Hill, it was believed that if any of Wadsworth's men escaped they would find refuge there.

Late that night they reached it without opposition and
found that the survivors of Wadsworth's party[1] had already been rescued by Captain Hunting[2] with a company of Indian scouts and a body of Prentice's horse.
This force had been on the eve of setting out from Charlestown to establish a fort at the fishing grounds on the Merrimac, but when the news of the attack on Sudbury became
known, Major Gookin, in charge of the party, dispatched
them immediately to the scene, and on reaching the mill
they were soon joined by Cowell and his command.[3]

---

[1] Massachusetts Archives, Vol. LXVIII, page 224. Petition of Daniel Warren and Joseph Pierce.

[2] Captain Samuel Hunting was born at Dedham, July 22, 1640. He
settled first at Chelmsford and later at Charlestown. He commanded
a company of friendly Indians during Philip's war; did good service at
Sudbury, and this fact aided greatly to abate the hostility felt by Massachusetts toward Indian allies. In the summer of 1676 this company
destroyed or captured a very large number of the enemy and performed
most effective work in the closing operations of the war. He was killed
by the accidental discharge of his gun, August 19, 1701.—Bodge,
page 289.

[3] Gookin's Christian Indians. American Antiquarian Society Coll.,
Vol. II, page 512.

Early on the following morning Captain Mason found and buried the bodies of the Concord men slain in the river meadow, and the united forces, confident in their numbers, soon after marched to Green Hill, where they gathered and buried the stripped bodies of Wadsworth, Brocklebank, and twenty-seven others of the ill-fated company. In the thickets, doubtless, there remained undiscovered the bodies of several others killed in their flight to the mill.

A few of the whites, probably of the Concord men, since of the eleven believed to have been slain the bodies of only five had been found, were taken prisoners and were said to have been put to the torture.

The Indians, after annihilating Wadsworth's force, drew off to the westward, and Lieutenant Jacob, in command of the garrison at Marlboro, saw them the next morning, two hours after sunrise, firing their guns, shouting "seventy-four times to signify to us how many were slain," and, after firing the remaining houses and seizing all the cattle, they departed.[1]

The loss of the Indians is not known. Gookin says that four dead Indians were found hidden in the brush but their losses were undoubtedly considerably greater. They boasted of their victory to Mrs. Rowlandson and one of them told her he had killed two Englishmen whose clothes were behind her. "I looked behind me and then I saw the bloody clothes behind me with bullet holes in them." They seemed very pensive after they came to their quarters, showing no such signs of rejoicing as they were usually wont to do in like cases, "but I could not

---

[1] Lieutenant Jacobs to Governor and Council. Massachusetts Archives, Vol. LXVIII, page 223.

perceive that it was from their own loss of men as I missed none except from one wigwam."

The appearance of Captain Hunting's force of Indian scouts on this occasion, was an event of great significance. The representations of Eliot, Gookin, Savage, Henchman and Prentice, strengthened by the example of Connecticut, had at last prevailed,[1] and their enlistment by the direct order of Governor Leverett and the Council marked a radical departure from the suspicious attitude so long maintained toward the friendly Indians and which had occasioned so many injustices and injuries. It meant that the lesson of Indian warfare had at last been grasped. The days of disastrous ambuscades had come to an end and their employment contributed not a little to the sudden collapse of the Indian resistance that soon followed.

-----

[1] Massachusetts Colony Records, Vol. V, pages 85, 92.

CHAPTER XIII

FOLLOWING the lead of Connecticut the Council of Massachusetts, urged by Reverend Mr. Rowlandson and Major Gookin, had, on the 3d of April, sent Tom Nepanet,[1] a Christian Indian, with a letter to Philip, Sagamore Sam and others, expressing the hope that terms of peace might be arranged, but more specifically, for the purpose of reclaiming the considerable number of captives that had fallen into their hands.[2] On the 12th, the messenger returned with their reply.[3]

"We now give answer by this one man, but if you like my answer send one more man besides this one, Tom Nepanet, and send with all true heart and with all your mind, by two men, because you and we know your heart great sorrowful with crying for your lost many, many hundred men, all your house and all your land, and women, child, and cattle, and all your thing that you have lost and on your back side stand.

(Signed)   "SAM SACHEM,

"KUTQUEN, and

"QUANOHIT, Sagamores,

"PETER JETHRO,

"Scribe."

---

[1] Nepanet, commonly called Tom Doublet, was a Christian Natick Indian.

[2] Massachusetts Archives, Vol. LXVIII, page 194.

[3] The original of this letter cannot be found but it is printed in full in Drake's Book of the Indians, Vol. III, page 90.

(Then follow messages to individuals.)

"MR. ROWLANDSON.—Your wife and all your child is well, but one child dye. Your sister is well and her three child."

"JOHN KETTELL.—Your wife and all your child is all well, and them prisoners taken at Nashaway is all well."

"MR. ROWLANDSON.—Se your loving sister his hand. C. Hanah, and old Kettle wif his hand. X."

"BRO. ROWLANDSON.—Please send thre pounds Tobacco for me, and if you can, my loving husband, pray send thre pound of tobacco for me.

"This writing by your enemies,

"SAMUEL USKATTNHGUN, and

"GUNRASHIT, two Indian Sagamores."[1]

While Nepanet was journeying to Boston, Mrs. Rowlandson was on her way with Philip and his warriors from the Connecticut River to Wachusett. They had forded Miller's Rvier, when an Indian came up to them saying she must go to Wachusett to her master as there was a letter come from the Council to the Sagamores about redeeming the captives, and that there would be another in fourteen days. "After many weary days" she writes, "I saw Wachusett Hill, but many miles off . . . going along having indeed my life, but little spirit, Philip came up and took my hand, and said, two weeks more and you shall be mistress again. I asked him if he spoke true? Yes, and quickly you shall come to your master again. . . . And after many weary days we came to Wachusett, and glad I was to see him."[2]

---

[1] Drake's Book of the Indians.
[2] Massachusetts Archives. Hutchinson Papers, Vol. II, page 282.

A few days later, Nepanet, accompanied by Peter Conway, another friendly Indian, arrived with a second letter from the Council, and a conference was held to which Mrs. Rowlandson was bid.

They bade her stand up and told her they were the General Court, and asked her what she thought her husband would give. She told them "twenty pounds," and the Christian Indians set out for Boston with the tentative offer from the Indians to ransom her for that sum, and expressing themselves sorry for the wrong done and that when the quarrel began with the Plymouth men they did not think there would be so much trouble.

On the 2d of May, in the early Sunday morning, they returned to Wachusett Hill accompanied by John Hoar.[1] The Indians treated him with rude horseplay, firing over and under his horse, and pushed him about.

After a conference, at which Mrs. Rowlandson's release was agreed upon, Hoar asked the sagamores to dinner, but "when we went to get it ready we found they had stolen the greater part of the provisions Mr. Hoar

---

[1] Mr. John Hoar of Boston met the Indian sachems for the purpose of negotiating for the redemption of the captives, particularly that of Mrs. Rowlandson, at a well-known gathering place of the tribes known since that event as "Redemption Rock." It lies near the northern boundary of the town of Princeton, Mass., and but a short distance east of the southerly end of Wachusett Pond. It is an isolated rock of large size lying upon the side of a cleared hill and close to the highway passing through the little hamlet of Everettville. From its summit a beautiful view of Mount Wachusett and the surrounding country may be had. Upon its western face it bears an inscription commemorative of the redemption. It may be reached by electric cars from Fitchburg or Gardner to Wachusett Park, and thence from the northern end of the pond by a walk of something less than a mile.

had brought with him, and we may see the wonderful
Providence of God in that one passage in that when
there was such a number of them together and all so
greedy for a little good food . . . that they did not
knock us on the head and take what we had, but instead
of doing us any mischief they seemed to be ashamed
of the fact and said it was the bad Indians that did
it."[1]

Negotiations for the release of other captives, and for
peace, still continued after her release, and on the 5th
of May we find the Council again writing to the sachems,
Philip, John, Sam, etc., "Received your letter by John
Hoar sent up with John and Peter," and they expressed
their disappointment that no answer was returned as to
the terms upon which they would release all the prisoners. "You desire not to be hindered by our men in
your planting, promising not to do damage to our towns.
This is a great matter and cannot be ended by letters
without speaking one with another." "If you will send
us home all the English prisoners it will be a true testimony of a pure heart in you for peace;" and they promised that if the councilors and sachems would come to Boston, Concord or Sudbury, the Council would speak to them
about their desires and they should safely come and go.[2]
Further correspondence[3] was carried on. John Hoar,
Seth Perry, Reverend Mr. Rowlandson, Peter Gardiner,[4]

---

[1] Mrs. Rowlandson's Narrative.

[2] Massachusetts Colony Records, Vol. V, page 83; also pages 93, 94.

[3] *Ibid.*

[4] Peter Gardiner of Roxbury embarked in April, 1635, on the *Elizabeth,* at London. He died November 5, 1698. His son Samuel was
killed by the Indians April 2, 1676.—Savage.

Jonathan Prescott[1] and others acting as intermediaries.

There is no doubt but that, while the main object was to secure the release of the captives, the authorities would gladly at this time, have made peace and held in abeyance the active prosecution of the war. The first object was finally accomplished and almost all the captives returned to their homes.[2] The negotiations as to peace failed utterly. What reason held the Indians aloof it is difficult to judge, for the suffering among them from the lack of food was now great, and their ammunition scarce.

It may be that they prolonged the negotiations for the sole purpose of gaining time, or from the belief that the English would pay but scant regard to the terms of any treaty, or that they relied on their own prowess and the prospect of the replenishment of their supplies from the crops planted in the valley and the opening of the fishing season, to achieve success. Possibly Philip was obstinate and the Narragansetts eager to revenge the death of Canonchet; all is conjectural.

It was commonly believed at the time, that these negotiations and the release of the captives, occasioned strained relations between Philip and the Narragansetts, on the one hand, and the Nipmuck tribes on the other.

Sagamore Sam and One-Eyed John declared later that they were inclined toward peace, and the former that he

---

[1] Jonathan Prescott was of Lancaster and driven thence to Concord by the Indians. His second wife was the daughter of John Hoar. He was a man of prominence, captain, and representative in 1692 at the first court under the new charter. He died after February, 1707.—Savage.

[2] New England Deliverances, by Rev. Thomas Cobbet of Ipswich. New England Register, Vol. VII, pages 209-219.

was the chief advocate of the release of the English captives, which Philip opposed.

Sam may have believed it would make for peace and more lenient terms for his own people if the worst came to pass, while Philip, with better judgment, declared that they would make better terms for their own people by retaining the English captives as hostages.

Sagamore Sam's family, like Philip's, was captured and sold into slavery and Sagamore Sam was hanged, his release of the captives serving him not a whit.

The negotiations into which both Connecticut and Massachusetts had entered, led to a policy of inaction, and, save for movements of convoys and reliefs, and the sending out of a force under Henchman, Brattle and Prentice, toward Mendon and Seekonk, the month of April and the early weeks of May were unmarked by any active organization of forces or aggressive movements on a large scale, an inactivity, however, which, when considered in relation to the Sudbury disaster is not without suspicion that the authorities, in view of the constant ambuscade and lack of success, were at their wits' end. Yet among the Indians, also, many were wavering, and some who had been actively hostile were already in communication with the English and professing friendship. "Tell James the Printer and others, to bring in the heads of Indians as a proof of this fidelity," wrote the Council to Major Gookin.[1]

While, throughout New England, the English held their hands during these negotiations, the Indians continued their attacks and depredations without cessation.

---

[1] Massachusetts Archives, Vol. XXX, page 207.

April 26th, while John Woodcock,[1] with his sons and several laborers were at work in a cornfield near Woodcock's garrison house,[2] a party of Indians concealed in a wooded swamp near the edge of the field fired upon them, killing Nathaniel Woodcock and one of the laborers and wounding John Woodcock and the other son.

Fleeing to the garrison the survivors barred the doors, and though the inmates of the house were but few, they succeeded in driving off the enemy after they had burned a nearby house.

On the 2d of May, Ephraim Kingsbury, a young unmarried man, was killed at Haverhill, and the same day the house of Mr. Kimball[3] at Bradford was burned, Kimball himself being killed and his wife and children carried away into captivity.[4]

It was to the south, within the confines of Plymouth colony, however, that the war parties were the most active. There, on May 8th, Tuspaquin and his band, to whom much of the mischief done in that region may be ascribed, fell upon Bridgewater, but the settlers, fore-

---

[1] John Woodcock is found at Springfield as early as 1635, before the settlement of the town by Pynchon, and built a house in the Agawam meadows on the west side of the river, which he abandoned on account of the freshets. He removed to Dedham in 1642 and thence perhaps to Rehoboth before 1673. His garrison house was within the bounds of Wrentham. Under date of July 5, 1670, he was allowed by the court "to keep an ordinary at the Ten Mile River (so called) which is on the way from Rehoboth to the Bay." He was representative from Rehoboth in 1691 and was living in 1694.

[2] Woodcock's garrison was a well-known place of rendezvous in the great Indian war, situated on what became the stage road running from Boston to Providence.

[3] Thomas Kimball was an early settler in that part of Rowley that was afterwards called Bradford.—Savage.

[4] This was the work of the eastern Indians.

warned of the coming attack, were found prepared, and the marauders were driven off; not, however, until they had burned thirteen dwelling houses. Three days later a party of warriors assaulted Halifax, an outlying part of Plymouth town, and destroyed some eleven houses and five barns, but the inhabitants, aroused by the sudden alarm, precipitately fled and reached a haven of safety. The Indians still continued in the neighborhood and a few days later returned, burning seven more houses and two barns. About the same time the remaining houses of Middleboro, then Nemasket, were destroyed.

May 20th, the Indians came into Scituate from the north, first burning the mill of Cornet Robert Stetson,[1] on the Third Herring Brook, about a mile north of the present village of Hanover Four Corners. They avoided the garrison of Joseph Barstow, and followed the general course of the North River into South Scituate (Norwell). They attacked the blockhouse located on the bank of the river, but were repulsed. Marching on they reached the garrison at Charles Stockbridge's[2] where a large force of the townsmen were assembled, and after a desperate fight, were driven off and no more seen in the town.

With the exception of several small forces from Con-

------

[1] Robert Stetson was of Scituate in 1634 and came from County Kent, England. He was a man of great public spirit, cornet of the first body of horse in Plymouth colony; representative 1654-62, and often afterwards. His service as one of the council of war during Philip's hostilities was active.—Savage.

[2] The Stockbridge garrison was in the present village Of Greenbush, and the house at present occupying its site contains some of the old garrison timbers. It stands close to the border of the mill pond made famous in the song of the "Old Oaken Bucket," the mill being on the opposite side of the road a few rods distant.

SITE OF THE BLOCK-HOUSE. SCITUATE. MASSACHUSETTS

necticut, who were constantly beating up the Narragansett country, and in Plymouth, where, as it has been seen, the Indians, divided into numerous parties, were occasioning widespread ruin, little was accomplished by the English during April and the early part of May.

Captain Denison of Connecticut returned to New London after an expedition into the Narragansett country, and reported that he had killed seventy-six hostiles,[1] but in general the inclement weather, the rough roads deep with mud, and considerable sickness, combined with the hope that peace might result from the negotiations, held the troops to the garrisons.

Only in the southeast, between Medfield and Providence, was there any considerable force of English engaged in active operations, whither on April 27th, the Council of Massachusetts had dispatched a considerable force under Henchman, consisting of three companies of foot commanded by Captains Sill, Cutler[2] and Holbrook,[3] and an equal number of horse under Brattle, Henchman and Prentice.

---

[1] Connecticut Archives. War, Vol. I, Doc. 66.

[2] Captain John Cutler, blacksmith, was of Charlestown. He was a deacon of the church. In 1681 he was a member of the Artillery Company, and was representative in 1680 and 1682. In Philip's war he was a captain and engaged on various occasions in conducting supply trains to the garrisons, and at the time of the destruction of Wadsworth at Sudbury, April 21, 1676, narrowly escaped being cut off with his company returning from Marlboro. He died September 12, 1694. —Bodge, page 285. Savage.

[3] Captain John Holbrook was of Weymouth in 1636. He was an enterprising man of business and a large dealer in real estate. He held the rank of lieutenant in the home company and was its commander at the time of Philip's war. He died November, 23, 1699, leaving a large estate.—Bodge, page 280.

On May 5th, near Mendon, the Natick Indian scouts accompanying the force came suddenly on a large party of Indians engaged in a bear hunt. The English horse immediately pushed forward, and, rushing upon the excited hunters while still intent upon the chase, killed and captured sixteen of them.[1]

At night the troops returned to their quarters at Medfield, "from whence they saw two hundred fires in the night, yet they could not afterwards come upon the Indians" who kept carefully out of their way, and the whole force soon after being "visited by an epidemical cold, at that time prevailing throughout the country," were (May 10th) temporarily disbanded.

By the middle of May it had become evident that negotiations for a general peace had accomplished nothing, and in the Bay towns and in the Connecticut valley, public opinion was beginning to press for aggressive operations. In the valley of the Connecticut, particularly, the troops and settlers were becoming restive under repeated and annoying attacks by small parties of Indians from the upper valley, whose constant presence around the towns prevented the planting of the crops and whose frequent seizures of cattle threatened the settlers with scarcity of food.

Captain Turner, left by Savage in command of the valley, had divided his meager force and lay, himself, with fifty-one men, at Hadley. Nine had been sent to Springfield, and at Northampton were forty-six. Many of his command were mere lads, and the whole force was so ill-armed and ill-equipped that Turner wrote to

---

[1] Massachusett Colonial Records, Vol. V, page 96. Hubbard.

the Council of Massachusetts (April 25th) complaining of the great distress from want of proper clothing. He himself, he declared, was weak and sickly, but he left it for their consideration whether he should be continued in command or another, more able-bodied, be appointed to succeed him.[1]

As the spring came on public opinion in the valley became more and more urgent for an attack upon the encampment at Peskeompskut (Turners Falls), but the Connecticut Council of War still believed in the possibility of a successful termination of the negotiations into which they had entered with the valley Indians, and urged the Rev. John Russell and Captain Turner to refrain from all aggressive movements until after the 5th of May.[2]

A petition of the Rev. John Russell to the Governor and Council of Massachusetts marks the eager desire of the men, both troops and settlers, to go out against the Indians. "We understand from Hartford some inclination to allow some volunteers to come up hither. We believe it is time to distress the Indians. Could we drive them from fishing and keep out small parties to harass them, famine would soon subdue them."

The Indians, in the meantime, relieved of anxiety by the withdrawal of Savage and by the failure of Turner to make any aggressive movement, had grown careless. They were in desperate need of food, their supplies of dried fish and corn had long since been exhausted. Game was scarce and the ground nuts were no longer fit for food. Planting for the new year had but just begun, and until

---

[1] Massachusetts Archives, Vol. LXVIII, page 228.
[2] Connecticut Colony Records, Vol. II, page 440.

O

the crops were ripe they must depend upon fishing, hunting and the spoil of English corn and cattle for existence.

The negotiations with Connecticut had tended to increase the sense of security. They were willing to bargain over the price to be paid for the redemption of captives and they took full advantage of the English willingness to negotiate, to gain time.

Their main strength, divided into three villages, was now concentrated about Peskeompskut, the great fishing ground of the valley Indians. One of these villages occupied the high ground on the right bank at the head of the falls, another was on the opposite bank, and a third on Smead's Island, a mile below. Here were gathered promiscuously not only many of the valley Indians but also considerable numbers of the Wampanoags, the Narragansetts, Nashaways, Quabaugs and a few of the far eastern Indians. Here also, besides the sachems of the valley tribes, were Pessacus and Pumham of the Narragansetts, and even the distant Tarratines of Maine were represented by a Minor sachem, Megunneway.

The greater number were undoubtedly women, children and old men, engaged in fishing and planting, while the warriors were continually coming and going in small parties.

Farther up the river, in the cleared fields of what had once been Northfield, was another settlement of the Squakheags, and in the country between still other small parties were planting their crops. Supplies of seed corn for the planting had been obtained, fish were abundant and the cattle plundered from the English by the roving parties of warriors afforded a welcome addition of milk and flesh.

So careless had they grown in their fancied security
that John Gilbert,[1] who had been taken prisoner at
Springfield the month before, had already escaped out
of their hands and brought considerable information as
to their doings and their attitude to Turner at Hadley.

Throughout the valley the desire to strike an aggressive blow was growing; when, on the 12th, learning that
the English had turned their cattle out to graze in the
meadows, a war party from Peskeompskut pushed rapidly down the valley and seized the whole herd, amount-
ing to seventy head of horse and cattle, and were gone
in safety with their booty before the English could reach
the scene. So great a seizure of their property lashed
the settlers into rage, and operations were already under
way, when, three days later, as Rev. John Russell wrote
to the Connecticut Council of War, "This morning about
sunrise, came into Hatfield, one Thomas Reed, who was
taken captive when Deacon Goodman was slain. He
relates that they are now planting at Deerfield and have
been so these three or four days or more; saith further
that they dwell at the Falls on both sides of the river;
and are a considerable number most of them old men
and women. He cannot judge that there are on both
sides of the river above sixty or seventy fighting men;
they are secure but scornful, boasting of the great things
they have done and will do. There is Thomas Eames'
daughter and child hardly used; one or two belonging
to Medfield, and I think, two children belonging to Lancaster. The night before last they came down to Hat-

---

[1] John Gilbert, aged eighteen, was the son of Thomas Gilbert of
Springfield. Mrs. Rowlandson found him above Northfield, sick and
turned out into the cold. She befriended him and got him a fire.

field upper meadow and have driven away many horses
and cattle, to the number of four score and upwards as
they judge. Many of these this man saw in Deerfield
meadow and found the bars put up to keep them in.
This being the state of things we think the Lord calls
us to make some trial which may be done against them
suddenly, without further delay; and therefore the con-
curring resolution of men here seems to be to go out
against them to-morrow night, so as to be with them,
the Lord assenting, before break of day."[1] But the
Connecticut Council, though it promised to send a company up the valley in support, stated its belief that an
attack while so many English captives remained in the
hands of the Indians, and negotiations were still pending,
was inadvisable.

[1] Connecticut Archives. War, Vol. I, Doc. 67a.

CHAPTER XIV

TURNER, well acquainted with Indian habits, realized that such a favorable condition for attack would not long continue, and that as soon at they had finished their planting and dried their fish, they would be on the warpath down the valley.

Help or no help, he resolved to wait no longer, and, calling for volunteers, determined to hazard the venture on the evening of the 18th. Nearly one hundred and eighty mounted men, one-half of them settlers who had supplied their own horses, gathered at Hatfield, and soon after sunset the gates of the stockade were thrown open and the force filed out.

Turner, himself, just arisen from his sick bed could hardly keep his saddle, and among his motley force, ill-equipped and ill-disciplined, were many young boys. It was an expedition fraught with great promises and great dangers. Success depended upon the complete surprise of the Indian encampment, for if the Indians should discover the movement and lead them into an ambush, then the character of the force under his command promised a terrible catastrophe, and the valley, left defenseless, would be harried from end to end.

Their path led them through the depths of the forest and along the meadows, past the ill-omened fields of Wequomps and Bloody Brook. It was near midnight when they entered the broad street of Deerfield and saw, on either hand, in the gloom, the skeleton outlines of blackened beams and tumbling walls that had once been the settlement of Pocumtuck. The moon, overcast with clouds, and the distant roll of thunder, proclaimed an approaching storm. They crossed the Pocumtuck River at the northerly end of the meadows, near the mouth of Sheldon's Brook, narrowly escaping discovery by an Indian fishing outpost at what is now Cheapside. They had made a detour to avoid it, but the noise of their passage, not far away, aroused the Indians who could be seen with flaring torches gathered at the fording place. Finally concluding that the noise was made by a herd of moose crossing the river, they withdrew and the English continued their march. The storm overtook them, drenching them to the skin, and they feared lest the lightning flashes should reveal them to the prying eye of some Indian scout, but the thunder and rain deadened the noise of their passage, and the Indians, unsuspicious of danger, had placed no outpost.

Pushing on they crossed Green River, and skirting the great ash swamp to the east, reached the high ground just under Mount Adams, at daybreak. Picketing their horses they forded the Falls River near its confluence with the Connecticut and climbed the steep hill above the upper encampment of the Indians.

Wet and tired, but full of hope, they had arrived in time. The storm had driven the Indians to shelter, and the camp, its occupants gorged with fish and the milk and flesh of captured cattle, lay silent below them. Neither guards nor dogs were stirring as they rushed in among the wigwams, firing through the frail bark or into the openings.

The attack, fierce and sudden, allowed no time for the Indians to rally. Confused and terrified they made but a feeble resistance. Many fell within the wigwams; others, shouting that the Mohawks were upon them, plunged into the river. "Many" says the writer of the Old Indian Chronicle, "got into canoes to paddle away, but the paddlers being shot, the canoes overset with all therein, and the stream of the river being very violent and swift . . . were carried upon the falls of water and from thence tumbling down were broken in pieces." Many sought refuge among the rocks under the banks, where Captain Holyoke,[1] discovering some old persons and children, set the example of indiscriminate massacre by "slaying five of them, old and young, with his sword." No discrimination was made, the same fate was dealt out alike to warriors, women and children. After the first confusion of surprise, the warriors were able to escape, but the women and children fell easy prey and were put to the sword or forced into the rushing river and swept over the falls. "The river Kishon swept them away, that ancient river, the river Kishon. O! my soul, they have trodden down strength," wrote Mather in exultation.

The wigwams were fired, with all the dried fish and ammunition, and two forges, used by the Indians for the repairing of their guns, were demolished. Only one of

---

[1] Captain Samuel Holyoke was the son of Elizur Holyoke of Springfield, and grandson of William Pynchon, the founder of the town. He was born June 9, 1647, and died October 21, 1676, soon after the Falls fight, his health having become impaired by the hardships of the campaign. See First Century of the History of Springfield, by Henry M. Burt, page 591.

the English had fallen, shot accidentally by a comrade. It seemed as if the victory had been cheaply won but the roar of the muskets and the cries of the assault had already aroused the other Indian camps, and on the other side of the river and on Smead's Island the warriors were astir and hastening to the assistance of their ill-fated comrades. Turner's men, tired with their long march, and carried away with the excitement of the assault, were now out of hand. No guards had been stationed at the ford where the Indians from Smead's Island could cross, and the delay in retreating gave the warriors an opportunity to come up. Swarming in on both flanks, they pressed upon the English in ever increasing numbers, a party even attacking the guard left in charge of the horses, until the approach of the main body of the English caused them to draw off. Turner led the van while Holyoke, in command of the rear guard, kept the Indians in check until the horses were gained.

The attack of the Indians meanwhile was growing every moment fiercer and more determined as they swept around the rear and left flank of the English and endeavored to break the column in two, while the confusion in the English ranks was intensified by the cry of a lad that Philip with a thousand warriors was coming down upon them. Holyoke's horse was shot and several warriors rushed in upon the captain, but he shot the foremost, and his men, hastening to his assistance, drove back the rest.

The rear guard was early cut off and Jonathan Wells,[1] a lad of seventeen, appealed to Turner to return to their

---

[1] Jonathan Wells was the son of Thomas of Hadley. An interesting account of his experiences at this time may be found on page 161 of the

RIVER BANK DOWN WHICH THE INDIANS WERE DRIVEN

At Peskeompskut (Turner's Falls), Massachusetts

aid, but the captain refused. "Better lose some than all," he replied and pushed forward; but the rear guard fought its way out in safety.

As the head of the column reached the Green River, at the mouth of Ash Swamp Brook, it was met by a fire from both banks, and Turner,[1] shot through the back and thigh, fell dead at the river's edge. The guides grew panic-stricken, each calling out to the troops to follow him to safety. The flight and pursuit continued through the woods and among the ruined houses of Deerfield to the place known as the Bars, in Deerfield South Meadow, the Indians easily keeping up with the troopers in the dense woods, firing upon the column from behind the trees and cutting off the stragglers.

Only the self-possession and courage of Captain Holy-

---

fist volume of Sheldon's History of Deerfield. He was commander of the military forces of Deerfield in Queen Anne's war and at the time of the attack upon that town by the French and Indians, February 29, 1704,1705, occupied a fortified house a few rods south of the stockade, in which those inhabitants who escaped capture or slaughter in the attack on the stockade, took refuge. Captain Wells led the relief force in the attack upon the retreating Indians in the North Meadow. He was, until his death, which occurred January 3,1738-39, a leader in the civil and military affairs of the town. He was representative; selectman for thirteen years, and the first justice of the peace in Deerfield. See Sheldon's History of Deerfield, Vol. II, page 357 of Genealogies.

[1] Captain William Turner came from South Devonshire to Dorchester, in Massachusetts, and was admitted freeman May 10, 1643. He removed to Boston, probably in 1664, and was there a member of the Baptist church. During this period of religious intolerance he was twice imprisoned. Early in Philip's war he raised a company of volunteers, but their services were refused and he denied a commission on the ground that most of the members were "Anabaptists." As early as February, 1676, however, the demand for soldeirs being then greater than before, Turner had taken the field with a company.—Bodge, page 232.

oke, who assumed command on Turner's death, saved the force from a terrible disaster. Forty-five were missing when they reached Hatfield late in the morning. Six of these, however, returned in the course of the next few days, among them Jonathan Wells, who, having attached himself in the retreat to one party, continued with them until they entered the swamp, when, seeing the Indians closing in, he left this company, who were all lost, and joined a small party taking another course. Wounded and exhausted he was obliged, soon after, to fall out of the ranks and spent several days hiding in the woods, and, though the Indians at times came close to his hiding-places, he fortunately escaped discovery.

The loss of the Indians has been variously estimated, some of the contemporary writers placing it as high as three or four hundred.

The Reverend Mr. Russell, a man not prone to exaggerate, declared that eyewitnesses said that there were one hundred dead Indians among the wigwams and along the banks.[1] William Drew,[2] and others, give the Indian loss as six score and ten. Their reports, however, should be received with caution, for it is not likely that, in the heat of such an engagement and the confusion into which the English forces fell, any accurate enumeration was possible. Indians who were afterwards taken, wrote Mather, affirmed that many of the Indians, driven down the falls, got safe on shore again, and that they lost not more than three score men in the fight, also that they

---

[1] Letter of Rev. John Russell to the Governor and Council of Connecticut (War, I, Doc. 74) contains an account of the expedition.

[2] William Drew of Hadley, and Robert Bardwell, afterwards of Hatfield, soldiers of Turner's company, are referred to here.

killed thirty-eight Englishmen, which was the exact number of the latter slain.[1] The author of the Old Indian Chronicle states "the English did afterwards find of their bodies, some in the river and some cast ashore, about two hundred."[2]

The Indian loss can reasonably be placed, therefore, at about one hundred, many of them women and children. The blow was a severe one to the Indians, not so much in the loss of life as in its physical and moral effect.

The flight of Turner's men before the furious onslaught of the Indians, marks the last partial success of the latter in the war. The war cry was again to be heard before the stockades of Hatfield and Hadley; a few more English were to fall in desultory conflicts about Narragansett Bay and in the Connecticut valley, but these record only the expiring efforts of a dying cause, the last impotent protest of a doomed race against extinction.

The sudden collapse of the Indian resistance came as a surprise to the whites, who looked forward to a prolonged and bloody struggle. The reasons, however, were not far to seek. Numerically much weaker than the English at the beginning, and more poorly armed and equipped, the Indians lacked the resources, which the English possessed in abundance.

Their hope of terrorizing into inaction the settlers in the valley, while they themselves planted and reaped their crops and laid in stores of fish for themselves and their confederates, had vanished. Their confidence in their own prowess had been rudely shaken and the plan, from which they had hoped so much, had failed. The

---

[1] Mather's Brief History, page 149.
[2] Old Indian Chronicle, page 261.

fallen warriors could not be replaced, and arms and ammunition could be obtained only in meager quantities and with great difficulty from adventurous traders, or from their opponents, as the spoil of victories; precarious sources of supply certainly, for such a life and death struggle as they were now waging. They were improvident and wasteful at best; and, unprovided with strongly fortified depots, their supplies were easily at the mercy of foes, who, though they might themselves be at times in want, found in the neighboring colonies all they could not themselves provide.

Disease, as before noted, had been rife during the winter, and the Indians, weakened by privations, had fallen easy victims to colds and the malignant fevers, to whose ravages even among the settlers Mather bears mournful testimony.

A not less important factor in the collapse of Indian resistance was their total lack of organization. Their variable temperament, traditional feuds and jealousies, combining to make concerted action impossible; not one, but many heads, essayed to direct the operations and every petty chief had his own plans and ambitions to further, and would sacrifice nothing for the common good.

The dissensions among the Nipmucks on the one hand, and the Wampanoags and Narragansetts on the other, had, during the last few months of the war, grown apace, and Philip had openly quarrelled with the Nipmuck chiefs over the surrender of the English captives. To add to the general demoralization the Mohawks had become openly hostile.

The English towns, palisaded and garrisoned, no longer offered an easy booty to their sudden raids, and the English commanders had learned the lesson of Indian tactics.

When, therefore, in the spring, the colonies put forth their full force and enlisted the friendly Naticks, Mohegans and Niantics, the weakened tribes were doomed.

May drew to a close amid active operations for a campaign in force. Conscious of the necessity of ending the war before the whole country should be brought to ruin, and no longer held back by apprehension as to the fate that might befall the captives, the authorities worked energetically levying men and impressing food and transport.

In the Connecticut valley guards and scouts were watching the trails against a counterstroke of the Indians, and Captain Newberry[1] with eighty men, sent by Connecticut at the request of Holyoke, marched up the valley and, leaving three troopers at Westfield as a reinforcement, for the Westfield volunteers had suffered heavily in the Falls fight, took up his quarters at Northampton on the 24th of May.

From here, a few days later, he wrote to the Connecticut Council of War that there were three hundred Indians at Quabaug; that if Major Talcott[2] would come or if the Council would send him a reinforcement of fifty men he would willingly go himself against them, and

---

[1] Captain Benjamin Newberry was of Windsor and commanded the military department of the Connecticut colony. He was representative at twenty-two sessions of the General Court; assistant in 1685, and member of the Council of War; captain of dragoons, and in November, 1675, was made second in command to Major Treat. His service in the field during Philip's war consisted of operations at Northampton and vicinity in the spring of 1676. He died September 11, 1689. See Ancient Windsor, Conn., by Henry R. Stiles, page 518. Colonial Records of Connecticut. Savage.

[2] Major John Talcott was a native of Braintree, England, and came to America in the ship *Lion* in 1632. He settled in Hartford where he

suggested that Samuel Cross' dogs[1] could be used advantageously.[2]

In the southeast, in the meantime, parties from Plymouth and Massachusetts were scouring the country between Plymouth, Rehoboth and Marlboro, and the Connecticut and Indian forces, under Captain Denison and Major Talcott, were constantly raiding the Narragansett country from their bases at Stonington and Norwich.

In Massachusetts Captain Brattle had again taken the field with a troop of horse and a large body of Natick Indians under Tom Nepanet. On the 24th, the same day that Newberry reached Northampton, Brattle, marching along the Pawtucket River "being on the Seaconck side," saw a considerable body of Indians on the opposite bank. Pushing forward with his troopers he forded the river above their camp and put them to flight with a loss of several killed and a number of prisoners.

In the letter in which the Massachusetts Council announced the success of Captain Brattle to Connecticut, they gave notice of their intention to send an expedition of five hundred men to attack the Indian encampments at Quabaug, Wachusett and Squakheag, by the 1st of June, and requested that Major Talcott with a consid-

---

became in 1654 deputy to the court at New Haven. He was elected treasurer of the colony May 17, 1660, which office he held until 1675, when he resigned the office and was appointed to the command of the army with the rank of major, and in June of that year took the field at its head. He received promotion to the rank of lieutenant-colonel, and died in Hartford July 23, 1688. See Talcott Pedigree, by S. V. Talcott, page 32 See Memorial History of Hartford County, Vol. I, page 263.

[1] Samuel Cross was of Windsor. He is called captain in the records. He died November 6, 1707.

[2] Connecticut Archives. War, Vol. I, Doc. 76.

erable force of troops and Indians should act with them. Talcott was already at Norwich preparing to march through the Narragansett country, when, in response to this letter, the Connecticut Council bade him leave Denison with seventy men at Norwich, and march with the rest of his force to Quabaug, where it was expected that Henchman would meet him.

While Massachusetts and Connecticut were making these preparations, which it was hoped would crush the Indians in Northern Massachusetts, the Indians in the valley, who had suddenly vanished toward the north after the Falls fight, had again taken the initiative. The scouts had reported no movements among them, but on the 30th of May they appeared before Hatfield in large numbers, burning some twelve outlying barns and houses and driving away a multitude of sheep and cattle. Twenty-five settlers and soldiers from Hadley immediately rowing across the river to the Hatfield side, in the face of a severe fire, pushed on across the meadows to the aid of the town. The Indians, sheltered behind trees and hidden in the long grass, poured in an unremitting fire, but with little effect, and the little band had almost reached the shelter of the stockade in safety when the Indians closed rapidly in, and firing at close range, endeavored to cut them off from both the stockade and the river.[1] Within the space of a few minutes five of their number fell, "among whom was a precious young man whose name was Smith (John Smith[2] of Hadley), that place having lost many in losing

---

[1] Hubbard, Vol. I, page 235.

[2] John Smith was the son of Samuel, and was the ancestor of Oliver and Sophia Smith, the founder of the "Smith Charities" and Smith College at Northampton.

that one man,"[1] and all would soon have been lost, when the gates of the stockade were thrown open and the Hatfield garrison, sallying out, drove back the Indians and saved the survivors.

Newberry in Northampton was early informed of the attack, and, fearful that an ambuscade awaited him on the direct road to Hatfield (and such was actually the case), crossed the river below Northampton, and marching up to Hadley, sought to cross the Connecticut River at that point, as had been done by the Hadley volunteers.

It was not a very certain way to bring relief as his passage across the river would expose him to a heavy fire without opportunity to reply, but it at least denoted a change from the usual haphazard rush into an ambuscade. Unfortunately for Newberry the lack of boats and the increased vigilance of the Indians prevented his repeating the feat of the Hadley men, and his force was still waiting on the bank[2] when the Indians, finding it impossible to break into the stockade, drew off with the approach of evening. Seven whites had fallen in the fight and five were wounded. The Indian loss was set down as twenty-five killed, but was undoubtedly less.

The news of the attack on Hatfield was already known throughout Connecticut, when, on the 2d of June, Major Talcott with two hundred and fifty whites and two hundred Mohegans, set out from Norwich with the expectation of effecting a juncture with Captain Henchman and the Massachusetts forces, at Quabaug. On the 4th he

---

[1] Mather's Brief History, page 151.

[2] Letter of Captain Newberry. Connecticut Colonial Records, Vol. II, page 450.

reached the Indian village of Wabaquasset.[1] Everywhere the country was deserted, no Indians were to be seen, but the green shoots of the young corn were showing in the cultivated clearings by the deserted wigwams, and, after trampling it down and firing the village, Talcott continued his march.

The next day he came suddenly upon a small encampment of Indians at Chabanakongomun, near the present town of Webster, and, killing nineteen of its occupants and capturing thirty-three others without loss to himself, passed on to Quabaug where he believed Henchman was awaiting his arrival. Henchman was not there, nor any news of him, but a small body of Indians, the scouts told Talcott, had encamped, unaware of his approach, only three miles away, and at midnight twelve of the English and a body of Indians marched out and succeeded in capturing two of them, both well supplied with fish and powder.[2]

The morning brought no news of Henchman, and Talcott, believing his own force not sufficient to attack the Indians at Wachusett, waited no longer but pushed on to Hadley which he reached the next day (June 8th). His march had been through a country made bare of supplies, and his force suffered severely, but Captain Denison with a convoy of powder and stores, sent at his request

---

[1] Wabbaquasset, "the mat producing country," so called from some marsh or meadow that furnished reeds for mats and baskets, was a tract west of the Quinnebaug River, north of a line running northwesterly from the junction of the Quinnebaug and Assawage Rivers, not far from Southbridge in Massachusetts.—Trumbull's Indian Names in Connecticut. Miss Larned's History of Windham County, Vol. I, page 1.

[2] Talcott's Letter to the Governor and Council of Connecticut. Connecticut Archives. War, Vol. I, Doc. 88.

P

from Hartford, joined him on the 10th and relieved his necessity. In the meantime, Captain Henchman with five hundred foot and horse and a party of friendly Indians, had left Concord in time to effect a junction with Major Talcott at Quabaug, but his progress was slow and information brought to him by Tom Nepanet and his Indian scouts who had come upon the trail of a party of Indians making for the fishing grounds at Washakim Ponds near Lancaster, caused him to turn aside in pursuit. He came upon them while fishing, killed seven and captured twenty-nine, most of the latter women and children, among them the wife of Muttaump and the wife and children of Sagamore Sam, who had gone, if we are to believe his own testimony, to secure the release of the English captives in the hands of the valley tribes.

The pursuit had taken Henchman considerably out of his way and he marched to Marlboro to replenish his ammunition and supplies, and then set out for Hadley.

The Indians, carefully watching Henchman's progress, had, strange to say, entirely missed touch with Talcott, and, confident that Henchman could not reach Hadley for several days, and ignorant of Talcott's arrival, massed their forces and came down the valley on the night of the 11th of June.

Dividing their forces they placed a strong party in the meadows at the north end of the stockade to intercept any English going out or any force attempting to enter the town from Hatfield. The remainder stationed themselves near the south end of the stockade with the intention of attacking from that direction and calling the attention of the garrison away from the north.

In the early morning three soldiers, having been warned not to go far afield, were finally allowed by the sergeant in charge to go out of the south gate. They had gone but a short distance when a warwhoop was heard and the men on guard saw them running back with a score of Indians at their heels. All three fell before the stockade was gained, but the alarm was given, and when the Indians at the north, thinking the garrison had been withdrawn to meet the attack at the south gate, rushed forward to take advantage of the confusion, they found the stockade lined with troops and friendly Indians. Ignorant as they were that five hundred men were within the stockade, the appearance of so large a force, which was evidently ready to sally out against them, so alarmed and disconcerted them that they hastily withdrew up the valley.

General Hoyt and Dr. Holland ascribe the appearance of General Goffe to the occasion of this attack.

It was the last action in the valley. Their counterstroke had failed, and, with the massing of such a large force of trained troops and friendly Indians, their position in the valley was rendered untenable. From that day they were seen no more in force.

Henchman arrived on the 14th, and two days later the combined force swept up the valley to Peskeompskut, Henchman along the east and Talcott along the west bank of the Connecticut. The weather was cold and chill, and three miles out of town a thunderstorm overtook and followed them up the valley. The Indian villages at the Falls were deserted but they found, along the banks of the river and in the neighboring swamps, the bodies of Turner and many of his men, and gave them decent burial. The rain continued to fall in torrents, they were wet to the skin, much of the ammunition was ruined, the bread grew musty in the dampness, it was all but impossible to make fire with the wood sodden with constant rain, and, after searching the woods to the east and west, the whole force returned down the valley.[1]

The terror that had hung over the settlers so long was lifted, the war was drifting back to the starting point, and along the shores of Narragansett Bay the Indian cause was entering on its death agony. The valley Indians, disheartened by their constant repulses and loss of supplies, and threatened by their old enemies the Mohawks, scattered, some far to the north, while others fled for refuge to the tribes in New Hampshire and Maine, who were still holding their own against the English.

---

[1] Connecticut War, Vol. I, Doc. 93.

CHAPTER XV

BEFORE the end of the month a force of thirty men, under Captain Swaine,[1] who had been left in command of the valley, marched up to the old Indian encampment on Smead's Island and destroyed the stockaded fort, one hundred wigwams and thirty canoes, and large quantities of supplies found buried in the Indian barns.[2]

On the 20th of June, Talcott was recalled by the Connecticut authorities and a week later, Henchman also left the valley for Boston, whither Brattle and Moseley had preceded him. On the 30th while on the march, he wrote to the Massachusett Council: "Our scouts brought intelligence that all the Indians were in continual motion, some towards the Narragansetts, others toward Wachusett, shifting gradually and taking up each others' quarters and lay not above a night in a place. The twenty-seven scouts have brought in two squaws, a boy and a girl, giving account of five slain. Yesterday they brought

---

[1] Captain Jeremiah Swaine was of Reading. When the forces for the Narragansett campaign were organized, he commanded, in lieu of Captain Appleton who was also major of the regiment, the First Company of the Massachusetts Line, as lieutenant. At the Narragansett fight he was wounded. In 1677 he commanded a company sent to Black Point in the Province of Maine, as part of a force to establish there a base of supplies, and in 1679 he was captain of the foot company in Reading. He also served as representative to the General Court. In 1733 his heirs received a grant of land in the Narragansett Township No. 3. (now Westminster, Mass.), in recognition of his services in Philip's war.—Bodge. Massachusetts Colony Records.

[2] Mather's Brief History, page 163.

in an old fellow, brother to a sachem, six squaws and children, having killed five men and wounded others. These and others inform that Philip and the Narragansetts were gone several days before to their own places."[1]

The information given to Henchman by his captives in respect to the departure of Philip, was correct. Accompanied by the remnant of the Wampanoags and many Narragansetts he had turned in desperation again toward his own country. Safety was no longer possible, either in the valley or at Wachusett. The Mohawks were threatening the valley Indians to the north, and the Nashaways, accusing him as the author of all their misfortunes, would doubtless purchase their safety with his head if the opportunity arose, and in the hope of regaining the fishing grounds and the corn buried in the Indian barns, and finding refuge in the wooded swamps along the coast, he had turned to the south.

His appearance in the south had already been made known to the Council of Massachusetts before the receipt of Henchman's letter, by a renegade Indian, the first of many traitors, sure indication of a dying cause, who had come into Rehoboth on the 28th and offered to conduct the English to the place not far distant where Philip with about thirty followers were encamped.

On receipt of this news the Council immediately dispatched Brattle toward Mount Hope with orders to pick up various forces along the way, and to be at Woodcock's garrison by midnight of the first. "There you shall meet with an Indian pilot and two file of musketeers, which pilot has agreed to bring you upon Philip who

---

[1] Letter of Captain Henchman, June 30. Hubbard, Vol. I, page 238.

hath not but thirty men, as he sayeth, and not ten miles from Woodcock's. In case the enemy should be past Mt. Hope and you can meet with the Plymouth forces you are to join with them."[1]

Brattle obeyed his orders to the letter, and with seventy-six men, and accompanied by Moseley and the Rev. William Hubbard,[2] followed their Indian pilot "only to find Philip newly gone."

Affairs had come to a desperate pass with him now and Philip's heart must have failed him as he took note of the growing weakness and disaffection of the tribes, but, whatever his failures as a leader may have been, he went on, neither faltering nor seeking peace, to the end.

Harassed and hunted as they were, there still remained opportunities for them to surprise and strike at isolated and outlying garrisons, or a careless settler, and even while Brattle and Moseley were searching for Philip, a small band, hovering on the outskirts of Swansea, shot down Hezekiah Willet[3] within sight of his father's

---

[1] Massachusetts Archives, Vol. LXIX, pages 24, 25.

[2] The Rev. William Hubbard was the author of "The History of The Indian Wars in New England," a contemporaneous record which is the chief basis of all accounts of those times. He was born in England, came to this country with his father, and was made freeman of Ipswich in 1653. He graduated in the first class from Harvard College, and November 17, 1658, was ordained in the ministry as colleague with the Rev. Thomas Cobbett of Ipswich. "He was many years the most eminent minister in the County of Essex; equal to any in the Province for learning and candour, and superior to all his contemporaries as a writer." He was held in the highest esteem and was appointed by the General Court to write the account of the Indian wars above mentioned, for which a grant of money was made him. He died September 24, 1704, aged eighty-three. See I Mass. Hist. Soc. Coll., Vol. X, pages 33, 34. Savage.

[3] Hezekiah Willet, born November 17, 1653, was the son of Thomas,

house, and striking off his head, carried it away as a trophy.

Hubbard, in recounting this exploit, says that the family frequently kept a sentinel in a watch tower built on the top of the house, whence they could discover any Indians before they came near, but not hearing of the enemy in those parts for a considerable time they grew careless, and within a quarter of an hour after young Willet went out of the door he was killed and a negro servant of the family who accompanied him, carried away into captivity.

Mather says there were omens of coming events. "On the 15th of June a bow had been seen in the sky and many strange and unnatural events occurred presaging great events," for "common observation verified by experience of many ages, show that great and public calamity has seldom come upon any place without religious warning."

The Connecticut forces left behind by Talcott had, during his absence, continually raided the Narragansett country "taking above thirty, the most of which being men are said to have been slain by them," in one expedition, and soon after capturing a party of forty-five "most of which probably were women and children but being all young serpents of the same brood, the subduing and taking so many ought to be acknowledged as another signal victory and pledge of Divine pleasure."

Supplies were pouring in from the neighboring colonies

---

an early settler of the Indian lands at Wannamoiset in Swansea (now Riverside, R. I.). He married, January 7, 1676, his first cousin Ann, daughter of John Brown the second, and was killed by the Indians July 1st following. "As hopeful a young gentleman as any in these parts."

of Connecticut and New York, and even distant Ireland sent a shipload of provisions. June 21st had been set apart as a day of humiliation and prayer; the 29th was proclaimed a day of public thanksgiving.

Major Talcott, recalled from the Connecticut Valley in the latter part of June, had reorganized his command at Norwich and before the 1st of July was again abroad in the Narragansett country accompanied by Captains Denison and Newberry with three hundred English and Indians. On July 2d, it being the Sabbath, and the sun about an hour high, the scouts from the top of a hill discovered a large Indian encampment in a cedar swamp at Nachek.[1] The English, who were all mounted, making a circuit, closed in upon the swamp from both sides and the rear, while the Pequots and Mohegans rushed down the hill. There was no escape from the trap. The Mohegans, joined by Captain Newberry and his men, sword in hand, glutted themselves with slaughter in the fastnesses of the swamp, while the Narragansetts, who sought safety in flight, were pursued and cut down by the troopers. Forty-five women and children were taken, and one hundred and twenty-six, including thirty-four warriors, were slain. Among the slain, Talcott reported, was "that old piece of venom, Sunk squaw Magnus," and "our old friend Watawaikeson,[2] Pessacus his agent, and in his pocket Captain Allyn's ticket for his free pas-

---

[1] This was on the south bank of the Pawtuxet River, below Natick. The exact place of this massacre is not known. It was seven miles from Providence.—Rider.

[2] The messenger between the Connecticut Council of War and Pessacus, in the peace negotiations.—Major Talcott to Connecticut Council, Connecticut Colony Records, Vol. II, page 458.

sage up to headquarters." Among the dead also was Stonewall John.[1]

No Englishman lost his life in this conflict, and only one friendly Indian. Resistance there had been none, and the whole affair was emphatically an indiscriminate massacre of those who possessed no means of resistance, and were mostly women, children and old men.

On the next day Talcott marched to Providence and received information that the enemy were there to make peace with some of the Rhode Islanders, "upon which information, being willing to set our seal to it, we posted away and drest Providence's necks, killing and capturing sixty-seven of the Indians we found there," among them Potuck, a minor sachem of the Narragansetts whose village was located on Point Judith.

Informed by one of his captives that Philip was at Mount Hope, Talcott would have gone in pursuit but could not persuade his Indians to accompany him. On account of the scarcity of provisions and the terms of some of his men having expired; he therefore turned homeward on the 4th, marching along the Bay by way of Point Judith to Stonington.

On this march an Indian prisoner, who had taunted his captors with the number of English and friendly Indians he had killed, was turned over by Talcott to the mercy of the Mohegans. "He boldly told them that he had with his gun dispatched nineteen English and that he had charged it for the twentieth, but not meeting with another, and unwilling to lose a fair shot, he had let fly at a Mohegan and killed him, with which, having made

---

[1] Drake's Book of the Indians, Book III, page 78.

up his number, he was satisfied. . . . This cruel monster has fallen into their power which will repay him seven fold."

"In the first place therefore making a great circle they placed him in the middle that all their eyes might at the same time be pleased with the utmost revenge upon him. They first cut one of his fingers round in the joint at the trunk of his hand, with a sharp knife and then brake it off, as men do with a slaughtered beast before they uncase him; then they cut off another and another till they had dismembered one hand of all its digits, the blood sometimes spurting out in streams a yard from his hand, which barbarous and unheard of cruelty the English were not able to bear, it forcing tears from their eyes, yet did not the sufferer ever relent or show any sign of anguish, for being asked by some of his tormentors how he liked the war . . . this unsensible and hard-hearted monster answered, he liked it very well and found it as sweet as Englishmen did their sugar. In this frame he continued until his executioners had dealt with the toes of his feet as they had done with the fingers of his hands, all the while making him dance round the circle and sing, till he wearied both himself and them. At last they brake the bones of his legs, after which he was forced to sit down which 'tis said he silently did, till they knocked out his brains"[1] Then, continues Hubbard, "Instances of this nature should be incentive to us to bless the Father of Lights who hath called us out of the dark places of the earth."

The blame for this act of barbarous cruelty does not

---

[1] Hubbard, Vol. II, page 64.

lie upon the Mohegans, with whom the torture of a prisoner was a custom sanctioned by immemorial usage, but
upon Talcott himself who, having the power to prevent
such a barbarity, lent to it the approval of his presence,
and as an Englishman had no excuse whatever.

In the meantime Captain Church, than whom no one
was more fitted by experience for the particular duties of
a partisan leader, had again appeared on the scene after
many months of inaction. He had not been on good
terms with the Plymouth authorities during the winter,
the fault lying as much with their constant interference
as in his own infirmities of temper, but his services had
now become invaluable for the partisan warfare into
which the conflict had degenerated. Some time before
they had asked him for advice as to the best means of
protecting the colony from the marauding bands who were
committing great destruction of property, and he had
proposed the raising of a body of volunteers and a large
number of Indians as scouts. They refused with asper-
ity and contempt to employ any Indians, and Church,
angry at the treatment accorded him, removed his family
to Duxbury despite the advice of his friends who had
urged him to leave his wife and family at Clark's garrison house at Plymouth.[1] Fortunate it was for them that
he refused, or they would have shared the fate of that
unfortunate family at the hands of Tatoson.

Late in June, while returning from Plymouth to Narragansett Bay around the Cape, he discovered, near Falmouth, two Indians personally known to him, engaged in
fishing. Calling them to go to a point clear of bushes

---

[1] Baylie's Memoirs of Plymouth, Part III, page 128.

near by, he landed and entered into conversation with them, and was told by one named George, that the Saconet tribe was weary of war and would gladly give up their arms if assured of amnesty.

Church proposed Richmond's Farm, near Falmouth, as a place of meeting in two days, and hastening to Plymouth returned with permission of the Governor to enter into negotiations with the Saconet queen, Awashonks. On reaching the place of meeting, the warriors, decked in their war paint, arose from the grass in a fierce manner. Turning quietly he asked them to lay aside their arms, which they did. When all were seated he poured some rum in a shell and drank it, and, to calm the suspicion of the queen, who suspected poison, poured out more and drank it from his hand as a cup.

After some mutual recriminations an agreement was reached, and though Major Bradford assumed an arbitrary attitude toward both Church and the Saconets, the Plymouth authorities, after an examination of Peter (Awashonk's son), and other Indian delegates, appointed a commission, consisting of Captain Church, Jabez Howland[1] and Nathaniel Southworth,[2] to confer with the Saconets. Church and Southworth, leaving the remainder of the commission at Sandwich, soon came to the shores of Buzzard's Bay, and hearing a great noise at a consid-

---

[1] Jabez Howland, son of John of the Mayflower, was of Duxbury and served during Philip's war as lieutenant in Captain Benjamin Church's company. After the war he settled in Bristol and became an innkeeper. He was representative in 1689–90.—Savage.

[2] Nathaniel Southworth, born in 1648, was first of Plymouth, then of Middleboro. He was a lieutenant in Philip's war. He was representative in 1696, and died January 14, 1711. His sister Alice was the wife of Captain Benjamin Church.—Savage.

erable distance from them upon the bank, were presently in sight of a "vast company of Indians of all ages and sexes, some on horseback running races, some at football, some catching eels and flatfish in the water, some clamming," etc. Church called and two of them rode up to see who it was. They were Awashonk's people, and, feasting with the queen and her councilors that night, they offered him their services against Philip.[1]

Plymouth accepted their submission, and a short time thereafter we find many of their number serving under Church, the offer of whose services as a leader of a force of volunteers and Indian scouts was accepted soon after the close of the negotiations with the Saconets. Thenceforth we find him the most active commander in the field, the runner to earth of the hostile sachems, tracking them into the deep recesses of the swamp with the unfailing keenness of a wolfhound, and recruiting Indians from the hostile forces by flattery and the promise of good pay. He played his part with skill and effect, but the task was no longer difficult, for traitors and deserters were saving their own lives by betrayals of their chiefs, and kept the whites well informed of the movement of every considerable body of their countrymen. Philip, worried and distressed by the numerous forces of the English in the field, had been driven for safety to the fastnesses of the great swamps that spread over all that part of Plymouth colony from Monponsit and Rehoboth on the north to Dartmouth on the south. He dodged his pursuers hither and thither, making no stand but seeking refuge in the inaccessible hiding places which the

---

[1] Church's Entertaining History, pages 21-30.

Indians knew so well. He was still able to strike, however, and in order to encourage his disheartened warriors
he endeavored to surprise Taunton on the 11th of July,
but the negro servant of Hezekiah Willet of Wannamoiset,
who had been taken prisoner at the time of his master's
death, and was acquainted with the Indian tongue, escaped and made known their design, and the inhabitants
drove off the attacking force before they had accomplished other mischief than the destruction of two houses.[1]

Three days later Bridgewater[2] was attacked, the Indians coming upon the north side of the town, but after
killing a few cattle they retired. The next day they came
again but with no better success, for though much exposed, Bridgewater was inhabited largely by a colony of
young men, who, from the outbreak of the conflict, had
refused to retire into Plymouth and give up their homes
when they had been solicited to do so.

It was the last feeble stroke for a lost cause. From
all sides the whites and large bands of Indians were hunting him down; traitors were many and Philip knew no
longer whom to trust. Powder and provisions were gone,
no shelter was secure from the eyes of the Mohegans,
Naticks and the renegades (and all who had hope of

---

[1] Hubbard, Vol. I, page 241. See also Mather's Prevalency of Prayer,
page 261.

[2] The house built for the first minister of the town, the Rev. James
Keith, almost directly opposite the north end of the most westerly bridge
across the river, is still standing, and not far from this was located the
church and cemetery, on what is now known as Howard Street, the site
being marked by a monument. Nearly a mile easterly from the minister's house, was one of the garrison houses, the location of this being
the only one that can now be identified. The village of that day was
identical with the present village of West Bridgewater and lay chiefly
along the north side of the Nunketetest or Town River.

mercy were seeking only an opportunity to give themselves up).

Moseley and Brattle and the other forces kept close upon his heels, searching out his hiding places and by their unflagging pursuit compelling him to constantly change his camp, while Major Bradford held the fording places of the Taunton River.

Through all the country around Rehoboth, through the great morass known as the Night Swamp, a marshy tract of some three thousand acres covered with tall marsh grass and wood, along the confines of the Metapoiset peninsula, amid the swamps that border on the Taunton River and around Assowomset Pond the English followed him. In a swamp near Dartmouth they came suddenly upon his camp; the fires were still burning and food was cooking in the kettles, the blankets and arms abandoned in wild haste, and the bodies of several of his warriors who had died of their wounds and lay unburied, told them how close they had been to him.[1]

On the 22d of July the Massachusetts forces returned to Boston, some to be disbanded, others to be sent to Maine and New Hampshire where the eastern war was raging with unabated fury. They had killed and wounded nearly one hundred and fifty Indians and their services were no longer required in the south, or in Massachusetts, where the Nipmucks had given way to despair.

The Councils of Massachusetts and Plymouth, in order to paralyze resistance, early in July offered an opportunity of surrender to those who might reasonably hope for pardon, by a proclamation that whatever Indians

---

[1] Hubbard, Vol. I, page 257.

HOUSE OF THE REVEREND JAMES KEITH
West Bridgewater, Massachusetts. He lived here during King Philip's War.
One of the very few houses of that date remaining.

within fourteen days next ensuing come into the English, might hope for mercy. By many the opportunity was gladly accepted, and the 6th of July witnessed the surrender of over three hundred of the Plymouth and Cape Indians, with several of their sachems.

Sagamore Sam of Nashaway, through whose efforts there is but little doubt that many of the English captives had been redeemed, was among those who offered submission, and with him Muttaump, John the Pakachooge, and other of the Nipmucks, and on the 6th of July these sachems entreated them piteously in the following letter:[1]

"Mr. John Leveret, my Lord, Mr. Waban, and all the chief men our brethren Praying to God: We beseech you all to help us: my wife she is but one, but there be more Prisoners, which we pray you keep well; Mattamuck his wife we entreat you for her, and not only that man, but it is the Request of Two Sachems, Sam Sachem of Weshakum, and the Pakashoag Sachem.

"And that further you will consider about the making Peace: We have spoken to the People of Nashobah (viz. Tom Dubler and Peter) that we would agree with you, and make a Covenant of Peace with you. We have been destroyed by your Souldiers, but still we Remember it now to sit still; Do you consider it again: We do earnestly entreat you, that it may be so by Jesus Christ. O! let it be so! Amen, Amen."

Sagamore Sam in the hope of mercy, wrote them again recalling his efforts in behalf of the English captives, but no word of hope was sent him or the others. The appeal

---

[1] Drake's Book of the Indians, Book, III. The original letter is not to be found.

Q

fell upon ears deaf to all mercy, and Sagamore Sam and the rest in despair fled to the Tarratines.

If the English were ready to extend mercy to some it was not to the chiefs and those most active in war, and their reply that "Treacherous persons that began the war and those that have been barbarously bloody must not expect to have their lives spared, but others that have been drawn into the war and acted only as soldiers and submit to be without arms and live quietly and peaceably in the future shall have their lives spared," closed the door of hope in the face of all the chief sachems of the tribes. They could make but little resistance, and the war had already degenerated into the hunting down of hostiles who, with but little food and ammunition, had hidden themselves in the thickets.

Amid the general rack and faint-heartedness some sterner natures fought resolutely to the end. Pumham, starved and surprised with a handful of warriors (many of them his relatives), near Dedham, by Captain Hunting and a mixed force of whites and Indians, July 27th, asked no quarter, but, mortally wounded by a shot in the back and unable to stand, retained his hatchet and fought to the death, for, catching hold of an Englishman who came upon him as he lay in the bushes, whither he had crawled for safety, he would have slain him had not another Englishman come to the rescue. His son was with him, says Hubbard, "a likely youth and one whose countenance would have besought favor for him had he not belonged to so barbarous and bloody an Indian as his father was." Fifteen of the band perished with their chief, and thirty-four others fell into the hands of the English.

Fugitive bands were constantly coming into the English lines. Some were seized by the way while others not only gave themselves up but brought in some chief known to be obnoxious to the whites, as a peace offering. In this way Matoonas was delivered into the hands of the English by Sagamore John, a sachem of the Nipmucks, who, with one hundred and eighty of his followers, gave himself up on the 27th,[1] and sought to ingratiate himself with the English by acting as executioner of Matoonas.

Pursued by the whites and friendly Indians, and, in some cases, attacked by their allies of a few days back, the plight of the tribes was pitiful in the extreme. It had become for the English merely a matter of "exterminating the rabid animals, which, by a most unaccountable condition from heaven, had now neither strength or sense left them to do anything for their own defense."

With the departure of the Massachusetts troops the task of stamping out the last embers of the war in Plymouth colony fell to the regular forces of Major Bradford and Captain Church's volunteers, while the Connecticut forces crushed all resistance among the Narragansetts.

Major Bradford's plan of campaign seems to have been limited to holding the fording places along the Taunton River and covering the towns, a strictly defensive policy of no value in bringing the war to a close. But if Bradford was inactive, not so Church. Doubtless Church magnified his own exploits, for his narrative, dictated forty years after the occurrence, is not remarkable for modesty, and the length of time which transpired between

---

[1] Hubbard, Vol. I, page 260.

the events and their narration did not lend itself to accuracy.

On the 25th of July, Church received his commission from Plymouth colony, and in command of some eighteen picked English volunteers and twenty-two Indians marched to Middleboro.

At dawn the next day, seeing the bivouac fires of a party of Narragansetts, he surrounded their camp and captured them all. Learning from his captives that another party of Narragansetts was near Monponsit Pond, he hastened back to Plymouth only to be foiled in his quest by the Plymouth authorities who bade him guard a convoy of supplies being sent to Major Bradford. On the march information reached him that Tuspaquin was encamped at Assawomset Pond, and sending the convoy on with a small guard, he marched with all speed to come upon him unawares. Leaving a small guard at the crossing of the Acushnet River, the remainder of the force pushed on a short distance and encamped, but, tired out with the labors of the last few days, the sentinels and all fell asleep. Church himself awoke before daybreak, and, alarmed by the danger to which they had exposed themselves, he sent a party to bring in the guards at the river, who came upon a party of Indians examining the trail over which Church had marched the day before. Finding the guards at the ford also asleep, they roused them, and in the course of the morning met and captured a number of Saconet Indians who had abandoned their countrymen when peace was made.

Ascertaining from a captured squaw that Philip and Quinnapin were only two miles away in a great cedar swamp, Church followed, and, concealing himself with

one comrade and an Indian in the meadows, saw the whole
body of the Indians defile before him. Church now divided his command, the Indians taking the road to the
west around the swamp and Church and his volunteers
setting out to the east, with the agreement that both parties should meet at John Cook's house at Acushnet.
When they met at the rendezvous it was found that the
English had killed three of the enemy and taken sixty-
three prisoners, mostly women who had been surprised
while gathering berries, and the Indians had killed and
captured the same number, among them Tyask's wife
and son, and secured many guns.[1]

Bradford was still at Taunton guarding the fords, and
Philip, harried by Church and unable to cross the river,
took refuge in the country bordering on the Taunton
River, moving up towards Bridgewater. The men of
Bridgewater were on the alert and a small party of them
ranging the woods discovered one of Philip's scouts and,
judging that a considerable force was near at hand, retreated in all haste to Bridgewater. On the next day
(the Sabbath) messengers were dispatched to Plymouth
to inform the authorities that the Indians were evidently
designing to cross the river near Bridgewater. Church
was at Plymouth at the time and, begging what provisions were necessary, immediately marched out and
reached Monponset Pond as the evening fell; his men
worn out by their rapid march in the heat of the day
could go no further. The messengers, however, pushed
on to Bridgewater with notice of his approach.

Early the next morning, July 31st, a force of twenty-

---

[1] Church's Entertaining History, page 32-37.

one men marched out from Bridgewater to meet him but, as fortune would have it, fell in with Philip and a mixed company of Wampanoags and Narragansetts in the act of crossing the Taunton River on a tree which had been felled for a bridge.[1]

A sharp conflict followed, but the Indians, fully exposed to the fire of the English, drew off, having lost several of their number, among them Akkompoin,[2] Philip's uncle. A number of captives also fell into the hands of the English, including, according to Mather, Philip's sister. Church, who was probably reconnoitering along the northern edge of the cedar swamp that extended towards Middleboro, heard the firing but as it lasted only a short time missed the direction, and as night was falling went on to the town.

On the following day, August 1st, he marched out very early in the morning with his own company of thirty English and twenty Indians, and accompanied by many of the townsmen, and soon came "very still to the top of the great tree which the enemy had fallen across the river, and the captain spied an Indian sitting upon the stump of it on the other side of the river and he clapped his gun up and had doubtless dispatched him but that one of his own Indians called hastily to him not to fire for he believed it was one of his own men, upon which the Indian upon the stump looked about and Captain Church's Indian seeing his face perceived his mistake

---

[1] This tree probably lay over the stream somewhere between what are now known as Covington's and Woodbury's bridges.

[2] II Mass. Hist. Soc. Coll, Vol. VII, page 157. This account was supposed to have been written by Comfort Willis, one of those who discovered the first Indian and who went as a messenger to Plymouth.

for he knew him to be Philip, clapped up his gun and fired, but it was too late, for Philip immediately threw himself off the stump, leaped down a bank on the side of the river and made his escape."[1]

Church, crossing the river,[2] threw out his men in a long line and marched swiftly forward, the Indians flying before him, but he picked up many of the women and children in the pursuit, among them Philip's wife, Woolonekanuske, and his only child, a son nine years of age. Following a newly made trail, Church and his men pushed forward, and after fording the river, in a short time overtook the women and children of Quinnapins' Narragansetts, who, faint and tired, had fallen behind. Learning from these captives that Philip was near by he resumed the pursuit and about sunset heard the Indians chopping wood for their camp fires in the midst of a swamp. When the night had fallen he drew his force up in a ring and sat down in the swamp without any noise or fire, and before dawn sent forward two scouts to reconnoiter; but Philip had done the same and his Indians, seeing Church's men, fled shouting to the Indian camp. Church pushed forward with all haste, but before he could come up with them Philip and his warriors had fled deeper into the swamp, leaving their kettles boiling and meats roasting upon the wooden spits. Confident that they would attempt to leave the swamp in some other direction, he

---

[1] Church's Entertaining History, page 38.

[2] The pursuit of Church after Philip, commencing at the fallen tree over the Taunton River not far from the present railway station at Titicut, passed westerly to the southward of Nippenicket Pond, through the northern part of Taunton, past Winniconnet Pond in Norton, then, bearing southwesterly, came into a swamp in the northern part of Rehoboth, where they came upon Philip as above related.

sent Lieutenant Howland with a party around one side of the swamp while he himself, after leaving a guard at the place where Philip had entered, in the hope that if he discovered Howland's force he would return on his tracks, marched around on the other side and joined Howland at the further end.

Philip, believing the English would follow him in the swamp, had laid an ambush also, at the same time sending a band of warriors, with most of the women and children, to make their way out in the opposite direction. The latter, however, came upon Howland and Church unexpectedly and one of the Christian Indians, at Church's bidding, shouting to them that "if they fired one gun they were all dead men," the English rushed forward and seized the guns out of their hands.

Having secured these prisoners, they then advanced and came upon Philip. Here a desperate fight was maintained for some time but Philip finally fled, and the English following fell into the ambuscade Philip had placed and one of their number, Thomas Lucas[1] of Plymouth was slain. Philip, Totoson and Tuspaquin, continuing their retreat, fell in with the party left at the entrance, but finally broke through and got safely away.

During the conflict, Church, with two companions, met three of the enemy, two of whom surrendered themselves and were seized by the captain's guard, but the other, a great stout, surly fellow, with his two locks tied up with red and a great rattlesnake's skin hanging to the back

---

[1] Thomas Lucas had a bad record for drunkenness, abusing his wife and reviling deceased magistrates. His name figures constantly in the court records.

of his head (whom they concluded to be Totoson) ran from them into the swamp.

The necessity of looking after his prisoners who now numbered over one hundred and seventy, and of procuring supplies, compelled Church to give over the pursuit. The prisoners were marched to Taunton where they "were well treated with food and drink and had a merry night of it."[1]

---

[1] Church's Entertaining History, page 38-41.

CHAPTER XVI

"YOU have made Philip ready to die, you have made him as poor and miserable as he used to make the English, for you have now killed and taken all his relations, but this bout almost broke his heart," said the Indian prisoners taken in this engagement, to Church.

That the arch enemy, who, in their eyes, more than any other individual, had been instrumental in bringing about this most devastating war, should at last experience the utmost misery and mental torture through his affections, could not fail to be a source of abundant satisfaction to the generation which saw in Philip nothing but a fiend. The old chronicles give us abundance of testimony on this point.

"Philip was forced to leave his treasures, his beloved wife and only son, to the mercy of the English. . . . Such sentence sometime passed upon Cain made him cry out that his punishment was greater than he could bear. This bloody wretch had one week or two more to live, an object of pity, but a spectacle of Divine vengeance, his own followers beginning now to plot against his life."[1]

"It must be as bitter as death to him to lose his wife and only son, for the Indians are marvelously fond and affectionate towards their children."[2]

The question as to the disposal of Philip's son and wife—whether they should be executed or sold into sla-

---

[1] Hubbard, Vol. I, page 263.
[2] Mather's Brief History, page 189.

very—was widely debated, the clergy (with a few exceptions), proving themselves, as usual, the most relentless of judges. Precedents of severity were diligently searched for in the Scriptures, and duly found. "We humbly conceive that children of notorious traitors, rebels and murderers, especially of such as have been principals and leaders in such horrid villainies, and that against a whole nation, yea, the whole Israel of God, may be involved in the guilt of their parents and may be adjudged to death, as to us seems evident by the scriptural instances of Saul, Achan, and Haman, the children of whom were cut off by the sword of justice for the transgressions of their parents, although concerning some of those children it be manifest that they were not capable of being co-actors therein,"[1] was the grim statement of Rev. Samuel Arnold.

"Philip's son makes me think of Hadad, who was a little child when his father, chief sachem of the Edomites, was killed by Joab, and had not others fled away with him I am apt to think that David would have taken a course that Hadad should never have proved a scourge to the next generation,"[2] wrote Increase Mather.

But there were some who were inclined to be merciful to Philip's son, and whose hearts were troubled, among them Eliot and Reverend Mr. Keith of Bridgewater, the latter of whom quotes II Chron. xxv, 4: "But he slew not their children, but did as was written in the law in the Book of Moses, where the Lord commanded, saying, the fathers shall not die for the children, neither shall the children

---

[1] Samuel Arnold, pastor of Marshfield, to John Cotton, September, 1676.

[2] Increase Mather to John Cotton, October 30. 1676.

die for the fathers, but every man shall die for his own
sins."

A letter of the Rev. John Cotton, written in the following March, contains the brief statement, "Philip's
boy goes now to be sold." Sent to Bermuda or the Spanish Indies the boy and his mother disappear from the
pages of history.[1]

With them vanished the race of Massasoit, the remembrance of whose friendship of forty long years, and their
own innocence, should have pleaded for them, and their
fate arouses a just indignation at the lack of manly generosity, which could stoop, in all self-righteousness, to such
an act of barbarity against this child and his mother.

Weetamoo, flying with a small remnant of her people,
took refuge in a dense swamp near Taunton early in
August, but an Indian deserter, in order to ingratiate
himself with the whites, carried the news to the people
of that place on the 6th, and offered to lead a force to the
encampment, which he declared was but a few miles distant. Twenty men immediately set out, and, surprising
the encampment, took over a score of prisoners, but
Weetamoo herself escaped. Attempting to cross the
Taunton River near its mouth, on a raft or some pieces
of broken wood, and either "tired or spent with rowing,
or starved with cold and hunger," her strength failed
and her naked body was brought to the shore by tide or
current. Some days later, "someone of Taunton finding
an Indian squaw in Metapoiset, newly dead, cut off her
head, and it happened to be Weetamoo, squaw sachem, her

---

[1] The discussion in regard to the disposal of Philip's wife and son,
and the ultimate outcome is to be found in full in Davis' Notes to Morton's New England Memorial. Appendix, page 454.

head,"[1] which, placed on a pole and paraded through Taunton, was greeted by the lamentations of the captive Indians who knew her, crying out that it was their queen's head. "A severe and proud dame she was," says Mrs. Rowlandson, "bestowing every day in dressing herself near as much time as any gentry in the land." Such treatment meted out to the dead body of a white woman would have sent Mather searching the Scriptures for a proper characterization of the barbarity and wickedness of the act.

On the 7th of August, Church again left Plymouth, and, falling in with Tatoson's band, dispersed them, and captured Sam Barrow,[2] who had participated in the massacre of the Clark family. They told him that "because of his inhumane murders and barbarities" the court allowed him no quarter. Stoically asking that he be allowed a whiff or two of tobacco it was given him, and after puffing away a moment or two he told them he was ready,

---

[1] Mather's Brief History, page 191.

Winanimoo, or Weetamoo, it is supposed was the daughter of Corbitant, sachem of Mattapoiset. In 1651 she was known as Nummumpaum, and was the wife of an Indian called Wecquequinequa, and enjoyed the title of squaw-sachem or "queen" of Pocasset. In 1656 she had become the wife of Massasoit's eldest son, Wamsutta, and called herself Tatapanum. After the death of Alexander, as he was then called, she married Quiquequanchett, and after his departure contracted a matrimonial alliance with Petownonowit, a man of considerable ability but who espoused the cause of the whites in Philip's war while she firmly allied herself to the Indian cause. She abandoned her husband and married Quinnapin, a Narragansett, cousin to Canonchet, chief of that tribe. With him she was present at the destruction of Lancaster and throughout the march which Mrs. Rowlandson accompanied as a captive, and from whose pen we have learned much of Weetamoo.—New England Register, Vol. LIV, page 261.

[2] He was said to have been Totoson's father.

whereupon one of Church's Indians dashed out his brains with a hatchet. Tatoson escaped the fate of most of his followers and fled with his son, a lad about eight years old, and an old squaw, to Agawom (in Rochester). Here, a short time after, "his son which was the last which was left of his family, fell sick" (and died), and "the wretch reflecting upon the miserable condition he had brought himself unto, his heart became as a stone and he died. The old squaw flung a few leaves and bushes over him and came into Sandwich," where she also died a few days after. Philip's hiding places around Assowomset Pond had now become untenable. Numerous bodies of mounted troops and friendly Indians guarded the fords and trails toward the north and scoured the country in all directions, and Philip, hunted for everywhere, fled southward in the hope, it is said, of reaching the Narragansett country. Church, who had left Plymouth on the 9th, was once again in pursuit, but lost the trail, and at fault as to Philip's whereabouts, after beating the woods around Pocasset, finally ferried his men across the east arm of Narragansett Bay into Rhode Island on the 11th. Leaving them encamped near the landing place, he took horse to Major Sanford's house,[1] some eight miles away, to see his wife, "who no sooner saw him than she fainted with surprise," and by the time she had revived, they espied two horsemen (Major Sanford[2] and Captain

---

[1] Major Sanford lived about half a mile south of the present Portsmouth line, in what is now Middletown, then Newport.

[2] Major Peleg Sanford was born at Newport, R. I., May 10, 1639. He was appointed captain of a troop of horse July 24, 1667, and became major in 1679 and later lieutenant-colonel. He was deputy to the General Court two years and for eight years assistant. He was

Goulding) riding rapidly up the road. They called out to him, "What would he give to hear some news of Philip?" They had ridden hard in the hope of overtaking him, for a Wampanoag had come down from Philip's camp to Sand's Point where, by signals and shouting, he attracted the attention of the English who rowed over and took him off. He told them that a short time previously Philip had killed his brother for giving advice that displeased him, and he had fled in fear of meeting the same fate.

Riding immediately to the camp where the Wampanoag had been taken they found him willing to guide them to Philip's hiding place. The whole force, marching with great rapidity, crossed the water at Bristol Ferry (then called Tripp's Ferry) which was at that point half a mile wide, and arrived shortly after midnight at their destination, a little upland in the north end of a miry swamp at the foot of Mount Hope. Church gave Captain Goulding[1] command of a small force, with orders, as soon as it was daybreak, to beat up Philip's hiding place and drive him into flight, and bade him pursue, shouting, in order that the Indians who fled silently might

---

general treasurer from 1678 to 1681, and Governor from 1680 to 1683. In 1687 he was member of the council of Sir Edmond Andros. He died in 1701 and his will was proved September 1st of that year. See Austin's Genealogical Dictionary of Rhode Island, page 171.

[1] Captain Roger Goulding was of Newport, R. I. It was he that came with his vessel to the rescue of Captain Church at Punkatees Neck early in the war. Plymouth colony granted him one hundred acres of land on the north side of Saconet as a reward for his helpfulness in the transportation of the military forces across the water. In 1685 he was deputy to the court, and from 1685 to 1691, with the exception of one year, he was "Major for the Island." He died before 1702. See Austin's Genealogical Dictionary of Rhode Island, page 84.

be known as enemies. Captain Williams[1] of Scituate was stationed on one side of the swamp, a soldier and an Indian being placed behind the trees at short intervals so as to cover the trails and paths leading out, with orders to fire at anyone that should come silently through the swamp. Church and Major Sanford then spread the remaining force on the other side and took their stand together. "I have so placed them it is scarce possible Philip should escape them," said Church to his companion. The same moment a shot whistled over their heads, then the noise of a gun towards Philip's camp followed immediately by the sound of a volley.

Goulding and his men, crawling along on their bellies, had advanced cautiously in the gray of the morning, and were close upon the sleeping camp when the captain came suddenly upon an Indian who appeared to be looking full at him. He fired immediately and the camp awoke to life in wild confusion.

Philip, seizing his pouch, gun and powderhorn, plunged at once into the swamp, clad in his small-breeches and moccasins, and running along one of the paths came directly upon Caleb Cook[2] and an Indian named Alderman (not the traitor, as has so often picturesquely been declared), but a subject of Awashonks. Cook's gun hung fire, for the morning air was heavy with mist, but the Indian sent one bullet through the heart and another two inches above it, "where Joab thrust his darts into rebellious Absolom," and Philip fell upon his face in the mud.

---

[1] Captain John Williams was of Scituate in 1643. He served in Philip's war in command of a company. He died June 22, 1694, aged seventy. He left no family.—Savage.

[2] II Mass. Hist. Soc. Coll., Vol. IV, page 63.

The greater part of the Indians escaped, for, perceiving that they were waylaid on the west side of the swamp they tacked short about. One of the enemy who seemed to be a great, surly fellow, shouted with a loud voice and often called out "Iootash, Iootash." In answer to Church's inquiry as to who it was that called out so, Peter (the Saconet) said that it was old Annawon, Philip's great captain, calling on his soldiers to stand to it and fight stoutly. The Indian whose shot had laid the sachem dead in the mire rushed to Church with the news, and when the whole force assembled Church informed them of Philip's fate. They greeted the news with cheers, and the friendly Indians, grasping the body by the leggings and small of the breeches, drew it out of the mud to the upland. "A doleful great naked dirty beast he looked like," says Church, "and for as much as he had caused many English to lie unburied and rot above ground, not one of his bones shall be buried." An Indian executioner, first addressing the dead Philip to the effect that he had been a very great man and made many a man afraid of him, beheaded and quartered the body in the manner of one executed according to the laws of England, for high treason.[1] Five of his men had fallen with him.

The troops, returning to Plymouth, brought the good tidings that the arch enemy was dead, and received each his four shillings sixpence.

Philip's dismembered body had been hung in quarters

---

[1] This account of Philip's surprise and death is taken mainly from Church's narrative.—Entertaining History, pages 42 to 45. The event was made known to the Governor and Council of Connecticut by a letter from Mr. Wm. Jones of New Haven. Connecticut Colony Records (Journal of the Council of War), Vol. II, page 471.

R

upon four trees, but his head, carried through the streets
of Plymouth on the 17th of August, was set upon a pole
where it remained for nearly a quarter of a century, and
about the year 1700, Dr. Mather, upon an occasion, "took
off the jaw from the exposed skull of that blasphemous
leviathan," while a hand, given to the Indian, Alderman,
and preserved in rum, was shown through the settlements
and won for its possessor many a penny. "He, like as
Agog, was hewn to pieces before the Lord. So let all
thine enemies perish, O Lord,"

His history and biography were written by contemporary enemies who regarded him as a Caananite and themselves as the elect of God. They were manifestly incapable of weighing testimony under such circumstances,
nor were they, individually, men from whom cool consideration or an impartial conclusion could be expected.
The records and the voluminous correspondence of the
time shed abundant light upon the events that led up to
the Indian war and those that attended it, and the reader
to-day, far removed from the narrow theological and racial standpoint of the contemporary writers, can lend
himself to fairer judgment.

Numerous legends, as little deserving of credence as
tales of Philip's cruelty and cowardice, abound; but much
has come to light of late years from which we can arrive
at some approximation as to his real character. Pride
and resentment against the English, and a sullen mis-
trust of their intentions, must have been as fire in his
breast under the nagging tyranny and the proclaimed
policy of stamping out the independence of the tribes,
and the systematic subversion of his authority by their
interference with every tradition and usage of Indian

THE PLACE OF PHILIP'S DEATH

The monument is placed on the firm land bordering the swamp, but a few rods distant from the spot where he fell.

life. No man with self-respect could defy the sentiment
of his own people in such circumstances. As a statesman
he had abilities of no small order. A man mean, cowardly
and of a weak and treacherous character could never
have won the sympathies of those tribes with whom his
own people had waged feuds of many generations, and,
until near the close of the war when despair seized them,
his influence remained strong and respected among the
chiefs, and particularly among the Narragansetts.

The weight of evidence is against the idea of a general
conspiracy, but Philip undoubtedly negotiated with many
of the tribes when it became evident that the conflict
could not be averted. As chief of the Wampanoags and
an independent sachem, Philip, if he deemed war with
the whites the only possible salvation for his race and
people, was fully justified in waging it and forming such
alliances as should insure its success.

As a warrior and a leader in battle he was probably
inferior to Canonchet and several other leaders. His abilities were rather those of an organizer and director. In
farsightedness, prudence and tenacity he was undoubtedly
superior to all, save possibly Pessacus. Had he been
able to win over all the tribes and hold his young men
in check until the plan of a simultaneous attack on the
outlying settlements could have been arranged, the war
would have assumed a far more formidable and dangerous
aspect.

The accusations of cowardice frequently made against
him are backed by no proof save the indefinite statement
that he was seldom recognized in the various conflicts.
Of cruelty no specific case has ever been cited, while it
is known that several families owed their lives to his

friendship, and while Mrs. Rowlandson wrote bitterly of the Indians in general she mentions Philip not unkindly.

That he was abandoned by so many of his tribe at the last and that there were not found wanting traitors among his own people, does not prove that he was held in contempt or hatred by them, as has often been stated, but that human nature is much the same among all races; and the death agonies of a lost cause breeds traitors and informers anxious to save their own lives and build their fortunes on the ruin of their former comrades. Neither the hero that sentimentalists, nor the fiend that Mather and Hubbard have painted for us, he was, from the Indian standpoint, a patriot. He fought uncompromisingly to the end against a fate that was certain and against a foe, which, representing a higher order of civilization than his own had attained, deserved to be victorious. The defeat of his cause and the doom of his people when it came in touch with European civilization was certain, whether by the quicker means of war or the slower process of decay. The circumstances that led up to the war and its conduct in many particulars were deplorable and were undoubtedly brought on more by the aggressions and petty tyrannies of the English than through any premeditated aggression of the Indians. At the same time it should not be forgotten that the point of view, social, economical and political, of the two races were so completely at variance that a conflict was almost inevitable, and that the colonists, harsh and repellant as their measure undoubtedly was, were more to be excused than their descendants. It was reserved for Andrew Jackson, President of the United States, to set an example of gross breach of faith and cynical violation of treaty rights be-

yond anything that can be urged against the New Englanders of Philip's time. Four days after Philip's death,
Quinnapin, the Narragansett, who had married Weetamoo after her last husband's apostacy of the Indian
cause, was captured, and, being taken to Newport, was
tried on the 24th and was shot the next day in company
with his brother.

Though resistance had ceased and the disbandment of
the forces was already begun, there were other remnants
and chiefs to be hunted down, and none so competent as
Church with his scouts and Indians to do it. A few days'
rest after the destruction of Philip, and Church was again
in the field in pursuit of Annawon, Philip's chief captain,
who had escaped from the Mount Hope swamp and was
reported to be near Rehoboth. Marching along the shore
Church's notice was attracted by some Indians paddling
a canoe from Prudence Island toward the promontory on
which the town of Bristol now stands. Following them
to their destination he captured them that night, and
learned that Annawon was encamped in the midst of
Squannakonk swamp a few miles north of Mattapoiset.

Church, with a few men, and an Indian who had requested liberty to go out and fetch his father, who, he
said, was about four miles away in the swamp with a
young squaw, set out at daybreak (August 28th). On
reaching the swamp the Indian was sent ahead, while the
remainder of the party hid themselves on either side of
the path. "Presently they saw an old man coming up
with a gun on his shoulder and a young woman following in his track. They let them come between them and
then started up and laid hold upon them both." The
young woman told Church that she belonged to Anna-

won's company, which numbered between fifty and sixty, and the old man, confessing the same, told Church that if he started presently and traveled stoutly he might reach Annawon's camp by sunset. It was just sunset when they at last saw the gleam of camp fires among the trees. The Wampanoags had built their fires at the bottom of a steep and rocky ledge,[1] and the pots and kettles were boiling and meat was roasting on the spits, while their guns, resting against a pole supported by forked sticks, were protected from the weather by a mat.

Church watched them from the top of the ledge, in doubt as to the course to be followed. He asked his captives if they could not get at the camp from the other side, but they answered, no; they had been warned to come over the rock, for anyone entering the camp from the other side would be shot. Finally, sending the old man and the girl down the rock to cover the noise of his own approach, he followed closely. The ruse succeeded and Church, stepping over Annawon's son who lay crouched upon the ground, secured the guns. The young Annawon, discovering him, whipped his blanket over his head and shrunk up in a heap, while the old captain, Annawon, started up and cried welcome. There was no resistance; Annawon, after an ejaculation of surprise and despair, asked them to share his food.

During the night, Church's men, worn out with fatigue,

---

[1] Annawon's Rock is located in the town of Rehoboth at the head of the great Squannakonk Swamp. It lies only a few rods south of the Providence and Taunton turnpike at a point about six miles from Taunton. The turnpike crosses the ledge of which this rock forms a part, and through which a cut has been blasted out to make a passage for the electric road. It may easily be reached by trolley from Taunton and Providence.

fell asleep, but the Indians made no attempt to escape. It was full moon and by its light Church watched Annawon pace moodily back and forth. Finally the old chief disappeared in the darkness of the swamp, but returned and, falling on his knees, offered Philip's royal belts of wampum, saying, "You have killed Philip and captured his country, for I believe that I and my company are the last that war against the English, so I suppose the war is ended by your means; these things belong to you."

Throughout the night they conversed in a friendly way, Annawon relating "what mighty success he had had formerly in wars against many nations when he served under Philip's father," and Church promised him his life.

On bringing his prisoners into Plymouth, Church was again requested to take the field for the purpose of effecting the capture of a well-known chief, Tuspaquin,[1] the "Black Sachem," Philip's brother-in-law, who was reported to be in hiding near by.

The directions given were erroneous, but Church, acting on information furnished by his own spies, and the reports that a large body of Indians were near Lippican doing great damage to the English in killing their cattle, horses and swine, searched them out and finding them "sitting round their fire in the thick brush," crept quietly upon and seized them all. Tuspaquin's wife and children were among the captives, some of whom told him that the sachem had gone down to Pocasset with a party to kill horses. Church said "he would not have him slain for there was a war broke out in the eastern part

---

[1] Tuspaquin was the sachem of Assowompset, and was at the head of the party who in the spring of 1676 so greatly annoyed the towns of Plymouth colony.

of the country and he would have him saved to go with them to fight the eastern Indians."

"The captain's leisure would not serve him to wait until they came in (though the Indians said they might come that night), therefore he thought upon this project: to leave two old squaws upon the place with victuals, and bid them offer Tuspaquin his own life as well as his family's if he would submit himself and bring in the two others with him and they should be his soldiers.[1]

We will let Hubbard narrate the event and the pretext for the breach of faith that followed. "Within a day or two after, the said Tuspaquin, upon the hopes of being made a captain under Church, came after some of the company and submitted himself in the captain's absence (Church had gone to Boston), and was sent to Plymouth; but upon trial (which was the condition on which his being promised a captain's place under Captain Church did depend) he was found penetrable by the English guns, for he fell down at the first shot, and thereby received the just reward for his wickedness." [2]

No wonder that Church, on his return, heard with "great grief" and indignation that both Annawon and Tuspaquin, "which were the last of Philip's friends," had been condemned by the court at Plymouth, and had been executed. He had pledged his word for their lives, and his authority to do so was not denied.

---

[1] Church's Entertaining History, page 52 and 53.
[2] Hubbard, Vol. I, page 275.

CHAPTER XVII

T HE drift of the war into the Wampanoag and Narragansett country, and the constant activity of the eastern Indians in northeastern Massachusetts and along the New Hampshire and Maine coasts, had drawn away the troops from the Connecticut Valley and left an opportunity for the escape of many of the Indians toward the west. All through July and August straggling bands, remnants of the Nipmuck and valley tribes, were making off in that direction seeking a refuge along the lower Hudson. Two hundred had been seen near Westfield on July 19th, and the request of the Rev. John Russell[1] to the Connecticut Council for troops testified to the growing alarm of the settlers, who feared hostilities might again break out in the valley and their crops be again destroyed.

After his successful campaign along the western shore of Narragansett Bay, Major Talcott had reorganized his force, and on the 18th of July again started out from New London over the same route, swinging to east around the head of the Bay. He searched the country around Taunton where Major Bradford and a large force had for some time lain more or less inactive, and then in obedience to orders marched north toward Quabaug

---

[1] Letter of Rev. John Russell to Connecticut Council of War. Connecticut Colony Records (Journal of the Council of War), Vol. II, page 464.

where he destroyed a considerable amount of corn stored in pits. Striking the trail of a large body of Indians making for the west, he followed toward the Connecticut.

On the day before Philip's death, August 11th, these Indians, over two hundred and fifty in number, crossed the Connecticut at Chicopee on rafts and passed Westfield the next day. A small body of settlers attempted to oppose them, but were driven off and the Indians continued their march, but Major Talcott, following fast in pursuit, finally overtook them August 15th, as they lay encamped on the bank of the Housatonic River within the limits of the present town of Great Barrington.[1] It was evening when he saw their camp fires blazing among the trees, and in the gathering darkness he determined to divide his force and to surround the whole party and attack them while they slept; but while Talcott and the troopers with him were making their way along the bank they came unexpectedly upon an Indian who had gone down to the river to fish. Lifting his head he looked into the faces of the English closing in upon him, and springing to his feet he shouted a warning to the camp that the English were upon them. One of Talcott's troopers immediately fired and killed him as he stood; the other division, hearing the shot and seeing the Indians leap up to fly, fired into them. Thirty-five of the Indians were killed, among them the sachem of the Quabaugs, and twenty were captured, but the meshes of the

---

[1] The Indian encampment was upon the western bank of the Housatonic River near the central bridge and within a quarter of a mile of the business center of Great Barrington. The spot is marked by a monument.

net were loose and the remainder, to the number of nearly two hundred, escaped to the Hudson.[1]

Many of the fugitives, though at first set upon by the Mohawks, were afterwards received and incorporated with them. Only one of Talcott's force, a Mohegan Indian, was killed in the conflict. Talcott followed the Indians no further, as he lacked supplies, but turned homeward.

While Talcott was following the scattered remnants of the valley tribes to the west, Captain Swaine, in accordance with orders from the Council of Massachusetts, collected a force from among the garrisons, and the settlers of Hadley, Hatfield and Northampton, marched up the valley to Deerfield and Northfield, and destroyed the growing corn.

In the north and east the conflict continued to flame well into the following year, but throughout the country where Philip's war had been waged, fighting had ceased. A few half-famished and hopeless vagrants, fearful of punishment, continued to roam the woods, and bands of friendly Indians continued to hunt them down throughout the year. As late as December, a band of sixty were run down and captured near Rehoboth, mainly through the efforts of Peter Ephraim, a friendly Natick,[2] and the punishments were continued well into the next year.

The Indians who had fled from New England to New York, including several chiefs, among them several chiefs of the Springfield Indians, and several Nonotuck and Pocumtuck chiefs, were the subjects of considerable

---

[1] Trumbull's History of Connecticut, New Edition, Vol. I, pages 292, 293. The information is from the manuscripts of Rev. Thomas Ruggles.

[2] Hubbard, Vol. I, page 285.

negotiations[1] between Andros and the Connecticut and Massachusetts authorities, who requested Andros to either send a force against those who were still at liberty or to allow them to do so, and they urged him to turn over to them for punishment those who had taken refuge in that colony and were in his hands. Andros was not overfond of the New Englanders, and little inclined to conceal his opinions, regarding them as constant and impertinent interferers in the affairs of his province. He did not approve of a New England expedition coming into New York in pursuit of the fugitives, as the Connecticut authorities desired. He had secured them, he wrote, but to all requests that they be surrendered he turned a deaf ear.

He may have thought that punishment enough had been inflicted. He certainly felt that his services in persuading the Mohawks to adopt a threatening attitude toward the New England Indians had received little recognition. A rough, choleric but honest soldier, his character has been persistently misrepresented by the majority of New England historians. His was a temperament certain to strike sparks when rubbed against the New Englander. In fact their mutual disposition, obstinate, recriminative and self-centered, was too near akin for cordial understanding or co-operation.

Of the remainder of the Nipmucks, their crops destroyed, their country overrun by the English and threatened by the Mohawks, many sought shelter among the Pennacooks and the Abenakis.

In July, Squando and Wannalancet had made a treaty

---

[1] Connecticut Colony Records, Vol. II, pages 469, 478, etc.

of friendship with the English and in the following month, as the other eastern Indians continued aggressive, came to Major Walderne[1] at Dover, to show the English that they had not re-engaged in hostilities.

Many of the Nipmucks, who considered it an admirable opportunity to accept, under the countenance of the other Indians, the terms of the proclamation made by the General Court in May, came with them, including Muttaump and Sagamore Sam, who hoped that in the company of those who were friends of the English, they might be overlooked or mercy extended. Vain hope, for the authorities knew of their presence, and Hathorne, Walderne and Captain Frost[2] of Kittery, had mutually agreed to seize all that "were met about Major Walderne's dwelling."

The details of what followed are obscure; the contemporary historians tersely describe the plan followed as a "contrivement." At any rate it succeeded and all the Indians were disarmed and seized on the 6th of September. The Rev. Jeremy Belknap[3] furnishes considerable detail as from eyewitnesses, to the effect that the Indians were induced to join in a sham fight, and, after considerable maneuvering, led to deliver the first fire, whereupon, their guns being empty, they were surrounded and disarmed.

---

[1] Major Walderne's report of the matter sheds little light on the details.—Massachusetts Archives, Vol. XXX, page 218.

[2] Charles Frost, born in Tiverton, England, came with his father, Nicholas, about 1637 and settled in Kittery. He was representative, captain and major, and chosen a counselor at the first election under the new charter. He was killed by Indians in ambush as he was going home from public worship on Sunday, July 4, 1697.

[3] Rev. Jeremy Belknap's History of New Hampshire, Vol. I, page 142.

The strategem adopted for the capture of these people was applauded by the colonists, but among the Indians, even by those friendly disposed, it was considered as a breach of faith and was not forgotten. Thirteen years later and Walderne paid the debt of vengeance for this and other acts as soldier and trader, and as they slashed his face and breast with their knives and weighed his severed hands in the scales as he had been wont to do in buying their beaver skins they told the dying man that thus they crossed out their old accounts.

A few days later Monaco and Old Jethro were captured, by what means we know not, only that "that abominable Peter Jethro betrayed his own father and other Indians of his special acquaintance, unto death."[1] "The vile and the wicked were separated from the rest," and, two hundred in number, were sent down to Boston where the General Court turned them over to the Council, declaring it to be "their sense that those who had killed Englishmen should be put to death, and not transported." On the 26th of September, Hubbard saw Monoco "with a few more Bragadozios like himself, Sagamore Sam, Old Jethro and the sagamore of Quabaug (Muttaump), going through Boston streets toward the gallows," with halters about their necks with which they were hanged "at the town's end." And with them,[2] to the death, in stern justice, went Samuel and Daniel Goble of Lancaster, condemned for the wanton murder of Indian women and children.[3]

As the war drew to a close, orders were given the con-

---

[1] Mather's Prevalency of Prayer, page 257.
[2] Judge Sewall's Diary.
[3] Massachusetts Archives, Vol. XXX, pages 209–211, 222.

stables to seize the bodies of all Indians remaining in the colonies after July, and the treasurers of the various colonies were to dispose of them for the benefit of the respective governments. All who had been concerned in the death of a colonist or the destruction of property (and to be suspected was often held to be concerned), were summarily executed. Most of those taken captive were sold as permanent bondsmen and the receipts from this source distributed to each colony proportionately, hundreds being shipped into slavery to the Spanish West Indies, to Spain, Portugal, Bermuda and Virginia. There is record of more than five hundred being sold into slavery from Plymouth alone.[1] Rhode Island, to her credit, abstained from this cruelty, and limited their bondage within the confines of the colony for a limited term of years. Some who had surrendered under the proclamation were given lands to dwell on, while young and single persons, particularly in Connecticut, were in many cases settled in English families as apprentices.[2]

Uncas had made hay while the sun shone, and many a hostile native had been added as warrior or servant to his tribe. He had rendered far greater service than he was ever given credit for, and to stand before the court at Hartford and be told that the success of the war was with the English, and that they meant to dispose of all the captives and enjoy its results, must have been as wormwood.[3] Suspected by the whites, he had aided in the ruin of his own race, and thenceforward he and his

---

[1] Baylie's Memoirs of Plymouth.

[2] Connecticut Colony Records, Vol. II, pages 481, 482 Massachusetts Colony Records, Vol. V, page 136.

[3] Connecticut Colony Records, Vol. II, page 473.

tribe had to accept with humility and subservience the rewards which ultimately fall to those weak allies who take the part of the conquering invader against their own people. A few generations and the Mohegans had disappeared as completely as their old foes the Narragansetts.

The loss suffered by the colonies was appalling. Connecticut alone had escaped the devastation that left vast tracts in the other colonies a wilderness, but even Connecticut had to mourn a fearful list of slain soldiers. In the four colonies, Plymouth, Massachusetts Bay, Rhode Island and Connecticut, over six hundred men had perished, or one in eleven of the population able to bear arms, in addition to many women and children. Over six hundred dwellings had been destroyed, with innumerable cattle, sheep and horses, and the greater part of a year's harvest. Thirteen settlements had been completely wiped out, and a great number had been partly destroyed, and the wilderness had again closed on many a scattered farm and hamlet; but the harvest, threatened with failure in the early summer, was abundant, and the suffering was not severe. No assistance had been asked for or given by the motherland; of men there had been enough.

The war cost the four colonies heavily. The commissioners reported that Plymouth colony had been put to an expense of not less than £100,000, an immense sum if we consider the feeble resources of the colony at that time. But if the whites had suffered, the Indians had been practically exterminated; their lands had passed to the whites; a few scantily inhabited villages were all that was left of the mighty tribe of the Narragansetts. The

was left of the mighty tribe of the Narragansetts. The valley Indians had disappeared and were seen no more save for a raid by some fugitive valley Indians, sallying forth from Canada, who over a year later, September 19, 1677, fell upon the inhabitants of Hatfield while they were building a house outside the stockade, and killing several, carried away as captives to Canada some twenty-four of the English, men, women and children, including several from Deerfield, most of whom were ransomed a few months later.

Never again did the southern New England tribes menace the people of these colonies. Their submission was that of death, and the feeble remnants lay quiescent amid the forays of the French and their Indian allies in the years to come, while New England rose rapidly from her ruins.

S

APPENDIX

APPENDIX

THE war waged along the coast of Maine, although contemporary with the outbreak in the southern colonies, was not directly a part of that conflict, but by its coincidence and the engagement in it of those who participated as contestants in the struggle in the lower colonies, it has come to be known as a part of that historic event, and its story may briefly be related in connection with it.

Within a few weeks after the uprising of the Indians in the Plymouth colony, news of events had been carried to the country lying to the northeast, now known as Maine, but at that time held under a patent issued to Sir Ferdinando Gorges, and ruled by a commission appointed by the king. This sparsely settled fringe of coast differed materially from the well-governed United Colonies. In extent it reached from Exeter and Dover (now in New Hampshire) to Pemaquid, a little plantation upon John's Bay just east of the Damariscotta River. The settlements or plantations within its confines were York, Wells, Cape Porpoise, Saco, Black Point (now Scarborough), Falmouth (now Portland), Arrowsick, Damariscotta, and a few scattered hamlets, all reached by the tides and practically connected for purposes of travel by the water, though Indian trails led along the coast. The Indians inhabiting this territory were the Penobscot, Kennebec, Pequacket and Ammoscoggin, commonly included under the general title of Abenakis or Tarratines, well equipped and hardy hunters. In New Hampshire were the Pennacook Indians, professed friends of the English.

During the continuance of the war in the United Colonies the local eastern Indians maintained a hostile atti-

tude and committed many depredations from the Piscataqua to the Kennebec, and by the summer of 1676 had
been reinforced by numbers of refugee Nipmucks who,
having lost their all and despairing of mercy, cast in their
lot with their northern neighbors, and inciting them to
further carnage and pillage, prolonged hostilities in the
north long after they had ceased elsewhere.

The English settlers of the northern border included
many of the rough and lawless element always to be found
in a frontier community governed by little other than the
laws of expediency; bent on immediate gain and heed-
less of the future. The same arbitrary and insolent interference with Indian rights and customs prevailed here
as in the south. The guns which had become a necessity
were continuously being demanded on the slightest pretext and suspicion, while in matters of trade the Indians,
without doubt, were constantly cheated and imposed upon.
Even Major Walderne, magistrate and austere Puritan,
tradition declares, used to place his hand in the scale
against the beaver skins, telling the Indians it weighed
a pound, and often failed to cross off their accounts when
paid him.

Acts of violence against the natives, particularly kid-
napping and selling them into slavery at the West Indies
were not uncommon, and these outrages were tenaciously
stored in Indian memories against the day of reckoning.
No wonder that when that day arrived with its afforded
opportunity, the score was settled to the fullest extent of
Indian ingenuity. The story as it has come down to us
is one of isolated border fights, a warfare of the woods and
thickets, in which the Indians, sometimes punished and
scattered, were more often successful.

The first depredation upon the northeastern frontier
began early in September, 1675, by a raid of the Indians
on the house of Thomas Purchase[1] in Pegypscot (Bruns-

---

[1] Thomas Purchase, says Savage, "was an adventurer of good dis-
cretion and perseverance, and was principal of the Pegypscot settlement

wick), when some of his cattle were killed but no violence offered to the inmates of the house. September 12th, the isolated house of Thomas Wakeley,[1] a resident of Falmouth on the Prescumpscut River about three-fourths of a mile below the falls, was attacked, and Wakeley, his son and his daughter-in-law, with three of their children were killed, their charred bodies being found in the ruins by a relieving party the following day. One daughter, about eleven years old, was carried into captivity, but after long wandering among the tribes, even as far south as the Narragansetts, was finally restored to the English by Squando. Three days before this attack a party of Englishmen going up the north shore of Casco Bay in a sloop and two boats to gather Indian corn came upon three Indians who were beating on the door of a house, and fired upon them killing one and wounding another. The third escaped, and, while the whites were scattered heedlessly about the field at their labors, rallied his friends, and attacking the settlers, drove them to their sloop and secured two boats loaded with the corn they had gathered. These Indians were followers of Madockawando, sachem of the Penobscots, and the attack upon them was declared by the Penobscot Indians to have been without provocation. This same month an attack was made upon Oyster River (now Durham, N. H.), where two houses belonging to settlers by the name of Chesley were burned. Two men passing along the river in a canoe were killed and two others carried into captivity.

These raids were quickly followed by attacks upon Exeter and Salmon Falls, and a little later houses were destroyed at Oyster River and two men killed. Small parties of Indians now prowled the woods in every direction, burning barns and houses, killing men and cattle and goading the English to desperation.

---

on both sides of the Androscoggin near its mouth." After the plundering of his house he removed to Lynn where he died in April, 1678.

[1] Thomas Wakeley was of Hinsgham when the house lots were drawn

On the 18th of September, Captain Bonython,[1] who lived on the east bank of the Saco River, warned by a friendly Indian of the approach of Squando's people, fled with his family, his house bursting into flames behind him. Warned by the flames, Major Phillips,[2] who lived on the opposite bank, immediately warned his neighbors, who fled to his garrison house to the number of fifty, and prepared for defense.

Setting fire to the neighboring houses, the Indians closed around the garrison calling out, "You cowardly English dogs, come out and put out the fire," but although Phillips himself was wounded, the garrison held them at bay and finally repulsed their attack with considerable loss,[3] but as the people would not remain, the garrison house was soon abandoned and a short time thereafter was burned. About the same time all the dwellings at Winter Harbor, abandoned by their owners, were plundered by the Indians and then given over to the flames, and five settlers going up the Saco River were attacked and killed.

Hearing of the defenseless condition of the settlers of Saco, Captain Wincoll of Newichawonock, with a company of sixteen men, proceeded by water around the coast to their assistance. On landing at Winter Harbor they were instantly fired upon from ambush and several of the party killed. These Indians gave the alarm to a

by the settlers, September 18, 1635, and he was made freeman March 3, 1636. He removed to Falmouth in 1661.

[1] Captain John Bonython was the son of Richard, who was a very early settler of Saco. His house, which was destroyed by the Indians, was located on the east side of the Saco River, not far from the present tracks of the Boston & Maine railroad. He died before 1684.

[2] Major William Phillips was of Charlestown where he was admitted to the church September 23, 1639, and made freeman Map 13, 1640. He removed to Boston, then to Saco, where he had mills, a mansion house, and a thriving settlement about him. He was a magistrate and an officer in the militia. After the destruction of his property he returned to Boston.

[3] Letter of Major Richard Walderne. Massachusetts Archives, Vol. LXVII, pages 26, 27.

larger number in the rear, and Wincoll's party[1] was at once surrounded by one hundred and fifty well-armed warriors. Taking refuge behind a pile of shinglebolts, the English fought with such desperation that the Indians were forced to retire with considerable loss,[2] but eleven inhabitants of Saco who attempted to aid Wincoll were utterly destroyed.[3] About this time an attack was also made upon Black Point, in which seven houses were burned and a number of the inhabitants killed.

The general leader of the Indians was Squando,[4] a sagamore of Saco, whose old friendship for the whites had been changed to hatred by several acts of insolence and injustice, but particularly by an outrage perpetrated by sailors from a vessel harbored in the Saco River. Perceiving the wife of Squando, with her infant child, crossing the river in a canoe, it seemed to these men a fitting opportunity to test the general belief that the young of the savages, like those of wild animals, would instinctively swim if thrown into the water. Upsetting the canoe the occupants were cast into the flood, but the mother, diving to the bottom, recovered the child, which, however, was shortly seized with an ailment and died. Squando never forgave the act.

---

[1] Captain John Wincoll, or Wincoln, was first of Watertown, where he was freeman in 1646, but he soon removed to Kittery, for which town he was representative to the General Court at Boston in 1653, 1654, 1655. In 1665 he was at Newichawanock (South Berwick), and was made a justice by the royal commissioners. He was representative again in 1665, 1667, 1667 and the holder of other honorable offices. He was injured by a fall from his horse and died October 22, 1694.—Savage.

[2] Saco Valley Settlements and Families, page 21.

[3] Hubbard Vol. II, p. 126.

[4] Squando, a Tarrantine sachem of the Socokis, was commonly called the Sagamore of Saco. Mather calls him "a strange, enthusiastical sagamore," who saw visions, while the historian Williamson says, "his conduct exhibited at different times such traits of cruelty and compassion as rendered his character difficult to be portrayed." Hubbard speaks of him as "that enthusiastical or rather diabolical miscreant, who hath yet put on a Garbe of Religion, and orders his people to do the like; performing religious worship amongst the Indians in his way, yet is supposed to have very familiar converse with the Devil, that appears to him as an Angel of Light, in some shape or other very frequently."

About the 1st of October, a large body of Indians attacked the house of Richard Tozer[1] at Salmon Falls, about a third of a mile north of the Plaisted garrison. Fifteen persons were in the house, most of whom succeeded in escaping to the garrison through the heroic efforts of a young girl of eighteen who held the door while the rest fled by the rear. She was finally struck down by the savages, who succeeded in entering, and left for dead, but recovered, and lived many years. A small child was, however, killed, and a girl of seven, who had been unable to keep up with the fugitives, was led away into captivity but shortly afterward restored.

The next day after burning Captain Wincoll's house and barn well stocked with corn, they drew away. On the 16th day of October, however, they returned in force and again fell on the house of Richard Tozer, killing Tozer and taking his son captive.

Lieutenant Roger Plaisted,[2] who commanded the small force at the garrison, hearing the sound of the firing, sent out seven men to reconnoiter and aid the inmates of the Tozer house. They had proceeded but a short way from the garrison, however, when they fell into an ambush which the Indians had prepared in the expectation of such an attempt, and were badly cut up. The following day Plaisted with twenty men set out with an ox team to bring in the bodies, exercising no precaution against

[1] Richard Tozer was first of Boston but removed to Kittery. He had a grant of land at Newichawonock of sixty acres, above the Salmon Falls. Here he built a garrison house. The site of this is now occupied by the dwellings of Mr. Charles Collins. Hubbard says this was a third of a mile north of the Plaisted garrison.

[2] Roger Plaisted of Kittery was intrusted with civil commissions as early as 1661. He was representative to the General Court in 1663–64, and again in 1673. He was made lieutenant in 1668 and was a brave and trustworthy officer.—Savage.

His garrison house was built on land purchased in 1669 from Captain John Wincoll and in a deed is called the "Birchen Point Lot." It was located in that part of Kittery known as Newichawonock, on the east side of the Salmon Falls River and just north of Salmon Falls Brook. His neighbors, Tozer and Wincoll, lived farther up the hill to the north. See Old Kittery and her Families.

LIEUTENANT PLAISTED'S BATTLEFIELD

The view is taken from the site of his garrison house and is near the spot where he fell

His grave and that of his son are marked by the three stones in the

middle distance.

surprise. Tozer's body was recovered and the party was returning to the swamp near the garrison where the other bodies lay, when the Indians, hidden among the rocks and trees, fired upon them from an ambuscade.

Plaisted, disdaining to fly, threw away his life in a vain endeavor to fight, almost singly, against overwhelming odds. Two of his sons and a number of his men were killed at the same time, and the survivors were able to cut their way out with only the greatest difficulty. After a continuous harassing of the settlements, the Indians withdrew, near the close of November, to their winter quarters at Ossipee and Pequacket.[1]

It is said that up to this time one hundred and fifty persons, Indians and whites, had been killed or captured between the Kennebec and Piscatauqua. A projected plan to attack the enemy in their winter quarters failed through the severity of the winter and the lack of sufficient snowshoes, but the neglect of the Indians to suitably provide for their winter wants so scourged them with famine and disease that they were driven to seek for a reconciliation. Accordingly they came to Major Richard Walderne[2] at Dover, early in January, 1676,

---

[1] Ossipee is located in Carroll County on the eastern border of New Hampshire, and still bears the same name. Pequacket is now Fryeburg, Maine, on the western border of Cumberland County and nearly on the line separating that state from New Hampshire, and about twenty-three miles in a northeasterly direction from Ossipee.

[2] Major Richard Walderne was born in Alcester, County of Warwick, England, September 2, 1615. He came to this country first in 1635, remaining two years, then returned to England. He settled permanently at Cochecho, now Dover, N. H., in 1640. He was a man of great influence, many times representative to the General Court, and often speaker. He was a captain in 1672 and in 1674 was made sergeant-major of the military forces of the province. In 1680 he became major-general. He was one of the councilors under the new form of government of New Hampshire in 1680, and the following year, after the death of President John Cutts, was at the head of the Province until the arrival of the Royal Governor. He was largely engaged in trade with the Indians and was a Puritan of the most austere type, which did not prevent him, if widespread tradition is to be believed, from cheating them in trade at every opportunity. He was an indifferent commander and negotiator. His trading and garrison house stood on the north side of

and entered into an armistice, bringing in some English captives.

July 3,1676, a treaty of peace[1] was signed at Cocheco (Dover) between a committee of the whites and several sagamores, the most important of whom was Squando, sagamore of the Sacos. Among those who came in were Simon and Andrew, the Christian Indians who, in the previous May, had attacked the house of Thomas Kimbal, of Bradford, killing him and carrying his wife and five children into captivity. They had, however, previously taken several other women whom they had treated not unkindly, and hearing of the negotiations, came in with the captives. Instead of improving the opportunity and securing their friendship, the English seized and threw them with others into the prison at York,[2] from which they speedily managed to escape.

The Indians living at the east of the Kennebec River, whose chief, Madockawando,[3] had been friendly to the settlers until the wanton destruction of his corn fields and

---

the Cochecho River on the west side of what is now known as Central Avenue in Dover, a little south of Second Street, and a suitable inscription noting its site is attached to the business block occupying its place. He was killed by the Indians in a most barbarous manner, June 27, 1689.

[1] Massachusetts Archives, Vol. XXX, page 206.

[2] The prison at York was built in 1653, an addition being made some time after. The whole of the original structure still exists in an excellent state of preservation.

[3] Madockawando was chief of the Penobscot tribe. He was a great "Pow Wow, " and Hubbard says of him, in connection with Squando, sagamore of the Saco tribe, "They are said to be by them that know them, a strange kind of moralized savages. Grave and serious in their speech and carriage and not without some show of a kind of Religion, which no doubt but they have learned from the Prince of Darkness (by the help of some Paptists in those parts), that can transform himself into an Angel of Light; under that shape the better to carry on the designes of his Kingdom. " The historians of the war have all observed that the prisoners under Madockawando were remarkably well treated. After the close of Philip's war no more is heard of him until 1691 when he again appears as a warrior in King William's war then being waged. He died in 1698. A daughter of his married the Baron de St. Casteen whose residence was on the Penobscot River where the present town of Castine is located. See Book of the Indians.

the attack upon the Indians found at Casco Bay in the month of September previous, had, after that event, retired to a fort they had at Totannock, at the confluence of the Kennebec with the Sebasticook, in the present town of Winslow, where the English also had a trading house.

Captain Sylvanus Davis,[1] the agent for Messrs. Clark and Lake, traders at Arrowsick, thought it prudent to bring down from Totonnock the powder and shot with other goods stored there, at the same time sending a message to the Indians inviting them in the interest of peace, to return to their former habitations near the coast.

The messenger intrusted with Captain Davis' message delivered it in an insolent and threatening manner, telling them if they did not come in and give up their arms the English would come and kill them all. Instead of complying they began to negotiate with the tribes farther east in order to resist any interference.

In the spring of 1676, John Earthy[2] of Pemaquid, had attempted to bring about peace, but the unrestrainable animosity of the settlers made success difficult.

Another conference had been held in the early spring (1676), but the Indians felt they had been hardly dealt with. "We were driven from our corn last year, by the people about Kennebec," they said, "and many of us died. We had no powder and shot to kill venison and fowl to prevent it. If you English were our friends as you pretend you are, you would not suffer us to starve

---

[1] Captain Sylvanus Davis was of Sheepscot in 1659 and was wounded at Arrowsick at the time Captain Lake was killed. He removed to Falmouth in 1680 and had command of the fort there in the next Indian war. He was captured and carried to Canada, May 20, 1690, and after his return in 1691 entered the Council by the Charter of William and Mary. He wrote an account of the conduct of the war which is in III Mass. Hist. Soc. Coll., Vol. I, page 101. He lived in Hull during the latter part of his life and died in 1704.—Savage.

[2] John Earthy of Pemaquid kept a public house, but little can be found regarding him. He appears as a witness to the treaty with the Indians, November 13, 1676.—Savage. Williamson states that it was Abraham Shurte of Pemaquid who was the negotiator.

as we did." However, a temporary peace was patched up and a promise obtained from these Indians that their influence should be exerted with the Androscoggins to bring about peace.

Unfortunately, during the winter, the cupidity of one Laughton, the master of a vessel harboring in those parts, who held a general warrant from Major Walderne to seize any Indians to the eastward, had induced him to carry away, for the purpose of selling into slavery, some of the natives he had invited on board his ship, and this act coming to the knowledge of the Penobscots, when they visited those parts, inflamed them to wrath. John Earthy and Captain Davis, seeking to pacify them, again visited Madockawando, and, among others, Assiminasqua[1] and Mugg, sachem of the Androscoggins, whose friendship had given place to hatred, in August, 1676, and endeavored to undo the mischief. Angry and distrustful they made bitter complaints of the wrongs they had suffered.

"It is not our custom when messengers come to treat of peace to seize upon their persons, as sometimes the Mohawks do; yea, as the English have done, seizing upon fourteen Indians, our men, who went to treat with you—setting a guard over them, and taking away their guns, and demanding us to come down unto you, or else you would kill us. This was the cause of our leaving both our fort and our corn, to our great loss."

An accusation that, Hubbard says, considerably embarrassed the English, who could only reply that they would do their best to find and return those Indians who had been kidnapped, and that the Indians should not blame the Government for the acts of irresponsible individuals.

"What shall we do, " they asked, "in the winter, when our corn is gone unless we have guns and powder? Answer yes or no; shall we have them?" The commis-

---

[1] Madockawando was his adopted son.

sioners could give no direct answer. They would confer
with the Governor and Council, and the chiefs grew angry,
and as the negotiations continued there came the news
that Squando had broken the treaty of July, 1676, and
had fallen on Cleve's Neck, Falmouth, now the city of
Portland. This action commenced on the 11th of August at the house of Anthony Brackett,[1] the day preceding that of Philip's death at Mount Hope, and was continued the following day, to the utter desolation of the
place. Brackett, with his wife and five children, was
carried into captivity, and Mrs. Brackett's brother was
killed. Several other settlers near by were killed and
their houses burned.

Immediately following the destruction of Falmouth, the
war advancing eastward into the Kennebec country, the
house of William Hammond,[2] a trader not much liked
by the Indians, was attacked, August 13th, and Hammond and fourteen of its inmates slain, the only person

---

[1] Anthony Brackett is found in Falmouth in 1662. Upon the renewal
of hostilities in the summer of 1676 he was living at his home on the
west side of the Back Bay at Falmouth (now Portland), and was, with
his family, captured on the 11th of August. His brother-in-law, Nathaniel Mitton, who resisted capture, was slain. While being conveyed
to the eastward, his captors being eager to share in the plunder of Arrowsick of which they had word, Brackett and his family with a colored
servant, managed to evade their captors; repairing an old birch canoe
which they found upon the shore with a needle and thread, they escaped
across Casco Bay to Black Point where they found a vessel bound for
the Piscataqua. Brackett served during the war, and afterwards as
lieutenant and captain, and was finally killed at his home during King
William's war, September 21, 1689. The cellar hole of his house still
remains and is located on Deering Avenue, a few rods beyond the railroad crossing just north of Deering's Oaks, one of the pleasure parks of
Portland.

[2] The sight of Hammond's fort and trading house, long in dispute,
has been definitely settled by the researches of Rev. Henry O. Thayer.
See Collections of Maine Historical Society, Second Series, Vol. I, page
261. He says, "It can be rebuilt in fancy upon that northeastern curve
of Long Reach where are now grouped the village dwellings of Day's
Ferry." Day's Ferry is recorded on the map as West Woolwich and is
three miles north of the ferry connecting Woolwich with Bath. "Hammond's Head," the site of the trading house, lies directly opposite Tele-
graph Point in North Bath.

escaping being a young woman. Distrusting the Indians, who had come as if to make a visit, she hid in the corn; hearing the shrieks and blows and divining their cause, she fled across country some ten miles, to Sheepscot, and gave the alarm.

The Indians then marched up the river and captured Francis Card[1] and his family, and passing down the Kennebec, crossed over to Arrowsick Island.

The cruelties attendant upon this attack are attributed to Simon, who had been lodged in the prison at York and had escaped. This attack resulted in the death and capture of over thirty of the English. The remainder of the inhabitants fled from the mainland to James Andrews, now Cushing Island in the Bay. Among them George Felt,[2] whose residence was at Mussel Cove two miles eastward from the neck.

Arrowsick Island[3] is a large tract of land some four

---

[1] See Francis Card's statement relative to the capture of Hammond's and Arrowsick, and the subsequent movements of the Indians. Hubbard, 1865 Edition, Vol. II, page 202. There is also a copy in Vol. LXIX of the Massachusetts Archives.

[2] George Felt was from Charlestown and in 1660 was a dweller at Casco Bay having in 1670 a residence at Mussel Cove. He was the owner of Lower Clapboard Island, the Brothers and Little Chebeague Islands in the Bay. Hubbard in his Indian Wars, says, "He had been more active than any man in those parts against the Indians." He was killed by them in the summer of 1676 on Peak's Island.—Felt Genealogy. History of Peak's Island.

[3] The long-lost site of the busy and populous trading house of Clark and Lake has been discovered by the Rev. Henry O. Thayer, and treated of in a paper read by him before the Maine Historical Society, and published in the first volume of the second series of their collections. This site may be reached by a drive of but little more than two miles from Woolwich, opposite Bath, and lies but a short distance to the north of Mill Island, on the west shore of the Back River. Traces of its buildings are still distinct. Thayer thus describes its discovery: "If Hubbard was correct the fortified post should have been within a mile of Mill Island. Search discloses it five-eighths of a mile from the present mill dam, a field by a cove, bearing notable traces of ancient occupation. Here relics have been gathered, implements found, bones exhumed, flagstones of old pathways uncovered. Here are cellars close by the water, a famed well of unknown antiquity. This place, made mysterious by curious relics and proof of early settlement, and long an enigma to the writer because not adjustable to the acquired history of the island,

SITE OF CLARK AND LAKE'S GARRISON AND TRADING POST

Arrowsick Island. Maine. The old cellars are marked by a growth of bushes along the water's edge.

miles in length, lying in the Kennebec River, between the main channel and the Back River, so called, its northern extremity being directly opposite the city of Bath. Upon it was the fortified trading house of Clark and Lake, two merchants of Boston. The Indians concealed themselves under the walls of the fort and behind a great rock near by. Early in the morning of August 14th, when, for some reason, the sentinel left his post, the gate of the fort being open, they rushed in and seized or killed the garrison. Captain Sylvanus Davis, who was in the fort, and Captain Lake,[1] with two others, secured a canoe at the water's edge in which they embarked, hoping to reach a neighboring island and escape, but they were quickly followed by four Indians in a canoe, who fired upon them just as they touched the rocky shore of Mill Island. Davis, badly wounded, managed to conceal himself in the crevices of the rocks and was overlooked by the pursuers. Lake was killed by a musket-shot while the two others eluded their pursuers and escaped unhurt. Before their departure the Indians destroyed everything of value in the neighborhood, including a mill and a number of buildings outside the fortification. A large amount of plunder was secured and the news of their success quickly spread abroad.

The number of persons killed or taken into captivity here and at Hammond's was fifty-three. About a dozen persons got away from Arrowsick in safety.

From Arrowsick the Indians proceeded to Sheepscot

---

is at the so-called Spring Cove, on the northeastern border. When found and its certified story told, it harmonized all parts of evidence. and completed the proof. Step by step, the lines of history followed, led hither to the mansion house of Clark   and Lake."

[1] Captain Thomas Lake came from London to New Haven, where he married, before 1650, the daughter of Deputy Governor Goodyear. He removed to Boston and was an eminent merchant there. In 1654 he purchased half of Arrowsick Island in the Kennebec River, and for many years had a trading house there with large transactions with the Indians. His body found by the expedition under Major Walderne in February following in a perfect state of preservation, was removed to Boston and buried in the Copp's Hill Burying Ground.

T

and Pemaquid, while a part of the force went over to
Jewell's Island, which was the refuge of a large number
of the inhabitants from the mainland and considered a
place of safety owing to its distance from the shore. The
sudden invasion of this supposed stronghold by the enemy,
caused great consternation among the refugees, who, however, though inadequately armed and not provided with
a suitable shelter, managed to beat them off.

Shortly after this on September 3d, a party of men
having gone upon Munjoy's Island,[1] to obtain sheep
which were required by their distressed families for food
(though forbidden to adventure themselves, by their commander), were set upon by a party of Indians in ambush,
driven into the ruins of an old stone house[2] and there
destroyed to a man, among them George Felt, "much
lamented," says Hubbard, "who had been more active
than any man in those parts against the Indians, but at
the last he lost his own life among them, in this too desperate an adventure."

In this month of September, the Pennacook and Wam-
esit Indians came in to Major Walderne at Dover, to the
number of four hundred, and with them many of the
southern refugees, and that "contrivement" or sham
fight strategem followed which has been related in the
previous chapter.[3]

The authorities regarded the entertainment, of the southern Indians by the Pennacooks and other tribes as a violation of the terms of the treaty, but the Indians themselves

---

[1] Munjoy's Island is now known as Peak's Island. It contains seven
hundred and twenty acres and lies about three miles off Portland in Casco
Bay. A narrow channel separates it from Cushing's Island.

[2] The stone house upon Munjoy's Island (now Peak's) was located at
its southwest point, about four rods northeast of the Brackett family
cemetery fence as it now exists. It was but a few rods from the shore
of the channel separating Munjoy's from James Andrews' Island, upon
the northern end of which the refugees from Falmouth first congregated.
It was built by George Munjoy and was occupied for several years by
John Palmer and his family until they were driven off by the Indians
in 1675.—History of Peak's Island.

[3] An account of what followed has been given on page 286.

were influenced by no other motive than hospitality, and believed the treaty embraced all who should accept its terms.

September 8th the authorities at Boston sent into the eastern country one hundred and thirty soldiers and forty Natick
Indians, under Captains Sill, Hathorne[1] and Hunting,[2]
which force was to be augmented by such troops as could be
raised in the province. They marched by land from Dover
to Black Point, thence went by vessel as far east as Casco
without discovering the enemy, although the work of destruction was going on all about them,[3] and they were compelled to retrace their steps without accomplishing anything.
A week later, October 12th, the Indians, one hundred strong,
under the leadership of Mugg,[4] attacked Jocelyn's[5] garrison

---

[1] Captain William Hathorne was born in Salem, April 1, 1645. In
the Narragansett campaign he was lieutenant under Captain Joseph
Gardiner and when that officer fell at the Swamp fight, succeeded to
the command. He died before 1679.—Savage.

[2] Captain Samuel Hunting, born July 22, 1640, was first of Chelmsford and later of Charlestown. He served during the war "with great
reputation as captain of the praying Indians who took up arms in our
cause against their countrymen." He and his men were of much service at the Sudbury fight and their conduct there did much to overcome
the popular prejudice against the friendly Indians as soldiers. He was
killed by the accidental discharge of his gun, August 19, 1701.—Savage.
Bodge, page 289.

[3] During the period covered by this expedition the Indians several
times assaulted Wells and Cape Neddeck, killing a number of settlers
and burning their dwellings. These places were directly on the line of
march of the expedition.

[4] Mugg, Mogg, Mogg Heigon, deeded in 1664 a tract of land lying
between the Kennebunk and Saco Rivers to Major William Phillips. In
the deed of conveyance he describes himself as "Mogg Heigon of Saco
River in New England, sunn and heyer of Walter Heigon sagamore of
sayd river." He was the subject of Whittier's poem, "Mogg Megone."
There appears to be some dispute as to his position. Drake (Book of
the Indians) says he was chief of the Androscoggins. Hubbard says,
"He was the principal minister of Madockawando." Willis calls him
"Prime Minister of the Penobscot sachem." He was alternately friend
or foe of the English settlers along the coast, and was killed at Black
Point (Scarborough), May 13, 1677, during an attack upon the garrison
there. See paper of Horatio Hight, read before the Maine Historical
Society, May 31, 1889, and published in the fifth volume of the second
series of their collections, page 345. Another Mogg Heigon was killed
with the Jesuit father, Rasle, by the English at Norigwok, August, 1724.

[5] Captain Henry Jocelyn, son of Sir Thomas of County Kent, came

at Black Point, but while Jocelyn, who was well acquainted with the savage leader, went forward to parley with them, the entire garrison, with such of the inhabitants as were within the fort, decamped by water, leaving Captain Jocelyn and his family at the mercy of the Indians. They were, however, kindly treated and soon liberated.

The winter of 1676-77 set in very early, and the authorities, supposing that the Indians were collecting at their fort at Ossipee, thought it best to attempt their capture. Accordingly Captains Hathorne and Sill were directed to march to that point. They set out from Newichawonock on the 1st of November; the snow was deep and the streams, not yet frozen, were crossed with difficulty. No Indians were found at Ossipee nor in the adjoining region, and the expedition returned having accomplished nothing but the destruction of the fort.

Immediately after the capture of Black Point, the English at Piscataqua had sent a small expedition under a young Mr. Fryer to Richmond Island to bring away whatever goods had escaped destruction. As they were loading their vessel, some being on shore and some aboard, they were surprised by the Indians and, unable to sail on account of the wind, and the cable being cut so that the vessel drifted ashore they were compelled after a short resistance, in which Fryer was wounded, to surrender. They were, however, kindly treated and allowed to send two of their number to Piscataqua to arrange for the ransom of the rest.

Unfortunately the party who bore the ransom, arriving a few days before the date set, fell in with another party of Indians who seized the goods and, through a mistake,

to Scarborough, probably in 1634, and entered into the service of Sir Ferdinando Gorges. He was one of the most active and influential men in the Province of Maine. After the loss of his garrison (which he was temporarily commanding in the absence of Captain Joshua Scottow), and his short captivity, he removed to Pemaquid where he was a justice and much engaged in public affairs, and where he died in the latter part of 1682 or early in h e following year. See New England Register, Vol. II, page 204; Vol. XI, page 31.

THE OLD JAIL AT YORK. BUILT 1653

killed one of the English, but on learning what the goods were for dismissed the two surviving English in safety.

On the 1st of November, Mugg came to Piscataqua, bringing in Fryer, who shortly afterwards died of his wounds. Mugg declared that the Indians were desirous of peace, and that the attack on the party bearing the ransom was a mistake committed by a party of Indians not acquainted with their mission.

Major-General Dennison, who was at Piscatauqua, alleging that he had not the power to make a treaty, immediately seized Mugg who was supposed to represent both the Androscoggin and the Penobscot Indians, and sent him to Boston, where, on the 6th of November, a treaty was signed between the Governor and Council on the one hand and Mugg, presumably acting for Madock-awando and probably for the Androscoggins, on the other.[1]

On the 21st, two vessels sailed for the Penobscot for the purpose of conveying back the captives released by the terms of the treaty, together with such arms and goods as were to be given in ransom. Madockawando was found ready to confirm the action of his subordinate, but he had with him only two prisoners.

Mugg, held as a hostage for the fulfillment of the terms agreed upon, learning that no captives, beyond the two held by his chief, were near by, offered to attempt a journey into the wilderness for the purpose of securing a number of captives that would probably be found there. The commander of the expedition agreed to wait for his return at the end of four days, that being the limit of the time required for the undertaking, and if at its ex-piration he had not appeared it should be assumed that he had either been killed by the natives or detained by them. The vessels awaited his appearance for a week beyond the allotted time, and then, fearing that wintry

---

[1] Hubbard, Vol. II, page 189. Also Drake's Book of the Indians, Book I.

conditions would prevent their return to Boston, sailed without him, stopping at Pemaquid where they found Thomas Cobbett,[1] the son of the Rev. Thomas Cobbett of Ipswich, who had long been mourned by his friends, and with this small number of captives returned to Boston. Mugg was not again seen by the English for some time, but it is reported that he greatly boasted of the trick by which he had outwitted the English and repaid them in their own coin.

Early in February, 1677, a force raised by the Council at Boston, consisting of two hundred men of whom sixty were Natick Indians, under the command of Major Walderne,[2] was sent by water to the eastward in the expectation that a systematic and organized attempt looking to the reduction of the enemy would meet with successful accomplishment. The expedition reached Arrowsick (after a stop or two, at one of which, near Falmouth, they had a skirmish with the sagamore, Squando, about the 21st. The country was clothed in its winter aspect and the ice in the bays and streams frustrated the major's plans. He decided, however, to leave a party at the lower end of Arrowsick to establish a garrison while he pushed on to Pemaquid,[3] having learned from some Indians at

---

[1] For an account of Thomas Cobbett's release from captivity see "A Narrative of New England's Deliverances," by his father, Rev. Thomas Cobbett of Ipswich, to be found in the New England Register, Vol. VII, page 215. Also Hubbard, Vol. II, pages 193–198.

[2] Hubbard & Williamson's History of Maine.

[3] Pemaquid is historically one of the most interesting localities of the Maine coast. It is the most easterly point touched by Philip's war. Its soil was the first on the mainland of New England to be pressed by English feet. In 1605 Captain George Weymouth, in his ship *Arch-angel,* landed here and took back with him to England five of the native Indians, one of whom, Squanto, was to play an important part in the history of the Pilgrims at Plymouth. Here in 1607 the settlement of the colony under the auspices of Sir John Popham was accomplished, only a few months later than the beginning of the settlement at Jamestown, Virginia. Here Captain John Smith in 1609 attempted the founding of a colony to succeed the Popham settlement, but none of the settlements remained permanent by reason of the many troubles between the English, Indians and French, the latter claiming it as a part of their

Arrowsick that the captives would be brought in later but were now near Pemaquid. Sailing on to that place, Walderne met Mattahando, one of Madockawando's lieutenants, with about twenty-five of his followers, who declared himself desirous of peace. Suspicious of his intentions, it was decided at a council to attempt to get possession of the captives and then to attack the Indians by surprise. The major finally went ashore with part of the ransom and while looking around found a lance-head under a board. Seizing it, he brandished it before their faces and accused them of treachery, and, waiving his hand to the men on the vessel to come to his assistance, he fell upon the Indians killing seven, among them the old chief, and seizing four others.

In April the noted Simon wrought mischief in Wells and York and in May a party of Indians laid siege to the garrison at Black Point, then commanded by Lieutenant Bartholomew Tippen,[1] which was obstinately defended for three days and resulted in the death of Mugg by Lieutenant Tippen, who, noting an Indian who was par-

---

territory of Acadia. A fort, called Shurt's Fort, was built here perhaps as early as 1624, succeeded by a new structure on the same site in 1677 called Fort Charles. The first must have been the scene of the fracas between Major Walderne and the Indians during Philip's war. This was followed by a third fort erected by Sir William Phips, and still later a fortification of stone erected on the same site in 1729, called Fort Frederick, was destroyed by the inhabitants during the Revolutionary war to prevent its falling into the hands of the British.

But the most interesting subject connected with the history of Pemaquid is the ancient city, whose very existence has been forgotten, and upon the site of which the small settlement of to-day stands. The evidence of ancient buildings in some four hundred cellar holes, still to some extent visible; remains of shipyards, docks, an old burying ground, and streets regularly paved with cobblestones and found about two feet below the present surface of the ground, are cause for speculation. This interesting spot lies upon a projecting point of land between John's Bay on the west and the ocean on the east, in the town of Bristol.—Ten Years at Pemaquid, by J. Henry Cartland.

[1] Lieutenant Bartholomew Tippen (commonly found recorded as sergeant) was of Exeter in 1675 and was commissioned in October, 1676, to command the forces in re-establishing the settlement of Scarborough. In 1680 he was representative.

ticularly bold in the attack, fired upon and killed him under the belief that he was Simon. On the death of Mugg the Indians hastily withdrew, a part of them going in the direction of York and killing several settlers in that quarter.

June 22d, a force of two hundred friendly Indians and forty soldiers, was sent under command of Captain Benjamin Swett[1] of Hampton, and Lieutenant James Richardson,[2] on an expedition to the Piscataqua. Anchoring off Black Point information was received of a force of the enemy in that vicinity and Captain Swett went on shore with a detachment of his men, and being joined by some of the inhabitants, marched some two miles from the fort in pursuit of an apparently fleeing band, which suddenly turned and gave furious battle, closing in and firing upon the English from an encompassing swamp as they climbed a hill, driving in turn the young and inexperienced soldiers of Swett's command before them. Twenty friendly Indians and forty of the English were left upon the ground, including Lieutenant Richardson and Captain Swett, who fell covered with wounds. This was the most sanguinary battle of the eastern coast.

During this season the Indians attacked many vessels

[1] Captain Benjamin Swett, born in England about 1626, came to Newbury with his father where they were living as early as 1642. He married there the daughter of Peter Weare. He was early chosen to fill places of trust in town and county and was appointed ensign of the Newbury Military Company as early as 1651. He removed to Hampton and was influential in civil and military affairs in Old Norfolk County. In 1675 he held the rank of lieutenant. In June, 1677, he was commissioned captain and ordered "to Goe forth on the Service of the Country agt the Eastern Indian Ennemy."—New England Register, Vol. VI, page 54. Massachusetts Archives, Vol. LXIX, page 132.

[2] Lieutenant James Richardson was first of Woburn but in 1659 removed to Chelmsford. He was with Captain Wheeler in the defense of Brookfield. He removed to Charlestown, May 1, 1676, and served with Captain Hunting in his mixed English and Indian Company in the summer and fall of that year at Pawtucket Falls (Lowell), where they built a fortification and maintained a garrison, of which Lieutenant Richardson was left in charge, as well as of the Christian Indians at Chelmsford. He was well acquainted with Indian ways and had great influence with the natives.—Bodge, page 346.

THE BATTLEFIELD, BLACK POINT
Captain Benjamin Swett was killed here.

lying apparently secure in the harbors, and more than twenty of them were taken. "Thus" says Hubbard, "was the summer spent in calamities and miserable occurrents among the eastern parts."

An attempt, made somewhat earlier than the time of the events now reached, to enlist the Mohawk tribes against the eastern Indians, by the advice of Governor Andros of New York, did not succeed, through the reluctance of the Mohawks to proceed to such a distance from their homes. It is probable that had it been possible to have accomplished this plan, the insane dread held by the New England Indians against this warlike tribe, would have speedily put an end to the war.

The disturbances in the east having dragged along until August, 1677, a sudden termination of hostilities was reached by an enterprise entirely unforeseen. Fearful that the Sagadahock province, which was a possession of the Duke of York, might, in its deserted condition, be seized upon by the French, Sir Edmond Andros, Governor of New York, sent an armed expedition to Pemaquid with orders to take possession of the country, build a fort, engage in trade with the natives and encourage intercourse between them and the English. By an agreement with the sagamores the release of fifteen captives was secured, as well as the release of all the vessels which had been detained by them. It is reasonable to conclude that the Indians were tired of the long-drawn-out hostilities and were glad to embrace an opportunity to retire without too great embarrassment.

No attempt to relate in detail all the incidents of the war along the Maine coast has here been made; some known to the writer have been omitted and undoubtedly many occurrences of these times are now absolutely unknown to any person. There were in this region but few of the conditions existing in the United Colonies. No well-fortified and defended towns to be set upon in warlike fashion by a furious enemy. No well-equipped force to surprise the Indian fastness in a moment of unwatchfulness. Here was border warfare only. The sharp and unexpected attack upon the undefended cabin of the settler; the still more unexpected surprise upon the little garrison, and always, common to all sections in which the English fought, the deadly ambush, offering a lesson which was apparently never learned.

The peace and tranquillity which prevailed throughout the following autumn and winter and the enjoyment of consequent harmony and safety throughout the eastern portion of the province, induced the other tribes to seek a like condition for themselves, and in the spring of 1678, the Government of Massachusetts appointed a commission, consisting of Major Nicholas Shapleigh[1] of Kittery, Captain Francis Champernoon[2] and Captain Nathaniel Fryer[3] of Portsmouth, to settle a peace between Squando and all the sagamores of the eastern country. The commissioners met the Indians at Casco[4] and entered into Articles of Peace, April 12, by which all captives were to be returned without ransom, all inhabitants in returning to their homes were to enjoy their possession unmolested, but as an acknowledgment of the Indian rights in the lands, they were to pay to them, year by year, as a quit-

[1] Major Nicholas Shapleigh, son of Alexander who built the first house at Kittery Point, was born about 1610, and after coming to this country lived first at Portsmouth, but became one of the most prominent citizens of Old Kittery. He served as selectman, deputy to the General Court, Provincial Councilor, County Treasurer, and was one of the commissioners to hold the first term of court in York County in June, 1653. He was appointed major in the militia in 1656, and was also a justice. He was extensively engaged in lumbering and milling. He was killed by an accident during the launching of a vessel, April 29, 1682.—Old Kittery and her Families, page 112.

[2] Captain Francis Champernoon was a nephew of Sir Ferdinando Gorges. He was of Kittery, 1639, Portsmouth, 1646, and York, 1665. He was captain in 1640 and afterwards major. He was one of the councilors of the Province of New Hampshire in 1684. His will was probated December 28, 1687.—Savage.

[3] Captain Nathaniel Fryer, mariner, was of Boston but removed to Portsmouth. He was representative in 1666, captain, and councilor in 1683. His death occurred August 13, 1705.—Savage.

[4] See Williamson's History of Maine, Vol. I, page 552.

rent, a peck of corn for every English family, and for Major Phillips of Saco, who was a great proprietor, one bushel.

The losses throughout the country east of the Piscataqua had been very great. About two hundred and sixty were known to have been killed or carried into captivity, and there were probably many others of whom no record was kept. Some of the settlements had been utterly destroyed and in others many dwellings burned, domestic animals killed and a great amount of property plundered and destroyed. The cost to the colony government amounted to over eight thousand pounds.

INDEX

INDEX

U

Similar titles
offered by
Digital Scanning, Inc.

The History of Philip's War
by Thomas Church
As Published in 1827.

TP: 158218089X ($19.95)
HC: 1582181306 ($29.95)

The History of King Philip
by John Abbott
As Published in 1857.

TP: 1582183147 ($19.95)
HC: 1582183155 ($34.95)

King Philip's War
by George Ellis and John Morris
As Published in 1906.
*Originally a part of the Grafton Historical Series.

TP: 1582184305 ($19.95)
HC: 1582184313 ($33.95)

To order any of the above titles:

* Contact your local bookstore and order through *Ingram Books*.
* **Contact the publisher directly (for general information or special event purchases):**

Digital Scanning, Inc.
344 Gannett Rd., Scituate, MA 02066
Phone: (781) 545-2100 Fax: (781) 545-4908
email: books@digitalscanning.com
www.digitalscanning.com